A Charlton Standard Catalogue

STORYBOOK FIGURINES

ROYAL DOULTON
ROYAL ALBERT
BESWICK

Seventh Edition

By
Jean Dale

Introduction
by
Louise Irvine

W. K. Cross
Publisher

The Charlton Press

TORONTO, ONTARIO • PALM HARBOR, FLORIDA

The Charlton Press

Editorial Office
P.O. Box 820, Station Willowdale B
North York, Ontario, M2K 2R1 Canada
Telephone (416) 488-1418 Fax: (416) 488-4656
Telephone (800) 442-6042 Fax: (800) 442-1542
www.charltonpress.com e-mail: chpress@charltonpress.com

EDITORIAL

Editor	Jean Dale
Editorial Assistant	Susan Cross
Graphic Technician	Davina Rowan
Colour Technician	Marina Tsoukis
Photography	Marilyn and Peter Sweet

ACKNOWLEDGEMENTS

The Charlton Press wishes to thank those who have helped with the seventh edition of Storybook Figurines, Royal Doulton, Royal Albert, Beswick, (A Charlton Standard Catalogue).

Special Thanks

The publisher would like to thank:

Louise Irvine for writing the introduction to this edition. Louise is an independent writer and lecturer on Royal Doulton's history and products and is not connected with the pricing in this price guide.

Hank Corley for his extensive work on the understanding of the Beswick Beatrix Potter series and their backstamps.

Carolyn Baker for all her work on the Beatrix Potter series in previous editions.

Our thanks also go to the staff of Royal Doulton, who have helped with additional technical information, especially **Fiona Hawthorne**, General Manager, Director and Relationship Manager (U.K.); **Sara Williams**, Product Manager, Royal Doulton, (U.K.); **David Lovatt**, Marketing Communications Design Manager (U.K.); **Josie Hunt** and **Julie Tilestone**, Doulton & Company Doulton Direct (U.K.); **Julie Mountford**, International Collectors Club (U.K.); **Marion Proctor**, Marketing Manager (Canada); **Janet Drift**, Director of Retail Sales (U.S.A)

Contributors to the Sixth Edition

The publisher would also like to thank the following individuals and companies who graciously supplied photographs or information or allowed us access to their collections for photographic purposes: **C. H. Crowley**, Essex, UK; **Simon Hadwick, Millennium Collectables**, U.K.; **William A. Haight**, Sarnia, Ontario; **David Hale Hand**, Fort Collins, CO; **Anita Hunter; Richard Kane**, Westlake, Ohio; **Judy Kula**, Flemington, New Jersey; **Mr. O'Neill**, U.K.; **Brenda and Ian Paterson**, Bedfordshire, UK

A SPECIAL NOTE TO COLLECTORS

We welcome and appreciate any comments or suggestions in regard to Storybook Figurines. If any errors or omissions come to your attention, please write to us, or if you would like to participate in pricing or supply previously unavailable data or information, please contact Jean Dale at (416) 488-1418, or e-mail us at chpress@charltonpress.com.

DISCLAIMER

While every care has been taken to ensure accuracy in the compilation of the data in this catalogue, the publisher cannot accept responsibility for typographical errors.

National Library of Canada cataloging in Publication

    Storybook figurines Royal Doulton, Royal Albert, Beswick: a Charlton standard catalogue

Annual.
7th
Continues: Charlton standard catalogue of Royal Doulton Beswick
.   storybook figurines (1995)
ISSN 1706-7146
ISBN 0-88968-260-7 (7th ed.)

1. Beswick (Firm) - Themes, motives - Catalogs. 2. Royal Doulton figurines - Catalogs. 3. Porcelain animals - England - Catalogs. 4. Porcelain animals - Prices - Catalogs. 5. Royal Doulton figurines - Prices - Catalogs. I. Dale, Jean, II. Charlton International Inc. III. Title. IV. Title: Royal Doulton Beswick storybook figurines.

NK4660.C5   738.8'2'0294   C2003-901662-5

**Printed in Canada
in the Province of Ontario**

PRICING, OLD, NEW AND THE INTERNET

The Old System

The first edition of Royal Doulton Beswick Storybook figurines, introduced in 1994, was priced in a manner similar to all the other catalogues we have published over the years.

We had developed four main streams of information upon which we relied for pricing.

(1) Auctions: Auction catalogues and their prices realized provide a wealth of information on what a collector or dealer is willing to pay for an item. We, of course, subscribe to and receive a variety of auction catalogues from all over the world.

(2) Dealers' direct main catalogues: There was always a number of active dealers in the direct mail field publishing and distributing detailed price lists. Incorporating these lists into our analysis was another important factor in arriving at a market price.

(3) Request: Two or three months before a print date, pricing requests were mailed to various dealers in different parts of the world requesting their opinion on market prices. These replies were tallied and incorporated into the above action.

(4) Newsletters: We subscribe to every and all newsletters that appear on the subject for which we are producing a price guide. Newsletters give a wealth of information on current happenings in various hobbies, but they also supply goodly quantities of pricing information.

The four streams were compiled into one, extreme high and lows removed, and the results averaged to arrive at a market value. After a while a trend would emerge indicating the direction of the market. We were then ready to build a pricing model that would allow us to arrive at a suggested evaluation.

Over the past three years dramatic changes have taken place in collecting, especially collectables produced in the 20th century, which have continuity between similar items. Posters, art pottery, art glass, Royal Doulton Storybook figurines, coins and stamps all belong to this category. They all have high artistic design content, produced in small but reasonable quantities and widely distributed throughout the world. They started life as ornaments or decoration for the home.

The Evolution

The impact the Internet would have on collectables was not fully anticipated. All the old avenues such as fairs, shows, dealer stores, retail outlets, direct mail and auction houses would come under severe pressure by the lowering of margins which the Internet fostered. This would have a direct impact on pricing.

When Royal Doulton Beswick Storybook, 6th edition was up for revision in the winter of 2002, the process began of gathering prices to generate the 7th. Our method of collecting pricing information had to change.

Why! Simply because of the tremendous growth of the internet, and looking deeper, the rapid growth of on-line auctions in which 20th century collectables fit so well. Our auction results multiplied more than a thousand fold.

Dealers' web sites have all but replaced direct mail. The direct mail houses of five years ago is the virtual store of 2003. Items, prices can all be changed daily, with little effort or cost.

Land based auctions still contribute to pricing for they, through their historical connection with the collectors, gather in the scarce and rare pieces. The value of which is helpful in establishing an overall price trend. Seldom does the rare trend higher, without the basic items being carried forward along in unison.

Now, following this far, you are starting to wonder what has changed from the old model to the new, it is the Internet component comprising two parts: on-line auctions and virtual stores, but must now be inserted into the equation.

Average items daily

Category	JAN. 2001	JAN. 2002	JAN. 2003
Beswick	**625**	**825**	**1,500**
Bunnykins	350	475	650
Coins	6,000	7,200	10,000
Disney	37,500	51,500	87,200
Harry Potter	2,300	12,000	15,300
Lalique	650	400	1,000
Moorcroft	250	300	400
Royal Doulton	**3,500**	**3,700**	**5,600**
Royal Worcester	600	800	1,200
Stamps	12,700	13,700	23,100
Star Wars	19,000	23,500	38,900

From the above table, which is based on only one on-line auction site, it is obvious that the growth of on-line auction items being offered in the collectable market is increasing at a rapid rate, Using the table and converting from a daily to an annual basis, clearly emphasizes the magnitude of the numbers involved.

Centering on Beswick, by January 2001 the projected annual rate of items offered for sale was 288,000. By January 2002, the number offered had risen to 301,100 and by January 2003, had increased again to over 547,500. Assuming only 25% sells, the number is still extremely large, 125,000 plus, when compared to a Royal Doulton Specialist Land-based auction which may sell 500 lots per auction twice a year.

The New System

(1) Auctions:

A. Land-based auctions: As before, we continually monitor auction results capturing the pricing data.

B. Virtual auctions: With the new on-line auctions, both dealers and collectors participate. Prices become a true indication at that moment of the value of the item,

(2) Virtual Stores: Dealers' virtual stores have replaced our previous direct mail component and dealer requests, for now their offerings are available 24-hours-a-day and are possibly changed on a daily basis.

(3) Newsletters: Newsletters still contribute in the previous way and must not be overlooked.

The price gathering process has changed dramatically. The analyzing of the data remains the same.

HOW TO USE THIS PRICE GUIDE

THE PURPOSE

The sixth edition of this price guide covers the complete range of children's figures issued by Royal Doulton, Royal Albert and Beswick with the exception of the Bunnykins figurines which are included in The Charlton Standard Catalogue of Royal Doulton Bunnykins, Second Edition. In the process we have taken liberties with the name of this catalogue, for all figures listed are certainly not derived from storybook characters. However, the great majority are, and thus we have carried the name forward.

As with the other catalogues in Charlton's Royal Doulton reference and pricing library, this publication has been designed to serve two specific purposes. First, to furnish the collector with accurate and detailed listings that provide the essential information needed to build a rewarding collection. Second, to provide collectors and dealers with current market prices for Royal Doulton and Beswick storybook figures.

STYLES AND VERSIONS

STYLES: A change in style occurs when a major element of the design is altered or modified as a result of a deliberate mould change. An example of this is The Duchess With Flowers (style one) and The Duchess With a Pie (style two).

VERSIONS: Versions are modifications in a minor style element, such as the long ears becoming short ears on Mr. Benjamin Bunny.

VARIATIONS: A change in colour is a variation; for example, Mr. Jeremy Fisher's change in colourways from spotted to striped leggings.

THE LISTINGS

The Beatrix Potter figures are arranged alphabetically. At the beginning of the Beatrix Potter listings are seven pages graphically outlining backstamp variations. Backstamps are illustrated for eleven major varieties covering over fifty years of production. In the Beatrix Potter pricing charts, the reader will see Beswick and Doulton model numbers, backstamp numbers and market prices.

The Brambly Hedge figures are listed by their DBH numbers. There are no backstamp variations known.

The Snowman series is listed in numerical order by the DS numbers. There are no backstamp variations.

All of the above listings include the modeller, where known, the name of the animal figure, designer, height, colour, date of issue, varieties and series.

CONTENTS

Benjamin, The Beswick Bear
Compton & Woodhouse

INTRODUCTION
By Louise Irvine

THE HISTORY OF STORYBOOK CHARACTERS FROM THE ROYAL DOULTON, JOHN BESWICK AND ROYAL ALBERT STUDIOS

For over a century, the Royal Doulton Studios have entertained us with storybook characters, particularly animals endowed with human personalities. In Victorian times, a group of frogs enacting a well-known fable raised a smile in much the same way as the antics of the BRAMBLY HEDGE™ mice amuse us today. The tales of BEATRIX POTTER™, with lots of different animals acting and conversing as if they were human, are as popular now as when they were first written in the early 1900s. Obviously the idea of a creature simultaneously human and animal is deep rooted in our literary culture, and it is interesting to trace when it first became apparent in the Doulton world.

The Doulton factory was founded in London in 1815, but for the first 50 years production was confined to practical pottery. In the late 1860s, Sir Henry Doulton established an art studio, employing students from the Lambeth School of Art to decorate vases, jugs and plaques in fashionable Victorian styles. Some artists specialised in figurative sculpture, notably George Tinworth, who was the first to seek inspiration from well-known stories. The Bible provided him with most of his subject matter, but he also enjoyed reading the fables of Aesop and La Fontaine. These moralistic tales feature foxes, mice, lions and other creatures exemplifying human traits, and they fascinated the Victorians, particularly after the publication of Darwin's theory of evolution. Tinworth modelled several fables groups in the 1880s, including "The Fox and the Ape," "The Cat and the Cheese" and "The Ox and the Frogs." Later he produced mice and frog subjects, based on his own observations of human nature, which reflect his perceptive sense of humour.

Mr. Toad disguised as a washerwoman

The potential for dressed-up animals to disguise a deeper message soon led to their widespread use in children's literature, notably "Alice's Adventures in Wonderland" and Lear's nonsense poems. In 1908, Kenneth Grahame wrote "The Wind in the Willows" to comment on the behaviour of the English aristocracy, but the exciting adventures of Mr. Toad subtly conceal the author's critical stance. The dapper toad in his pinstripes and tails was modelled shortly afterwards by Lambeth artist Francis Pope, and a companion piece shows Mr. Toad disguised as a washerwoman in order to escape from prison.

Figures like these probably encouraged Beatrix Potter to approach the Lambeth studio in 1908 with a view to having her own animal characters immortalised in ceramic. Miss Potter published several illustrated stories about her favourite animals after the success of "The Tale of Peter Rabbit"™ in 1902, and some characters had already appeared as cuddly toys and decorative motifs on clothes, etc. Unfortunately an earlier contract with a German china firm made any arrangement with Doulton impossible, but she tried on a later occasion to have figures made of her characters at Grimwade's factory in Stoke-on-Trent. They suggested that Doulton's other factory in Burslem would be the best place to have the figures decorated, but again plans fell through. It was not until after Miss Potter's death that her dream was realised when the John Beswick factory in Longton began making little figures inspired by her books.

The John Beswick factory was founded in 1894 to produce ornamental jugs, vases and other decorative fancies. By the 1940s the Beswick artists had established a reputation for quality animal modelling, particularly portraits of famous horses by Arthur Gredington. In 1947, Gredington demonstrated his versatility when he modelled "Jemima Puddleduck" at the suggestion of Lucy Beswick, the wife of the managing director. She had been inspired by a visit to Beatrix Potter's Lake District home, where many of the tales are set. The success of this first study led to an initial collection of ten Beatrix Potter characters, including "Peter Rabbit," "Benjamin Bunny" and "Mrs. Tiggy-Winkle."

Launched in 1948, the new Beatrix Potter figures were welcomed with enthusiasm, and it was not long before Gredington was at work on another collection of character animals, this time from a British animated film. The "Lion" cartoon by David Hand was released in 1948, and "Zimmy Lion" became a new star for the Rank Film Organisation. Sequel cartoons introduced "Ginger Nutt," "Hazel Nutt," "Dinkum Platypus," "Loopy Hare," "Oscar Ostrich," "Dusty Mole" and "Felia Cat," all of which were modelled in 1949 as the DAVID HAND'S ANIMALAND™ series. David Hand had formerly worked for the Walt Disney studios, directing Mickey Mouse shorts, as well as the major films "Snow White" and "Bambi," and it was not long before these cartoons also inspired a collection of Beswick figures. Arthur Gredington modelled the little figures of "Snow White and the Seven Dwarfs" whilst Jan Granoska, a trainee modeller, was given the task of portraying Mickey Mouse and friends, plus some characters from "Pinocchio" and "Peter Pan." Although Miss Granoska was only at the Beswick studio for three years, she was responsible for some of their most desirable figures.

Music (of sorts!) is being played by the BEDTIME CHORUS™, a group of enthusiastic children accompanied by a singing cat and dog. These were amongst the first character figures to be modelled by Albert Hallam, who gradually took over responsibility for this area in the 1960s. As head mouldmaker, Hallam had made many of the production moulds for Gredington designs, so he was already familiar with the subject matter. He continued the Beatrix Potter collection, adding characters such as "Old Mr. Brown" and "Cecily Parsley," and in 1968 he launched a new Disney series based on their newest cartoon hit, "Winnie the Pooh and the Blustery Day."

The late 1960s was a time of transition for the company as Ewart Beswick was ready to retire but he had no heir for his successful business. Fortunately the Royal Doulton group was in the midst of an expansion programme and they acquired the Beswick factory in 1969. They soon benefited from Beswick's expertise in the field of character animals.

When Albert Hallam retired in 1975, Graham Tongue became the head modeller at the Beswick Studio under Harry Sales, the newly appointed design manager. Harry Sales was primarily a graphic artist and he dreamed up many new ideas for the Beatrix Potter range, which Graham Tongue and others modelled during the 1980s. This was becoming increasingly difficult as the most popular characters had already been modelled. Favourites, such as "Peter Rabbit" and "Jemima Puddleduck," were introduced in new poses, and he came up with the idea of double figures, for example "Mr Benjamin Bunny and Peter Rabbit" and "Tabitha Twitchet and Miss Moppet."

As well as developing the established figure collections, Harry Sales delved into lots of other children's books for inspiration. He re-interpreted the timeless characters from classic tales such as "Alice's Adventures in Wonderland" and "The Wind in the Willows," and he worked from contemporary picture books, notably Joan Walsh Anglund's "A Friend is Someone Who Likes You" or Norman Thelwell's "Angels on Horseback." Whenever possible, Harry liaised closely with the originators of the characters he portrayed. He spent many happy hours of research at Thelwell's studio, studying his cartoons of shaggy ponies with comical riders, and he also worked with Alfred Bestall, the illustrator of the Rupert Bear adventures in the "Daily Express" newspaper before embarking on this series in 1980.

With their outstanding reputation for developing character animals, it is not surprising that Royal Doulton artists were invited to work on the publishing sensation of the 1980s, the Brambly Hedge stories by Jill Barklem. Within three years of their launch the "Spring," "Summer," "Autumn" and "Winter" stories had been reprinted 11 times, translated into ten languages, and had sold in excess of a million copies. Readers young and old were captivated by the enchanting world of the Brambly Hedge mice, as indeed was Harry Sales, whose job it was to recreate the characters in the ceramic medium. In his own words, "The first time I read the books and studied the illustrations I felt that I was experiencing something quite unique. Over a period of many years designing for the pottery industry one develops an awareness, a feeling for that something special. Brambly Hedge had this."

Ideas flowed quickly and eight leading characters were chosen from the seasonal stories for the initial collection, which was launched in 1983. Such was the response that they were soon joined by six more subjects, making a total of 14 by 1986, when Harry left the company. Graham Tongue succeeded him as design manager and continued to add new Brambly Hedge figures from the original stories. Miss Barklem's later titles, The Secret Staircase, The High Hills and The Sea Story, provided inspiration for some of his figures; for example, Mr and Mrs Saltapple who supply the Brambly Hedge community with salt in The Sea Story.

Encouraged by the amazing success of the Brambly Hedge collection, Royal Doulton's marketing executives were soon considering other new storybook characters. Like millions of TV viewers, they were spellbound by the magical film, The Snowman, which was first screened in 1982. Based on the illustrated book of the same name by Raymond Briggs, the animated film about a snowman who comes to life has become traditional Christmas entertainment in many parts of the world. The absence of words gives the tale a haunting quality, and there is hardly a dry eye in the house when the little boy, James, awakes to find his Snowman friend has melted away after an exciting night exploring each other's worlds. Fortunately the SNOWMAN™ lives on in more durable form in the Royal Doulton collection. Again Harry Sales was given the challenge of transforming this amorphous character into ceramic, whilst remaining faithful to Briggs' original soft crayon drawings. He succeeded in this difficult task by adding additional curves to the contours of the figures which gives them a life-like appearance. The first four figures were ready and approved by Raymond Briggs in 1985, and the collection grew steadily until 1990, latterly under the direction of Graham Tongue.

The 1990s saw Graham Tongue and his team of artists develop the Beatrix Potter collection for the 100th birthday of "Peter Rabbit" and, in 1994, the centenary of the Beswick factory was marked with the launch of the "Pig Promenade," featuring a special commemorative backstamp.

This series is just one of three new collections of novelty figures, and it is refreshing to see this traditional type of Beswick ware being revitalised by a new generation of artists. Amanda Hughes-Lubeck and Warren Platt created the LITTLE LOVABLES™, a series of cute clowns with special messages, such as "Good Luck" and "Congratulations," and they also worked with Martyn Alcock on the collection of ENGLISH COUNTRY FOLK™, which has been very well received.

The collecting of Beatrix Potter and Brambly Hedge figures has reached epidemic proportions in recent years, and there is now a growing awareness of the desirability of all their storybook cousins, hence the need for this much expanded price guide.

COLLECTING BEATRIX POTTER FIGURES

A number of factors have combined recently to make Beatrix Potter figures the "hottest" collectables of the day. The 100th birthday of "Peter Rabbit" was celebrated amidst a storm of publicity in 1993, and the centenary of the John Beswick factory in 1994 focused a lot of collector attention on its products. 1997 saw more celebrations as Beatrix Potter figures had been in continuous production at Beswick for fifty years.

A group of Beatrix Potter books with the figures beside

The market has been stimulated by regular withdrawals from the range and prices are rocketing for the early discontinued figures. Most collectors will need a bank loan to purchase "Duchess with Flowers," the first Beatrix Potter figure to be retired, if indeed they are lucky enough to find one for sale.

Ever since the Beswick factory launched their Beatrix Potter collection in 1948, most of the figures have been bought as gifts for children. However, many young fans have grown up to find they have some very valuable figures, with early modelling and backstamp variations, and they have begun collecting in earnest to fill the gaps and find the rarities. Figures marked with a Beswick backstamp are most in demand, as this trademark was replaced with the Royal Albert backstamp in 1989. The Royal Albert factory, another famous name in the Doulton group, produces all the Beatrix Potter tableware, and the change of backstamps was made for distribution reasons. The most desirable Beswick marks are the gold varieties, which predate 1972, and these are often found on early modelling or colour variations, which also attract a premium price, for example "Mrs Rabbit" with her umbrella sticking out and "Mr Benjamin Bunny" with his pipe protruding.

As well as seeking out discontinued figures and rare variations, it is advisable to keep up to date with new models as they are introduced. A complete Beatrix Potter figure collection will encompass more than 100 of the standard-size models, around three inches tall, and thirteen large models, which are about twice the size. "Peter Rabbit," the first of these large size models, was launched in 1993 with a special commemorative backstamp from the John Beswick studio, and it changed in 1994 to a Royal Albert mark. The Royal Albert mark was used on most Beatrix Potter figures between 1989 and 1998 when new John Beswick backstamps were introduced.

If owning all the Beatrix Potter figures is beyond the realms of possibility, whether for financial or display limitations, then why not focus on particular types of animals or characters from your favourite tales. There are twenty mice figures to find, a dozen cat characters and more than twenty rabbits, half of which feature "Peter Rabbit." There are also discontinued character jugs, relief modelled plaques and a ceramic display stand to look out for, so happy hunting.

COLLECTING BRAMBLY HEDGE FIGURES

Since their introduction in 1983, the Brambly Hedge mice have overrun households in many parts of the world. They are scurrying about the shelves as Royal Doulton figures and even climbing up the walls on decorative plates. Far from being undesirable, these particular mice are considered indispensable members of the family. Children frequently receive them as gifts from doting grandparents, but adults have also been seduced by the cosy, timeless mouse world which Jill Barklem has created. The mood of rustic nostalgia has all been painstakingly researched. The interiors of the field mice homes are of the sort common in English farmhouses at the end of the 19th century, and the food served is genuine country fare, based on old recipes and tested in Jill Barklem's kitchen. The Brambly Hedge residents were all expertly drawn with the aid of her two mouse models, a keen understanding of zoology and a knowledge of historical costume.

The same attention to detail went into the Royal Doulton figures designed by Harry Sales. As he explains, "One important feature in the concept was that I chose poses which, when the figures are together, appear to be reacting to one another. I can imagine the fun children and the young at heart will have arranging the figures in conversational situations." Essentially this sums up the collectability of the Brambly Hedge mice, and as there are only 25 figures in the first series, they can all be displayed effectively together on one shelf. There are, however, a couple of unusual modelling variations to look out for as "Mr Toadflax's" tail was altered shortly after its introduction, plus some colour variations. Royal Doulton retired the first Brambly Hedge collection in 1997, but a new collection of figures was introduced in 2000 to celebrate the 20th anniversary of Brambly Hedge.

COLLECTING SNOWMAN FIGURES

Initially, the seasonal appeal of the Snowman tended to limit his collectability, as most purchases were made around Christmas time, and he was more popular in areas which regularly experience snow. Having said this, for some fans the wintry connotations were overshadowed by the inherent quality and humour of the models and there are now keen collectors in sunny Florida as well as in Australia, where beach barbecues are typical Christmas celebrations.

Between 1985 and 1990, young children regularly received the new Snowman models in their Christmas stockings, and the characters have been widely used as holiday decorations. Like the Brambly Hedge models, they were designed to interact, and the little figure of James, gazing up in wonder, can be positioned with various Snowman characters, whilst the band works very well as a separate display grouping. There are 19 figures and two musical boxes to collect in the first series, and as the range was withdrawn in 1994, they can now be quite difficult to locate. In fact, prices have been snowballing, particularly for the figures that were not in production for long, notably "The Snowman Skiing." The antics of the Snowman were revived in 1999 for a limited edition collection commissioned by Lawleys By Post.

COLLECTING STORYBOOK CHARACTERS

The Beatrix Potter, Brambly Hedge and Snowman stories have already been discussed in some detail, as there are so many figures to collect in each of the categories. However, the Beswick artists have also sought inspiration in other children's stories, some better known than others.

The American author-illustrator, Joan Walsh Anglund, enjoyed quite a vogue in the 1960s following the publication of "A Friend is Someone Who Likes You" (1958). Three of her drawings of cute children with minimal features were modelled by Albert Hallam for the Beswick range in 1969, but they were withdrawn soon after, making them extremely hard to find today.

The bizarre cast of characters from Alice's Adventures in Wonderland has offered a lot more scope for collectors. First published in 1865, this classic tale has entertained generations of young readers and inspired many artistic interpretations. In the early 1900s, Doulton's Lambeth artists modelled some fantastic creatures from the tale, notably the pig-like "Rath" from the "Jabberwocky" poem. The Burslem studio designed an extensive series of nursery ware and, more recently, a collection of character jugs based on the original illustrations by Sir John Tenniel, who firmly fixed the appearance of the Wonderland characters in the public imagination. Harry Sales also consulted the Tenniel illustrations in 1973 when designing Beswick's ALICE IN WONDERLAND™.

Curiously the figures inspired by another great children's classic, The Wind in the Willows, did not have the same appeal. Christina Thwaites, a young book illustrator, was commissioned to produce designs for a collection of wall plates and tea wares, and her watercolours of "Mr Toad," "Ratty," "Mole," "Badger" and others were interpreted by the Beswick modellers. Four figures were launched in 1987 and two more in 1988 as part of a co-ordinated giftware range with the Royal Albert backstamp, but they were withdrawn in 1989. Consequently "Portly and Weasel," the later introductions, were only made for one year, and will no doubt prove particularly hard to find in the future. Royal Doulton has recently embarked on a new Wind in the Willows collection, which is distributed by Lawleys by Post in a limited edition of 2,000.

With the WIND IN THE WILLOWS™ collection, the Royal Doulton artists have come full circle, reflecting the enthusiasm of their predecessors at Lambeth, notably Francis Pope who modelled two superb figures of "Mr Toad" shortly after the book was published. Obviously storybook characters, particularly animals in human guises, have timeless appeal.

COLLECTING CARTOON CHARACTERS

Cartoon characters, whether they be from animated films or comic book strips, are becoming a popular field for collectors. A major reference book on the subject, together with introductions such as the Hanna Barbera and Disney collections have already generated even more interest. Now is the time to start collecting, if you have not already done so.

The characters from David Hand's Animaland are virtually unknown today, but following their film debut in 1948, they were sufficiently well known to inspire Beswick's first series of cartoon figures. Modelled in 1949 and withdrawn in 1955, "Zimmy the Lion" and his seven friends now have a different kind of notoriety, stealing the show when they come up for auction.

In contrast, Mickey Mouse is the best known cartoon character in the world. Within a year of his 1928 screen debut in "Steamboat Willie," his image was being used to endorse children's products, and by the 1950s there were more than 3,000 different Mickey Mouse items, including plates, dolls, watches and clothes. With all this merchandising activity, it is not surprising that the Beswick studio sought a license for portraying Mickey and his friends in ceramic.

A range of nursey ware was launched in 1954, along with figures of "Mickey" and his girlfriend "Minnie," "Pluto" his dog and his crazy friends "Goofy" and "Donald Duck." Characters from some of Walt Disney's feature-length cartoons completed the original WALT DISNEY CHARACTERS™ set of 12 figures. "Peter Pan," the newest Disney hit in 1953, inspired four characters, "Peter" himself, "Tinkerbell," "Smee" and "Nana," whilst the classic "Pinocchio" (1940) provided the puppet hero and his insect conscience "Jiminy Cricket." Surprisingly only "Thumper" was modelled from another favourite film, "Bambi" (1942), although the fawn appears on the tableware designs. The response to the initial Disney collection encouraged the Beswick factory to launch a second set the following year, featuring "Snow White and the Seven Dwarfs" from Disney's first feature symphony. All the Disney characterisations are superb, making them extremely desirable amongst collectors of Beswick and Disneyana and they are all hard to find, even though they were produced until 1967.

The 1960s saw the rise of a new Disney star, Winnie the Pooh, who became a very popular merchandising character after his cartoon debut in 1966. The Beswick factory was quick off the mark, launching an initial collection of six characters from the film in 1968, followed by two more in 1971. "The Bear of Little Brain" originated in bedtime stories about nursery toys told by A. A. Milne to his son Christopher Robin in the 1920s, and he was visualised in the resulting books by the illustrator E. H. Shepard. To celebrate the 70th anniversary of the first "Winnie the Pooh" book, Royal Doulton launched a second series of figures in 1996 and these have been a great success. Royal Doulton continue to work closely with the Walt Disney company today and they have launched two exciting figurine collections featuring Disney "Princesses" and "Villains" exclusively for sale in the Disney stores. The other new Disney collections have been distributed through specialist china shops, notably the "101 Dalmatians" series, which was inspired by the live action film, and the second series of "Snow White and the Seven Dwarfs," which was prompted by the 60th anniversary of the film. A new Disney series featuring Mickey Mouse and his gang, was launched during 1998 so don't miss the opportunity to add these to your cartoon collection.

The massive marketing campaigns for Disney characters have made them household names all over the world. British cartoon characters, by comparison, are less well known internationally. The "Daily Express" newspaper was slow to capitalise on the success of "Rupert the Bear," who has been the star of their children's comic strip since 1920. Originated by Mary Tourtel, the Rupert stories were enlivened by Alfred Bestall who took over the daily drawings in 1935. Rupert enjoys the most extraordinary adventures with his friends Bill the Badger, Algy Pug and Pong-Ping, always returning safely to his comfortable family home in Nutwood. Rupert Bear annuals sold in millions from the mid 1930s, and his exploits were adapted for TV in the 1970s, but his following is essentially British. No doubt it was for this reason that the five figures in the original RUPERT THE BEAR™ collection, designed by Harry Sales in 1980, were relatively short lived. However, the second Rupert Bear collection, launched in 1998, is proving very popular with Lawleys By Post customers.

A similar fate befell the NORMAN THELWELL™ figures, which were in production from 1981 to 1989. Norman Thelwell was a humorous illustrator for "Punch" magazine, who made his reputation with comical observations of young riders and their mounts. "Angels on Horseback," published in 1957, was the first compilation of his successful cartoons, and many other popular books followed. Thelwell worked closely with Harry Sales to create the most effective figures, both in ceramic and resin, and the results are guaranteed to raise a smile without breaking the bank.

After a gap of nearly 15 years, famous British cartoon characters are back on the drawing board at the Royal Doulton studios once again. "Denis the Menace" and "Desperate Dan," stars of the long-established children's comics, "The Beano" and "The Dandy," have been immortalised as character jugs. This is the first time large-size character jugs have been used for portraying cartoons, although there are similarities to the set of six THUNDERBIRDS™ busts modelled by jug designer Bill Harper to celebrate the 30th anniversary of this children's TV show in 1992.

COLLECTING CHARACTER ANIMALS

In the 1880s Doulton's first artist, George Tinworth, was modelling groups of mice engaged in popular human pastimes, and nearly a century later Kitty MacBride did much the same thing with her "Happy Mice." The appeal of these anthropomorphic creatures is timeless, and collectors have responded with enthusiasm from Victorian times to the present day. Admittedly, developing a taste for Tinworth's sense of humour will prove very expensive, with models costing several hundreds of pounds each, but the KITTY MACBRIDE™ whimsical mice are still relatively affordable.

Kitty MacBride was a writer and illustrator who began to model little clay figures of mice in 1960. Initially they were sold through a London dealer, but when she could not keep up with the demand she asked the Beswick factory to produce 11 of them commercially, which they did between 1975 and 1983.

The Beswick studio has had a considerable reputation for character animals since the launch of the Beatrix Potter collection in 1948. However, the modellers have not only interpreted illustrations from famous books, from time to time they have envisaged their own comical creatures. Albert Hallam was responsible for a succession of animals with human expressions in the late 1960s. Similar humanising traits can be found in the LITTLE LIKEABLES™ collection, which was produced briefly in the mid 1980s. Robert Tabbenor's animals play up the humour of their situation, notably the carefree frog, "Watching the World Go By," whilst Diane Griffiths takes a more sentimental approach, using human feelings to describe her cartoon-like animals.

The fun has continued in recent years with a collection of "Footballing Felines," produced in 1999, and the on-going series of "English Country Folk," depicting appropriate animals with human manners and costumes. However, the last laugh is reserved for the "Pig Promenade." The absurdity of nine different breeds of pigs playing musical instruments makes this one of the most hilarious series of character animals.

MAKING STORYBOOK CHARACTERS

All the current storybook characters are made at the John Beswick factory in Longton, which became part of the Royal Doulton group in 1969. They have over fifty years' experience in the production of humorous figures and character animals, and essentially the methods have not changed since the earliest days of the Beatrix Potter figures.

First of all the designer has to familiarise himself thoroughly with the character to be portrayed, reading the story and studying the illustration. Having chosen the most suitable pose for interpretation in ceramic, he will produce reference drawings for the modeller. Often he can only see one side of the character in the original illustration, so he has to improvise for his three-dimensional model.

In consultation with the designer, the modeller will create the figure in modelling clay, and if satisfactory, a set of master moulds will be made in plaster of Paris. The number of mould parts will depend on the complexity of the figure, and sometimes the head and arms have to be moulded separately. Two or three prototype figures will be cast from the master mould for colour trials and subsequent approval by the original artist or his agent.

In the case of the Beatrix Potter figures, all the models are scrutinised by the licensing agents, Copyrights, working on behalf of Miss Potter's original publishers, Frederick Warne. Raymond Briggs, who was responsible for the Snowman, is generally quite relaxed about letting experts in other media interpret his drawings. He thought Royal Doultons models were marvellous and really captured the spirit of the story, although he maintained he would "jolly well say so" if he thought they had got it wrong! Jill Barklem, the creator of Brambly Hedge, likes to get very involved in the licensing of her characters, and design manager Harry Sales spent a lot of time working with her on the finer points of detail. Sometimes slight modifications need to be made to the model or the colour scheme before the figure is approved by all concerned.

The next stage is to produce plaster of Paris working moulds from the master, and supplies are sent to the casting department. An earthenware body is used to cast all the character figures produced at the John Beswick studio, and it is poured into the mould in liquid form, known as slip. The moisture in the slip is absorbed into the plaster of Paris moulds and a "skin" of clay forms the interior.

Once the clay has set to the required thickness, the excess clay is poured out and the mould is carefully dismantled. Any separate mould parts, such as projecting arms, will be joined on at this stage using slip as an adhesive, and the seams will be gently sponged away. The figure is then allowed to dry slowly before it goes for its first firing. The high temperature in the kiln drives out the moisture in the body and the figure shrinks by about 1/12th of its original size, forming a hard "biscuit" body.

Skilled decorators will paint the figure, using special under-glaze ceramic colours. They work from an approved colour sample and great care is taken to match the colours to the original book illustrations. A second firing hardens on the colour before the figure is coated with a solution of liquid glaze. When the figure is fired in the glost kiln, it emerges with a shiny transparent finish which enhances and permanently protects the vibrant colours underneath. After a final inspection, the figures are dispatched to china shops all over the world where they will capture the hearts of collectors young and old.

RESIN FIGURES

Several collectables manufacturers began experimenting with new sculptural materials in the 1980s and developed different types of resin bodies that allow more intricately modelled detail than conventional ceramic processes. Royal Doulton launched its new "bonded ceramic body" in 1984, and two storybook collections were included in its Beswick Studio Sculptures, as the range was known. Seven subjects were chosen from the "Tales of Beatrix Potter" and two from the Thelwell series. Production was short-lived, despite the minute detailing of the animals' fur and the tiny pebbles and grasses in their habitat, which would have been impossible to achieve in traditional earthenware. Royal Doulton ceased production of resin at the end of 1985, but designs have been commissioned from resin specialists, notably the "Paddington Bear" and "St. Tiggywinkles series."

YEAR CYPHERS

Beginning in 1998 a cypher was added to the base of each figurine. The cypher for 1998 was an umbrella, for 1999 the Top Hat as worn by Sir Henry Doulton, for 2000 a fob watch, for 2001 a waistcoat, for 2002 a boot and for 2003 a pair of gloves.

1998 Umbrella   1999 Top Hat   2000 Fob Watch

2001 Waistcoat   2002 Boot   2003 Gloves

THE DOULTON MARKETS

INTERNATIONAL COLLECTORS CLUB

Founded in 1980 The Royal Doulton International Collectors Club provides an information service on all aspects of the company's products, past and present. A Club magazine, "Gallery," is published four times per year with information on new products and current events that will keep the collector up-to-date on the happenings in the world of Royal Doulton. Upon joining the club, each new member will receive a free gift and invitations to special events and exclusive offers throughout the year. To join the Royal Doulton Collectors Club, please contact the club directly by writing to the address opposite or calling the appropriate number.

International Collectors Club
Sir Henry Doulton House
Forge Lane, Etruria
Stoke-on-Trent, Staffordshire
ST1 5NN, England
Telephone:
    U.K.: 8702 412696
    Overseas: +44 (0) 1782 404045
    On-line at www.doulton-direct.co.uk
    E-mail: icc@royal-doulton.com

VISITOR CENTRE

Opened in the Summer of 1996, the Royal Doulton Visitor Centre houses the largest collection of Royal Doulton figurines in the world. Demonstration areas offer the collector a first hand insight on how figurines are assembled and decorated. Also at the Visitor Centre is a restaurant and a retail shop offering both best quality ware and slight seconds. Factory tours may be booked, Monday to Friday.

Royal Doulton Visitor Centre
Nile Street, Burslem
Stoke-on-Trent, ST6 2AJ, England
Visitor Centre: Tel.: +44 (0) 1782 292434
             Fax: +44 (0) 1782 292424
Factory Store: Tel.: +44 (0) 1782 292451

WEBSITE AND E-MAIL ADDRESS

Websites
    www.royal-doulton.com
    www.doulton-direct.com.au
    www.royal-doulton-brides.com

E-mail:
    Visitor Centre: visitor@royal-doulton.com
    Consumers Enquiries: enquiries@royal-doulton.com
    Museum Curator: heritage@royal-doulton.com
    Doulton-Direct: direct@royal-doulton.com

ROYAL DOULTON FACTORY SHOPS

Royal Doulton Group Factory Shop
Lawley Street, Longton
Stoke-on-Trent, ST3 2PH, England
    Tel.: +44 (0) 1782 291237

Royal Doulton Factory Shop
Forge Lane, Etruria
Stoke-on-Trent, ST1 5NN, England
    Tel.: +44 (0) 1782 284056

Royal Doulton Factory Shop
Victoria Road, Fenton
Stoke-on-Trent, ST4 2PJ, England
    Tel.: +44 (0) 1782 291869

DOULTON CHAPTERS

Detroit Chapter
Ronald Griffin, President
629 Lynne Avenue
Ypsilanti, MI. 48198-3829

Edmonton Chapter
Mildred's Collectibles
6813 104 Street,
Edmonton, AB Canada

New England Chapter
Lee Piper, President
Meridith Nelson, Vice President
Michael Lynch, Secretary
Scott Reichenberg, Treasurer
E-mail: doingantiq@aol.com

Northern California Chapter
Edward L. Khachadourian, President
P. O. Box 214, Moraga, CA 94556-0214
Tel.: (925) 376-2221
Fax: (925) 376-3581
E-mail: khach@pacbell.net

Northwest, Bob Haynes Chapter
Alan Matthew, President
15202 93rd Place NE, Bothell
WA 98011 Tel.: (425) 488-9604

Rochester Chapter
Judith L. Trost, President
103 Garfield Street, Rochester
NY 14611 Tel.: (716) 436-3321

Ohio Chapter
Reg Morris
5556 Whitehaven Avnue
North Olmstead, Ohio 44070
Tel.: (216) 779-5554

Western Pennsylvania Chapter
John Re, President
9589 Parkedge Drive
Allison Park, PA 15101
Tel.: (412) 366-0201
Fax: (412) 366-2558

THE DOULTON MARKETS

LAND AUCTIONS

AUSTRALIA

Goodman's
7 Anderson Street
Double Bay, Sydney, 2028, N.S.W., Australia
Tel.: +61 (0) 2 9327 7311; Fax: +61 (0) 2 9327 2917
Enquiries: Suzanne Brett
www.goodmans.com.au
E-mail: info@goodmans.com.au

Sotheby's
1180122 Queen Street, Woollahra
Sydney, 2025, N.S.W., Australia
Tel.: +61 (0) 2 9362 1000; Fax: +61 (0) 2 9362 1100

CANADA

Empire Auctions

Montreal
5500 Paré Street, Montreal, Quebec H4P 2M1
Tel.: (514) 737-6586; Fax: (514) 342-1352
Enquiries: Isadore Rubinfeld
E-mail: montreal@empireauctions.com

Ottawa
1380 Cyrville Road, Gloucester, Ontario
Tel.: (613) 748-5343; Fax: (613) 748-0354
Enquiries: Elliot Melamed
E-mail: ottawa@empireauctions.com

Toronto
165 Tycos Drive
Toronto, Ontario, M6B 1W6
Tel.: (416) 784-4261; Fax: (416) 784-4262
Enquiries: Michael Rogozinsky
www.empireauctions.com
E-mail: toronto@empireauctions.com

Maynards Industries Ltd.
415 West 2nd Avenue, Vancouver, BC, V5Y 1E3
Tel.: (604) 876-1311; Fax: (604) 876-1323
www.maynards.com
E-mail: antiques@maynards.com

Ritchie's
288 King Street East, Toronto, Ontario M5A 1K4
Tel.: (416) 364-1864; Fax: (416) 364-0704
Enquiries: Caroline Kaiser
www.richies.com
E-mail: auction@richies.com

Waddingtons
111 Bathurst Street, Toronto, Ontario M5V 2R1
Tel.: (416) 504-9100; Fax: (416) 504-0033
Enquiries: Bill Kime
www.waddingtonsauctions.com
E-mail: info@waddingtonsauctions.com

UNITED KINGDOM

BBR Auctions
Elsecar Heritage Centre, Nr. Barnsley
South Yorkshire, S74 8HJ, England
Tel.: +44 (0) 1226 745156; Fax: +44 (0) 1226 351561
Enquiries: Alan Blakeman
www.bbauctions.co.uk
E-mail: sales@bbauctions.com

Bonhams

Bond Street
101 New Bond Street, London W15 1SR, England

Chelsea
65-69 Lots Road, Chelsea, London SW10 0RN, England

Knightsbridge
Montpelier Street, Knightsbridge, London, SW7 1HH
Tel.: +44 (0) 20 7393 3900; Fax: +44 (0) 20 7393 3905
Enquiries:
Decorative Arts; Joy McCall
Tel.: +44 (0) 20 7393 3942
Contemporary Ceramics: Gareth Williams
Tel.: +44 (0) 20 7393 3941
Doulton Beswick Wares: Mark Oliver
Tel.: +44 (0) 20 7468 8233
www.bonhams.com
E-mail: info@bonhams.com

Christie's

London
8 King Street, London, SW1, England
Tel.: +44 (0) 207-839-9060; Fax: +44 (0) 20 7839-1611

South Kensington
85 Old Brompton Road, London SW7 3LD, England
Tel.: +44 (0) 20 7581 7611; Fax: +44 (0) 20 7321-3321
Enquiries:
Decorative Arts: Michael Jeffrey
Tel.: +44 (0) 20 7321 3237
www.christies.com; E-mail: info@christies.com

Potteries Specialist Auctions
271 Waterloo Road, Cobridge, Stoke-on-Trent
Staffordshire, ST6 6HR, England
Tel.: +44 (0) 1782 286622
Fax: +44 (0) 1782 213777
Enquiries: Stella Ashbrooke
www.potteriesauctions.com
E-mail: enquiries@potteriesauctions.com

Sotheby's

London
34-35 New Bond Street, London W1A 2AA, England
Tel.: +44 (0) 20 7293 5000; Fax: +44 (0) 20 7293 5989

Olympia
Hammersmith Road, London, W14 8UX, England
Tel.: +44 (0) 20 7293 5555; Fax: +44 (0) 20 7293 6939

Sotheby's (cont.)

Sussex
Summers Place, Billingshurst, Sussex
RH14 9AF, England
Tel.: +44 (0) 1403 833500
Fax: +44 (0) 1403 833699
www.sothebys.com
E-mail: info@sothebys.com

Louis Taylor
Britannia House
10 Town Road, Hanley
Stoke-on-Trent, Staffordshire, England
Tel.: +44 (0) 1782 214111
Fax: +44 (0) 1782 215283
Enquiries: Clive Hillier

Thomson, Roddick & Laurie
60 Whitesands
Dumfries DG1 2RS
Scotland
Tel.: +44 (0) 1387 279879
Fax: +44 (0) 1387 266236
Enquiries: C. R. Graham-Campbell

Peter Wilson Auctioneers
Victoria Gallery, Market Street
Nantwich, Cheshire CW5 5DG, England
Tel.: +44 (0) 1270 610508
Fax: +44 (0) 1270 610508
Enquiries: Peter Wilson

UNITED STATES

Christie's East
219 East 67th Street, New York, NY 10012
Tel.: +1 212 606 0400
Enquiries: Timothy Luke
www.christies.com

William Doyle Galleries
175 East 87th Street, New York, NY 10128
Tel.: +1 212 427-2730
Fax: +1 212 369 0892

Sotheby's Arcade Auctions
1334 York Avenue, New York, NY 10021
Tel.: +1 212 606 7000
Enquiries: Andrew Cheney
www.sothebys.com

VIRTUAL AUCTIONS

Amazon.com ® Auctions
Main site: www.amazon.com
Plus 4 International sites

AOL.com Auctions ®
Main site: www.aol.com
Links to – E-bay.com
– U-bid.com

E-BAY ® The Worlds On-Line Market Place™
Main site: www.ebay.com
Plus 20 International sites

YAHOO! Auctions ®
Main site: www.yahoo.com
Plus 15 International auction sites

FAIRS, MARKETS AND SHOWS

AUSTRALIA

Royal Doulton and Antique Collectable Fair
Marina Hall, Civic Centre
Hurstville, Sydney

CANADA

Christie Antique Show
Christie Conservation Park
Highway 5
near Dundas, Ontario
always May and September
Gadsden Promotions Ltd.
P.O. Box 490, Shelburne, ON. LON 1S0
Tel.: (800) 667-0619
Fax: (519) 925-6498
Website: www.antiqueshows.canada.com

UNITED KINGDOM

20th Century Fairs
266 Glossop Road, Sheffield S10 2HS, England
Usually in May or June
For information on times and dates:
Tel.: +44 (0) 114 275 0333
Fax: +44 (0) 114 275 4443

Doulton and Beswick Collectors Fair
National Motorcycle Museum, Meriden
Birmingham
Usually March and August
For information on times and dates:
Doulton and Beswick Dealers Association
Tel.: +44 (0) 181 303 3316

DMG Antiques Fairs Ltd.
Newark, the largest in the UK with usually six fairs
annually. For information on times and dates for this
and many other fairs contact:
DMG
Newark, P.O. Box 100, Newark
Nottinghamshire NG2 1DJ
Tel.: +44 (0) 1636 702326
Fax: +44 (0) 1636 707923
www.antiquesdirectory.co.uk

U.K. Fairs
Doulton and Beswick Fair for Collectors
River Park Leisure Centre, Winchester
Usually held in October.
For information on times and dates contact:
Enquiries U.K. Fairs; Tel.: +44 (0) 20 8500 3505
www.portia.co.uk
E-mail: ukfairs@portia.co.uk

LONDON MARKETS

Alfie's Antique Market
13-25 Church Street, London; Tuesday - Saturday

Camden Passage Market
London; Wednesday and Saturday

New Caledonia Market
Bermondsey Square, London; Friday morning

Portobello Road Market
Portobello Road, London; Saturday

UNITED STATES

Atlantique City
Atlantic City Convention Centre
Atlantic City, NJ

International Gift and Collectible Expo
Donald E. Stephens Convention Centre
Rosemont, Illinois

For information on the above two shows contact:

Krause Publications
700 East State Street, Iola, WI 54990-9990
Tel.: (877) 746-9757
Fax: (715) 445-4389
www.collectibleshow.com
E-mail: iceshow@krause.com

Doulton Convention and Sale International
Fort Lauderdale, Florida, U.S.A.
Usually February.
For information on times and dates:

Pascoe & Company
575 S.W. 22nd Ave., Miami, Florida 33135
Tel.: (305) 643-2550; Fax: (305) 643-2123
www.pascoeandcompany.com
E-mail: sales@pascoeandcompany.com

Royal Doulton Convention & Sale
Cleveland, Ohio
Usually August. For information on times and dates:
Colonial House Productions
182 Front Street, Berea, Ohio 44308
Tel.: (866) 885-9024; Fax: (866) 854-3117
www.Colonial-House-Collectibles.com
E-mail: yworry@aol.com

FURTHER READING

Storybook Figurines

Beatrix Potter Figures and Giftware edited by Louise Irvine
Beswick Price Guide by Harvey May
Brambly Hedge Collectors Book by Louise Irvine
Bunnykins Collectors Book by Louise Irvine
Cartoon Classics and other Character Figures, by Louise Irvine
Charlton Standard Catalogue of Bunnykins by Jean Dale and Louise Irvine
Charlton Standard Catalogue of Border Fine Arts Storybook Figurines, by Marylin Sweet
Royal Doulton Bunnykins Figures by Louise Irvine

Animals, Figures and Character Jugs

Character Jug Collectors Handbook by Kevin Pearson
Charlton Standard Catalogue of Beswick Animals by Callows and Sweets
Charlton Standard Catalogue of Royal Doulton Animals by Jean Dale
Charlton Standard Catalogue of Royal Doulton Figurines by Jean Dale
Charlton Standard Catalogue of Royal Doulton Jugs by Jean Dale
Collecting Character and Toby Jugs by Jocelyn Lukins
Collecting Doulton Animals by Jocelyn Lukins
Doulton Figure Collectors Handbook by Kevin Pearson
Doulton Flambé Animals by Jocelyn Lukins
Royal Doulton Figures by Desmond Eyles, Louise Irvine and Valerie Baynton

General

Charlton Standard Catalogue of Beswick Pottery by Diane and John Callow
Discovering Royal Doulton by Michael Doulton
Doulton Burslem Advertising Wares by Jocelyn Lukins
Doulton Burslem Wares by Desmond Eyles
Doulton for the Collector by Jocelyn Lukins
Doulton Kingsware Flasks by Jocelyn Lukins
Doulton Lambeth Advertising Ware by Jocelyn Lukins
Doulton Lambeth Wares by Desmond Eyles
Doulton Story by Paul Atterbury and Louise Irvine
George Tinworth by Peter Rose
Hannah Barlow by Peter Rose
John Beswick: A World of Imagination. Catalogue reprint (1950-1996)
Limited Edition Loving Cups by Louise Irvine and Richard Dennis
Phillips Collectors Guide by Catherine Braithwaite
Royal Doulton by Julie McKeown
Royal Doulton by Jennifer Queree
Royal Doulton Series Ware by Louise Irvine (Vols. 1-5)
Sir Henry Doulton Biography by Edmund Gosse

Magazines and Newsletters

"Beswick Quarterly" (Beswick Newsletter) Contact Laura J. Rock-Smith: 10 Holmes Ct., Sayville,
    N.Y. 11782-2408, U.S.A. Tel./Fax 516-589-9027
"Collecting Doulton Magazine", Contact Barry Hill, Collecting Doulton, P.O. Box 310,
    Richmond, Surrey, TW10 7FU, England
"Cottontails" (Newsletter of Bunnykins Collectors' Club), Contact Claire Green: 6 Beckett Way
    Lewes, East Sussesx, BN7 2EB, U.K.: E-mail: claireg@btinternet.com
"Rabbitting On" (Bunnykins Newsletter) Contact Leah Selig: 2 Harper Street, Merrylands 2160,
    New South Wales, Australia. Tel./Fax: 61 2 9637 2410 (International), 02 637 2410 (Australia)

ALICE IN WONDERLAND

EARTHENWARE SERIES 1973-1983
RESIN SERIES 1997-1997
EARTHENWARE SERIES 1998-2000

ALICE IN WONDERLAND
EARTHENWARE SERIES 1973-1983

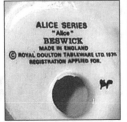

2476
ALICE™
Style One

Designer:	Albert Hallam and Graham Tongue
Height:	4 ¾", 12.1 cm
Colour:	Dark blue dress, white apron with red trim
Issued:	1973 - 1983
Series:	Alice

U.S.	**$500.00**
Can.	**$650.00**
U.K.	**£250.00**
Aust.	**$700.00**

2477
WHITE RABBIT™
Style One

Designer:	Graham Tongue
Height:	4 ¾", 12.1 cm
Colour:	White rabbit wearing a brown coat and yellow waistcoat
Issued:	1973 - 1983
Series:	Alice

U.S.	**$550.00**
Can.	**$675.00**
U.K.	**£275.00**
Aust.	**$600.00**

2478
MOCK TURTLE™

Designer:	Graham Tongue
Height:	4 ¼", 10.8 cm
Colour:	Browns and grey
Issued:	1973 - 1983
Series:	Alice

U.S.	**$325.00**
Can.	**$450.00**
U.K.	**£150.00**
Aust.	**$450.00**

2479
MAD HATTER™
Style One

Designer:	Albert Hallam
Height:	4 ¼", 10.8 cm
Colour:	Burgundy coat, yellow and blue check trousers, yellow and red bowtie, grey hat
Issued:	1973 - 1983
Series:	Alice

U.S.	**$375.00**
Can.	**$500.00**
U.K.	**£225.00**
Aust.	**$525.00**

2480
CHESHIRE CAT™
Style One

Designer:	Albert Hallam and Graham Tongue
Height:	1 ½", 3.8 cm
Colour:	Tabby cat
Issued:	1973 - 1982
Series:	Alice
U.S.	**$550.00**
Can.	**$775.00**
U.K.	**£350.00**
Aust.	**$800.00**

2485
GRYPHON™

Designer:	Albert Hallam
Height:	3 ¼", 8.3 cm
Colour:	Browns and greens
Issued:	1973 - 1983
Series:	Alice
U.S.	**$225.00**
Can.	**$325.00**
U.K.	**£150.00**
Aust.	**$350.00**

2489
KING OF HEARTS™

Designer:	Graham Tongue
Height:	3 ¾", 9.5 cm
Colour:	Burgundy, yellow, white, blue and green
Issued:	1973 - 1983
Series:	Alice
U.S.	**$150.00**
Can.	**$225.00**
U.K.	**£ 90.00**
Aust.	**$225.00**

2490
QUEEN OF HEARTS™
Style One

Designer:	Graham Tongue
Height:	4", 10.1 cm
Colour:	Blue, green, yellow, white and burgundy
Issued:	1973 - 1983
Series:	Alice
U.S.	**$150.00**
Can.	**$225.00**
U.K.	**£ 90.00**
Aust.	**$225.00**

ALICE SERIES
"Dodo"
BESWICK
MADE IN ENGLAND
© ROYAL DOULTON TABLEWARE LTD. 1975
REGISTRATION APPLIED FOR.

ALICE SERIES
"Fish Footman"
BESWICK
MADE IN ENGLAND
© ROYAL DOULTON TABLEWARE LTD. 1975
REGISTRATION APPLIED FOR.

ALICE SERIES
"Frog Footman"
BESWICK
MADE IN ENGLAND
© ROYAL DOULTON TABLEWARE LTD. 1975
REGISTRATION APPLIED FOR.

2545
DODO™
Style One

Designer:	David Lyttleton
Height:	4", 10.1 cm
Colour:	Browns and greens
Issued:	1975 - 1983
Series:	Alice
U.S.	**$300.00**
Can.	**$450.00**
U.K.	**£200.00**
Aust.	**$475.00**

2546
FISH FOOTMAN™

Designer:	David Lyttleton
Height:	4 ¾", 14.6 cm
Colour:	Blue, gold, white and brown
Issued:	1975 - 1983
Series:	Alice
U.S.	**$375.00**
Can.	**$550.00**
U.K.	**£225.00**
Aust.	**$575.00**

2547
FROG FOOTMAN™

Designer:	David Lyttleton
Height:	4 ¼", 10.8 cm
Colour:	Maroon jacket with yellow trim, blue trousers
Issued:	1975 - 1983
Series:	Alice
U.S.	**$375.00**
Can.	**$550.00**
U.K.	**£225.00**
Aust.	**$575.00**

ALICE IN WONDERLAND
RESIN SERIES 1997-1997

The Alice in Wonderland resin series does not carry a backstamp. It was sold as a set through Lawleys By Post.

ALICE™
Style Two

Modeller:	Adrian Hughes
Size:	4", 10.1 cm
Colour:	Pale blue, white, red and green
Issued:	1997 - 1997
U.S.	**$35.00**
Can.	**$50.00**
U.K.	**£20.00**
Aust.	**$50.00**

CHESHIRE CAT™
Style Two

Modeller:	Adrian Hughes
Size:	4", 10.1 cm
Colour:	Ginger, blue, red, and brown
Issued:	1997 - 1997
U.S.	**$35.00**
Can.	**$50.00**
U.K.	**£20.00**
Aust.	**$50.00**

DODO™
Style Two

Modeller:	Adrian Hughes
Size:	4", 10.1 cm
Colour:	White, blue, yellow and black
Issued:	1997 - 1997
U.S.	**$35.00**
Can.	**$50.00**
U.K.	**£20.00**
Aust.	**$50.00**

MAD MATTER™
Style Two

Modeller:	Adrian Hughes
Size:	4", 10.1 cm
Colour:	Brown, green, and blue
Issued:	1997 - 1997
U.S.	**$35.00**
Can.	**$50.00**
U.K.	**£20.00**
Aust.	**$50.00**

QUEEN OF HEARTS™
Style Two

Modeller:	Adrian Hughes
Size:	4", 10.1 cm
Colour:	Red, white and black
Issued:	1997 - 1997
U.S.	**$35.00**
Can.	**$50.00**
U.K.	**£20.00**
Aust.	**$50.00**

WHITE RABBIT™
Style Two

Modeller:	Adrian Hughes
Size:	4", 10.1 cm
Colour:	White, brown and green
Issued:	1997 - 1997 edition of 2,500
U.S.	**$35.00**
Can.	**$50.00**
U.K.	**£20.00**
Aust.	**$50.00**

ALICE IN WONDERLAND
EARTHENWARE SERIES 1998-2000

LC 1
THE MAD HATTER'S TEA PARTY™

Modeller:	Martyn Alcock
Size:	5" x 8 ½", 12.7 x 21.6 cm
Colour:	Green, yellow, red and blue
Issued:	1998 in a limited edition of 1,998
Series:	1. Alice's Adventures
	2. Tableau

Beswick Number	Price U.S. $	Can. $	U.K. £	Aust. $
LC 1	250.00	350.00	150.00	350.00

Note: Issued to commemorate the centenary of Lewis Carroll's death.

LC 2
ALICE™
Style Three

Modeller:	Martyn Alcock
Size:	4 ½", 11.9 cm
Colour:	Pink and white
Issued:	1999 in a limited edition of 2,500
Series:	Alice's Adventures
U.S.	**$125.00**
Can.	**$175.00**
U.K.	**£ 75.00**
Aust.	**$150.00**

Note: Issued, numbered, sold as a pair with the Cheshire Cat.

LC 3
CHESHIRE CAT™
Style Three

Modeller:	Martyn Alcock
Size:	3 ½", 8.9 cm
Colour:	Ginger striped cat
Issued:	1999 in a limited edition of 2,500
Series:	Alice's Adventures
U.S.	**$125.00**
Can.	**$175.00**
U.K.	**£ 75.00**
Aust.	**$150.00**

Note: Issued, numbered and sold as a pair with Alice.

LC 4
QUEEN OF HEARTS™
Style Three

Modeller:	Martyn Alcock
Size:	5 ¼", 13.3 cm
Colour:	Red, dark blue, yellow and pink
Issued:	2000 in a limited edition of 2,500
Series:	Alice's Adventures
U.S.	**$ 85.00**
Can.	**$125.00**
U.K.	**£ 50.00**
Aust.	**$150.00**

BEATRIX POTTER
FIGURINES

NOTES ON COLLECTING BESWICK BEATRIX POTTER FIGURES

by Frank W. Corley

The key to serious collecting of Beswick Beatrix Potter figures is making sense of the somewhat confusing series of changes to many of the original figures that took place between 1970 and 1975. In retrospect, these changes portray a particularly turbulent transition period during which the old Beswick corporate culture was being supplanted by that of Royal Doulton, the new owners as of 1969. Although the changes were little noticed by customers and collectors at the time, in later years they have had the effect of shifting the emphasis in Beswick Beatrix Potter collecting to the changes rather than the original figures. The many versions, variations and multiple associated backstamps of many of those thirty-seven original figures apparently were the consequence of well-intended management steps to improve the production side of things at Royal Doulton's newly-acquired Stoke-on-Trent plant. While we do not have an insider's account of the rationales underlying the then-new management's initiatives, the evidence that came off the production line in that period strongly suggests that major decisions were made in several areas, though unevenly implemented.

Decision 1: do something about the untidy plethora of gold oval backstamps:

* the lettering on the gold oval backstamps, which had replaced the gold circle (and gold parallel lines) in 1955, had evolved into a rather sloppy assortment of styles — large script, small script, large block letters, hand-made block letters, reverse slant script and two more styles of smaller size block letters. While the gold oval was a constant, the lettering style was associated only with figures introduced in a particular year, rather than with the whole range of production. It seems as if whenever new figues were introduced someone was told to go off in a corner, speak to no one, and design a new lettering format; that format was then used for that/those figure(s) from then on. Perhaps the grossest example involves the three 1955 figures (Duchess [with flowers], Pigling Bland, and Tommy Brock), with their very crude hand-made block letters.

* In any event, Beswick went off the gold standard at the end of 1972 in favour of a new, standardized brown-lettered backstamp, the initial version of which, like all its gold predecessors, did not carry a copyright date (the Charlton BP-3a).

* a copyright date was added in 1975, a decision that probably was driven by legal considerations (the BP-3b).

Decision 2: improve production efficiency for certain figures by simplyfying their moulds:

* at the expense of a loss in aesthetic appeal Benjamin Bunny's shoes, Mrs. Rabbit's umbrella and Mr. Benjamin Bunny's pipe were moulded to their bodies to reduce susceptibility to damage in the production process and to improve yields; also, the top of Tommy Brock's spade handle was eliminated and a minor change made to the tip of the bottle in Appley Dappley's basket for similar reasons.

Decision 3: simplify the decoration process and improve the eye-appeal of certain figures by lightening the colours:

* the colours of Squirrel Nutkin's coat and nut were lightened, Little Pig Robinson's striped tunic was replaced with a blue textured one, Pigling Bland's and Mr. Benjamin Bunny's dark maroon coats were changed to lilac, the top of Tabitha Twitchett's striped dress and the patterned dress of Goody Tiptoes became plain, and, Mr. Jackson's skin became brown instead of green.

Decision 4: standardise hand painting to improve quality control and decrease the range of hand painting variation:

* broad 'discretion' in the hand painting phase, which had been a Beswick hallmark since the Beatrix Potter line was introduced, was curtailed. This discretion had resulted in strikingly different variations of some figures in the same time frames. For example, Timmy Tiptoes was produced with both red and pink jackets; the pattern of Mrs. Tiggy-winkle's dress was sometimes diagonal, sometimes square; Mr. Jeremy Fisher usually had spots on his legs but sometimes had stripes; and, Miss Moppet was sometimes mottled, sometimes striped and sometimes in between. Although the catalogues mistakenly continue to describe "variation one" as ending and "variation two" as originating in the 1972-1975 time frame, in fact, what happened was that the standardisation process simply eliminated one of the two existing variations, with the surviving version labeled as the second despite the fact that it had existed all along. Thus, Timmy Tiptoes'

red jacket, Mrs. Tiggy-winkle's diagonal dress pattern, Mr. Jeremy Fisher's spots and Miss Moppet's mottled fur were eliminated, apparently in the interests of standardisation.

* the size of Tommy Brock's eye patch is in a category similar to the above. For the sixteen or so years prior to the transition period the size of Tommy Brock's eye patches varied within fairly small limits — mainly half-way between the two now familiar extremes, and alway curling inward towards the centre of his forehead with a somewhat feathery appearance; they all had open spade handles. Those differences in eye patch size would probably have gone unnoticed except that during the transition an initial decision was made to use a very small eye patch as well as a closed spade handle. A year or two later, the eye patch part of the decision was reversed in favour of a very large eye patch. Both of the new styles are readily recognisable by their exaggerated sizes — one small, one large — crisp rather than fuzzy appearance and the fact that they point in a straight line towards the ears rather than curling inward towards the centre of the forehead. In the actual production process, the patch changes, the spade handle change and the backstamp change were uncoordinated, resulting in multiple combinations of eye patch styles, spade handle configurations and backstamps.

* a number of less obvious colour standardisation changes were made to address long-time variations not much noticed by the collecting world until recent years:

    * Timmy Tiptoe's brown and grey fur variations became grey only;

    * Benjamin Bunny's light tan/light green jacket variations changed to a rich dark brown during the transition— and then to a luxurious cream in the later years of the Royal Albert period;

    * Other changes: Mrs. Rabbit (dress colours), Goody Tiptoes (dress colour, pattern and a longer base), Old Mr. Brown (colour of squirrel), Amiable Guinea Pig (jacket colour), Aunt Petitoes (dress colour), Pigwig (skin and dress colours), and, Sir Isaac Newton (jacket colour, scarf pattern).

* in addition to the foregoing colour standardisation changes, but several years later, the dark blues of the following figures were changed to a light blue: Peter Rabbit, Tom Kitten, The Old Woman Who Lived in a Shoe, Anna Maria, Cecily Parsley, and, Mrs. Flopsy Bunny. The reason for this is not clear but it has been suggested that it was done out of paint formulae considerations. But, curiously, the dark blue of Mrs. Rabbit and the Bunnies was not changed. Distressingly, all these light blues evolved into sickly pale blues during the Royal Albert period.

It would appear that undertaking to tune-up the entire range of Beatrix Potter production, while probably successful from a management point of view, resulted in some figures being produced in multiple versions, variations and backstamps before things settled down. In particular, for figures undergoing both a mould change and a decorating change synchronisation of the two changes was not in the cards. The result is a collector's dream: multiple mould, colour, pattern and design changes with up to three backstamp possibilities — BP-2, BP-3a and BP-3b.

Changes to the gold circle (BP-1a) backstamps prior to the 1955 introduction of the gold oval (BP-2):

* The 1955 change to the gold oval backstamp to accommodate small base figures was preceded by a gold parallel lines style with the words Beswick and England one atop the other in tiny gold block letters. When Tailor of Gloucester was introduced in 1949 there were obvious problems in accommodating the Beswick-England gold circle, plus the other backstamp information, in the limited space available on Tailor of Gloucester's small base. Beswick's solution was to create what Charlton calls the BP-1b backstamp. An unknown, but small, quantity of Tailor of Gloucester, first version, may have been produced with the gold circle but the new backstamp quickly replaced it. Several of the original ten 1948 figures also have shown up with the BP-1b design but Tailor of Gloucester is the only one on which it was used with any consistency. Use of the BP-1b backstamp was discontinued in 1951.

* The gold oval modification. Beswick was presented with a similar small base problem in 1951 when Mrs. Rabbit was introduced. However instead of using the rather unattractive gold parallel line design a gold oval modification of the original gold circle, now known as the Charlton BP-2 backstamp, was developed. An unknown but small quantity of Mrs. Rabbit, first version, were produced with the gold circle.

* In 1954, another small base figure, Johnny Town-Mouse, was introduced and relative scarcity of that figure with the gold circle suggests that the new gold oval was used early-on, despite the fact that it — the BP-2 — did not become official for all standard range figures until a year later.

* The relative scarcity of gold circles for the other three 1954 figures (Miss Moppet, Flopsy, Mopsy and Cottontail and Foxy Whiskered Gentleman) suggests that in addition to the gold circle the gold oval was heavily used prior to 1955.

* While general use of the gold oval (BP-2) for all standard range figures did not begin until 1955, it seems probable that use of the BP-1b for Tailor of Gloucester was ended in 1951 in favour of the new gold oval.

Other notes:

* The metamorphoses of Benjamin Bunny are of particular collector interest: leaving aside the shoe and ear mould changes the early catalogue descriptions had version one wearing a pale green jacket, version two a brown jacket and version three a light tan jacket; the pompon on the tam was orange with red stripes. In fact: version one varied between pale green, light tan and in between; version two started out the same as version one, but very quickly changed to brown, with a solid orange pompon; version three started out as brown and remained that colour until it became cream sometime in the Royal Albert period. In sum, three mould versions, three backstamp possibilties, two pompon colour schemes, and, three jacket colours overlapping and occurring within a span of about three years! Are there exceptions to the above? Of course, that's what hand painting is all about!

* Mrs. Tiggy-Winkle: while there are dress pattern differences in the early years they seem minor and insufficient to justify a version one vs. version two distinction.

* Timmy Willie: the multicoloured base on some of the early figures — mainly BP-1's — is very attractive and is an example of desirable decorator discretion. The multicoloured base variation is a must for the serious collector!

* Sally Henny Penny: some of the BP-3a's and early BP-3b's have red hearts rather than checks on the breast feathers, and, a tiny red tongue in an open mouth. Note: the open mouth appears to be a matter of whether the mould used was new and clean or clogged from repeated use; in any event, there are definitely open mouth versions.

* Louise Irvine B1 and B3 backstamps: when brown backstamps were introduced in 1973 the Beswick designers of the five latest figures at that time — Appley Dappley, Pickles, Pig-Wig, Mr. Alderman Ptolemy and Sir Isaac Newton — had apparently anticipated the change over and had produced slightly different variations of the new brown backstamp design. The first three figures were similar to the new design in all respects except that the figure names are all in capital letters; this anomaly, Irvine's B-1 category, applies to all of the no copyright date figures (BP-3a's) as well as some copyright date figures (BP-3b's). The last two figures also used the new brown lettering format except that the words "made in England" are used versus the single word "England"; this is Irvine's B-3 category and again the anomaly applies to both no copyright date and copyright date versions. The B1/B3 anomalies disappeared sometime after 1975.

SCARCEST BESWICK BEATRIX POTTER FIGURES
THE RAREST OF THE RARE

Abbreviated Relative Scarcity Lists of Beswick and
Royal Albert Beatrix Potter Figures/Versions

To arrive at a comfortable perspective on scarcity and value of Beswick/Royal Albert Beatrix Potter figures a collector needs to acquire a data base of the relative number of each figure, version and variation produced. The lists which follow are shortened versions of complete lists that were created as tools for estimating relative scarcity, which is the key to value. In the form presented they represent raw data based on presumed years in production broken down not only by figure, version and variation but also by backstamp.

The data are considered raw because years-in-production is only the starting point in determining relative value. Years- in-production does not mean equal numbers of different figures produced the same number of years. For example, Duchess (with flowers) was in production for thirteen years, Duchess (with pie) for four; yet, the first Duchess appears to be the scarcer figure – although, it may not be, And, Peter Rabbit in a given year surely was produced in far greater quantities then, say, Mrs. Flopsy Bunny.

The term scarcity is used in preference to rarity because, while the difference between the terms may be minimal in an academic sense, scarcity seems more data driven and to connote a number, whereas rarity tends to imply a judgment of the collector community, hence connoting value.

The term value, while related to scarcity, is related to the number of active collectors in search of a particular figure at a particular time; it is inherently relative, reflecting a judgment of the collecting community at a particular time, or, in a particular auction. Also, even though a figure might be quite scarce in an absolute sense its value will decrease as the number of collectors possessing it increases: supply and demand, pure and simple.

In the real world, collectors searching for items being resold in various secondary markets see scarcity as a reflection of what is appearing in the markets they see, with the number of a particular figure likely to appear in a particular secondary market at a particular time related, in a broad sense, to the actual number originally produced. Many other factors contribute to local scarcity: geographic distribution when initially marketed; susceptibility of particular figures to breakage, changes in the kinds of things people collect; the age factor where old figures simply disappear, etc.

Although hard data to determine scarcity is not available, the auction sites have compensated to a degree by vastly increasing the number and variety of figures available on the secondary market. How? By simply pulling out of attics, basements, closets, shoe boxes, etc. figures that otherwise would remain unavailable to collectors. In its short lifespan eBay has done a remarkably efficient job of matching up the relatively limited pool of collectors with an increased quantity of available figures. As a result prices/values have decreased substantially. Assuming willing-buyer, willing-seller transactions are the final arbiter of true value, tracking eBay transactions can provide a serious collector with an authoritative range of a figure's current value.

Except: Except that sometimes there may be an intrinsic value based on real scarcity that escapes the perception of the collecting community as well as that of dealers and investors. For example, Mr. Jackson, variation one (green frog) is easily among the scarcest Beswick Beatrix Potter variations yet its price is relatively modest.

Except: Except that different collectors collect different parts of the Beswick figure/version/variation/backstamp spectrum. That is, many Beswick Beatrix Potter collectors collect only a portion of the figures available, or, ignore the different versions and variations and backstamps.

Except: Except that there are overlapping collector communities that distort availability of certain type figures. For example, cat collectors search out Ginger and Simpkin, mouse collectors search out Anna Maria and rabbit collectors collect Peter, Benjamin etc. – all to the exclusion of the full range of Beatrix Potter figures.

Except: Except that auction sales prices seem to vary seasonally: a high value figure listed without reserve during a holiday period might sell for a deceptively low price.

Except. Except that scarce figures tend to have greater value than scarce versions or variations which, in turn, tend to have greater vakue than scarce backstamps – all other thinks being equal:

* figure scarcity – figures which have appeared in only one version or variation are inherently of greater value than multi-version/variation figures because many collectors do not collect multiple versions/variations.

* version/variation scarcity – the appeal and collectability of individual versions or variations of multiple version/variation figures is related to unique discernable differences – something that can be seen by a viewer. Thus, for example, a version two or version three Benjamin Bunny is collectable in its own right because the differences can be seen,

* backstamp scarcity – since different backstamps can be detected only through handling, the appeal of a figure having a short run with a particular backstamp tends to be esoteric and limited

to a smaller segment of the collector community. Nonetheless, scarce backstamps, particularly the first backstamp used on a figure/version/variation, are highly collectable. It is just that there are few collectors willing to pay the price scarcity might otherwise command. This abbreviated list shows mainly backstamps with one year of less production.

Caveat: in using auction prices as a guide to value, take the long view, because auction prices can vary widely from one week to the next.

In the absence of better data, using the number of years a particular figure/version/variation was in production is a reasonable starting point for estimating the number of figures that exist in a global, collecting sense. Hence, a good clue to current relative scarcity. Another caveat: unsuccessful figures such as Duchess (with flowers) never in their best years were produced in numbers comparable to, say, Peter Rabbit in his worst year, sales-wise.

Following is an abbreviated listing of the scarcest figures/versions/variations, plus the old Beswick figures retired early. Parts I to III are abbreviated listings of original Beswick, Royal Albert and new Beswick figures and major versions/variations thereof, in descending order of scarcity. Part IV is a combined listing and Part V lists scarce backstamps.

Ideally there should be a separate (and later) step in which the raw data would be "massaged" to take account of (1) different levels of production of individual figures, (2) individual figure susceptibility to damage and (3) an "age factor" where over a time a number of figures simply disappear beyond the reach of collectors. Such an effort would result in more accurate final scarcity rankings.

Corley's Short List of Scarce Beswick/Royal Albert Beatrix Potter Figures

I – OLD BESWICK

Figure	Version/Variation	Years in production
Mr. Benjamin Bunny	v 1b	<1 (rare)
Mr. Jeremy Fisher Digging		1
Mr. Tod		1
Johnny Town-Mouse with Bag		1
Mr. Jackson (green frog)	v 1	1
Little Pig Robinson Spying		2
Tom Kitten and Butterfly		2
Tom Thumb		2
Mr. Benjamin Bunny	v 2a	2
Benjamin Bunny	v 2	2 – maybe as many as 4
Tommy Brock	v 3	2 – maybe as many as 3
Cecily Parsley	v 2	3
Benjamin Bunny Sat on a Bank	v 1	3
Benjamin Bunny Sat on a Bank	v 2	3

Plus, the 12 old Beswick figures retired early:

Duchess (with Pie)	4
Old Mr. Pricklepin	6
Susan	6
Ginger	7
Thomasina Tittlemouse	8
Simpkin	9
Pig-Wig	11
Pickles	12
Sir Isaac Newton	12
Duchess (with flowers)	13
Amiable Guinea Pig	17
Anna Maria	21

II – ROYAL ALBERT

Note: bold face type = originally issued as old Beswick

Figure	Years
Susan	<1 (small handful)
Thomasina Tittlemouse	<1 (scarce)
Old Mr. Pricklepin	<1 (scarce)
Mrs. Rabbit and Peter	2
Peter with Postbag	3
Peter with Daffodils	3

III — NEW BESWICK

Note: bold face type = originally issued as old Beswick or Royal Albert

Figure	Version/Variation	Years in Production
Peter Ate a Radish		>0 (tiny handful)
And This Pig Had None		>0
Benjamin Ate a Lettuce Leaf		>0
Mrs. Flopsy Bunny		>0
Pigling Bland	v 2	>0
Peter and the Red Pocket Handkerchief		<1
Peter with Daffodils		<1
Mrs. Rabbit Cooking		<1
Jemima Puddle-Duck and Foxy Whiskered Gentleman		<1
Old Mr Brown		<1
Jeremy Fisher Catches a Fish	v 1	<1
Tom Kitten	v 2	<1
Two Gentleman Rabbits		1
Mrs. Tiggy-Winkle Buys Provisions		1
Head Gardener		1
Little Pig Robinson	v 2	1*
Peter Rabbit Gardening		>1
Hunca Munca		>1
Lady Mouse		<2
Ribby		<2
Mr. Drake Puddle-Duck		<2
Rebeccah Puddle-Duck		<2*
Squirrel Nutkin	v 2	<2
Mrs. Tiggy-Winkle	v 2	<2
Mr. Benjamin Bunny	V 2b	<2*
Hunca Munca		2
Peter Rabbit Digging		2
Hunca Munca Sweeping		2*
Mrs. Rabbit and Peter		2
Mr. Jeremy Fisher	v 2	2

Note: the four asterisked figures were re-issued in the closing months of 2002 with new "P" numbers and with BP-11 John Beswick signature backstamps. All four were originally old Beswick figures which also had been produced as Royal Albert and as new Beswick figures; they had been discontinued after varying periods of production with the Beswick BP-10 series backstamps.

IV – COMBINED : OLD BESWICK< ROYAL ALBERT AND NEW BESWICK

Figure	Old Beswick Years	Royal Albert Years	New Beswick Years	O/A Total Years
Jeremy Fisher Catches a Fish (v-1)	0	0	<1	<1
Two Gentlemen Rabbits	0	0	<1	<1
Mrs. Tiggy-Winkle Buys Provisions	0	0	<1	<1
Head Gardener	0	0	<1	<1
Mr. Benjamin Bunny (v 1b)	1	0	0	<1
Mr. Jackson (green frog) (v 1)	1	0	0	1
Mr. Peter Rabbit Gardening	0	0	>1	>1
Hunca Munca, style two	0	0	2	2
Peter Rabbit Digging	0	0	2	2
Mr. Benjamin Bunny (v 2a)	2	0	0	2
Benjamin Bunny (v 2)	2	0	0	2
Mrs. Tiggy-Winkle Washing	0	0	<3	<3
Tom Kitten in the Rockery	0	0	3	3
Johnny Town-Mouse Eating Corn	0	0	3	3
Yock-Yock in the Tub	0	0	3	3
Timmy Willie Fetching Milk	0	0	3	3
Farmer Potatoes	0	0	3	3
Mrs. Tittlemouse, style two	0	0	3	3
Amiable Guinea Pig, style two	0	0	3	3
Tommy Brock (v 3)	3	0	0	3
Benjamin Bunny Sat on a Bank (v 1)	3	0	0	3
Peter with Daffodils	0	3	<1	<4
Jeremy Fisher Catches a Fish (v 2)	0	0	4	4
Fierce Bad Rabbit (v 1)	4	0	0	4

Plus, the 12 old Beswick figures retired early:

Figure	Old Beswick Years	Royal Albert Years	New Beswick Years	O/A Total Years
Duchess (with pie)	4	0	0	4
Susan	6	<1	0	<7
Old Mr. Pricklepin	6	<1	0	<7
Ginger	7	0	0	7
Thomasina Tittlemouse	8	<1	0	<9
Simpkin	9	0	0	9
Pig-Wig	11	0	0	11
Pickles	12	0	0	12
Sir Isaac Newton	12	0	0	12
Duchess (with flowers)	13	0	0	13
Amiable Guinea Pig	17	0	0	17
Anna Maria	21	0	0	21

V - BACKSTAMP SCARCITY

BP-1a (gold circle) backstamps

Figure	Version/Variation	Years Produced
Duchess (with flowers)		<1 (tiny handful)
Tommy Brock	v 1 and v 2	<1 (tiny handful)
Pigling Bland	v 1	<1 (tiny handful)
Tailor of Gloucester		<1* (very rare)
Johnny Town-Mouse		<1* (very rare)
Mrs. Rabbit	v 1	<1* (rare)
Miss Moppet	v 1 and v 2	1 (very scarce)
Flopsy, Mospy and Cottontail, style one		1 (very scarce)
Foxy Whiskered Gentleman		1 (very scarce)

* Difficulties with fitting the gold circle on small base figures first surfaced in 1949 with Tailor of Gloucester and led to the ultra small-type (and unattractive) gold parallel lines backstamp. A similar problem arose in 1951 with the introduction of Mrs. Rabbit, which led to the so-called "flattened circle" (oval) modification of the gold circle. In 1955 this special oval backstamp became standard and is now known as the BP-2. Another small base figure, Johnny Town-Mouse, apparently began using the gold oval soon after its introduction in 1954; its gold version is very rare.

BP-1b (gold parallel lines) backstamps

Figure	Version/Variation	Years Produced
Tailor of Gloucester		2 (scarce)

BP-2 (gold oval) backstamps

Figure	Version/Variation	Years Produced
Pig-Wig		<1 (tiny handful)
Benjamin Bunny	v 2	<1 (rare)

BP-3a (brown no copyright date) backstamps

Figure	Version/Variation	Years Produced
Mr. Benjamin Bunny	vers. 2 / var. 2	1
Sally Henny Penny		1
Sir Isaac Newton		2
Mr. Alderman Ptolemy		2

BP-5 (gold backstamp Royal Albert) backstamps

Figure	Version/Variation	Years Produced
Jemima Puddle-Duck		1 (scarce)
Peter Rabbit	v 2	1 (scarce)
Benjamin Bunny	v 3	1 (scarce)
Hunca Munca, style one		1 (scarce)
Flopsy, Mopsy and Cottontail, style one		1 (scarce)
Mrs. Rabbit and Bunnies		1 (scarce)

BP-6 (brown Royal Albert) backstamps

Figure	Version/Variation	Years Produced
Susan		<1 (small handful)
Thomasina Tittlemouse		<1 (scarce)
Old Mr. Pricklepin		<1 (scarce)

BP-8a (Beswick Ware) backstamps

Figure	Version/Variation	Years Produced
Jemima and Her Ducklings		<1 (tiny handful)
Mrs. Tiggy-Winkle Washing		<1 (about 1700)

BP-10a/b/c (Beswick) backstamps

Note: excepting Peter Rabbit Gardening all of these figures were introduced as either old Beswick or Royal Albert figures.

Figure	Version/Variation	Years Produced
Peter Ate a Radish (10b)		>0 (tiny handful)
And This Pig Had None (10a)		>0
Benjamin Ate a Lettuce Leaf		>0
Mrs. Flopsy Bunny (10b)		>0
Pigling Bland (10c)	v 2	>0
Peter / Red Pocket Handkerchief (10a)		<1
Mrs. Rabbit Cooking (10b)		<1
Tom Kitten (10c)	v 2	1
Old Mr. Brown (10a)		1
Jemima Puddle-Duck and Foxy Whiskered Gentleman (10b)		1
Peter with Daffodils (10b)		1
Peter Rabbit Gardening (10b)		>1

BP-11 (Beswick) backstamps (Oct.-Dec. 2002 reissues)

Figure	Version/Variation	Years Produced
Little Pig Robinson	v 2	<1 (3 months)
Mr. Benjamin Bunny	v 2b	<1 (3 months)
Hunca Munca Sweeping		<1 (3 months)
Rebeccah Puddle-Duck		<1 (3 months)

BEATRIX POTTER BACKSTAMPS

BP-1   **BESWICK GOLD CIRCLE AND
BESWICK GOLD PARALLEL LINES
ISSUED 1948 TO 1954**

The Beswick-England gold circle backstamp (BP-1a) was the primary backstamp used from the introduction of the first ten figures in 1948 through 1954. However, three small base figures introduced during that period could not easily accommodate the full gold circle and forced changes in the backstamp design.

The first small base figure, Tailor of Gloucester, introduced in 1949, resulted in the creation of a special backstamp especially for that figure – the BP-1b gold parallel lines backstamp which has the words Beswick and England in very small type. While the BP-1b was used in small quantities on several other figures, such usage was likely simply a matter of production line convenience.

The second figure presenting problems for the full gold circle was Mrs. Rabbit, introduced in 1951. In this instance instead of using the unattractive BP-1b parallel lines design the gold circle was "modified" into a gold oval – which is now called the BP-2. In addition, it appears likely that use of the BP-1b on Tailor of Gloucester was discontinued at this time in favour of the gold oval.

The third small base figure, Johnny Town-Mouse, introduced in 1954, apparently used the new gold oval almost from the start of production and probably led to the decision to simplify the backstamp situation by using the gold oval (BP-2) design for all figures starting in 1955. This much is clear: there are only a tiny handful of gold circle backstamps on the three small base figures introduced prior to 1955 – and all of these are probably pre-production prototypes produced prior to the start of the regular production.

It should be noted that a tiny handful of each of the three figures introduced in 1955 – Tommy Brock, Duchess with Flowers, and Pigling Bland – were produced with the gold circle backstamp. In all likelihood, all of these are pre-production prototypes produced in 1954 for marketing purposes.

BP-1a (gold circle). The first variety has the words "Beswick" and "England" forming a circle; the word "copyright" may or may not appear. While this variety was used on a total of 24 figures plus one variation, it is found only in miniscule quantities on six of these:

Duchess with Flowers
Johnny Town-Mouse
Mrs. Rabbit
Pigling Bland
Tailor of Gloucester
Tommy Brock

BP-1a Beswick Gold Circle

The following is a list of the 18 figures which regularly used the BP-1a backstamp:

Benjamin Bunny, first version
Flopsy, Mopsy and Cottontail, style one
Foxy Whiskered Gentleman, first version, first variation
Hunca Munca, style one
Jemima Puddle-Duck, first version, first variation
Lady Mouse
Little Pig Robinson, first variation
Miss Moppet, first variation
Mr. Jeremy Fisher, first version, first and second variations
Mrs. Tiggy-Winkle, first version, first variation
Mrs. Tittlemouse, style one
Peter Rabbit, first version, first variation
Ribby
Samuel Whiskers
Squirrel Nutkin, first version, first variation
Timmy Tiptoes, first variation
Timmy Willie
Tom Kitten, first version, first variation

BP-1b (gold parallel lines). The second variety has the words "Beswick" and "England" arranged in parallel lines, one atop the other; the word "Copyright" appears in script. This variety was created for use on Tailor of Gloucester but was used in error on several other figures incuding:

BP-1b Beswick Gold Parallel Lines

Benjamin Bunny, first version
Little Pig Robinson, first variation
Peter Rabbit, first version, first variation
The Tailor of Gloucester, first version
Tom Kitten, first version, first variation

BP-2   **BESWICK GOLD OVAL**
                           ISSUED 1955 TO 1972

BP-2a The gold oval was in use for 18 years, between 1955 and 1972, on 38 figures plus 4 versions/variations. The last gold oval figure, "Pig-Wig," was introduced in late 1972. The tiny number of gold oval Pig Wig's produced suggests that they were the usual pre-production prototypes and that, because plans to introduce the brown line backstamp in 1973 were at full throttle, all 1972 regular production Pig-Wig's received the no-copyright-date variety of the new backstamps. The following is a list of figures that can found with a BP-2 backstamp:

BP-2 Beswick Gold Oval

Amiable Guinea-Pig, style one
Anna Maria
Apply Dappley, first version
Aunt Pettitoes
Benjamin Bunny, first and second versions
Cecily Parsley, first version
Cousin Ribby
Duchess, style one (with flowers)
Flopsy, Mopsy and Cottontail, style one
Foxy Whiskered Gentleman, first version, first variation
Goody Tiptoes
Hunca Munca, style one
Jemima Puddle-Duck, first version, first variation
Johnny Town-Mouse
Lady Mouse
Little Pig Robinson, first variation
Miss Moppet, first variation
Mr. Benjamin Bunny, first version
Mr. Jeremy Fisher, first version, first variation
Mrs. Flopsy Bunny
Mrs. Rabbit, first version
Mrs. Tiggy-Winkle, first version, first and second variations
Mrs. Tittlemouse, style one
Old Mr. Brown
Old Woman Who Lived in a Shoe, The
Peter Rabbit, first version, first variation
Pickles
Pigling Bland, first variation
Pig-Wig
Ribby
Samuel Whiskers
Squirrel Nutkin, first version, first variation
Tabitha Twitchit, first variation
Tailor of Gloucester, first version
Timmy Tiptoes, first and second variations
Timmy Willie From Johnny Town-Mouse
Tom Kitten, first version, first variation
Tommy Brock, first version, first and second variations

BP-2b   **Transitional Gold/Brown**
                           Issued 1971 - 1972

BP-2b Between BP-2 and BP-3 there exist transitional backstamps. These appear on a very limited number of figures. The backstamp is part gold and part brown line; usually "Beatrix Potter" and the figure's name appear in gold with the last three lines in brown.

Part gold, part brown line backstamp

The following is a list of figures known to carry the transitional backstamp:

Flopsy, Mopsy and Cottontail
Mr. Benjamin Bunny, first version
Mrs. Tittlemouse, style one
Peter Rabbit, first version, first variation
Squirrel Nutkin, first version, first variation
Timmy Tiptoes, first variation

BP-3   **BESWICK BROWN LINE**
                           ISSUED 1973 TO 1988

BP-3a Potter's, no date, issued 1973 to 1974
(no copyright date)
Used on 41 figures, plus 9 versions/varieties

The overall BP-3 category groups eight minor backstamp varieties into three major categories, as set forth below. In each category, the words "Beswick" and "England" appear in brown lettering either in a straight line or with "Beswick" atop "England," depending on the size or shape of the base. Over a period of 16 years BP-3 category backstamps were used on a total of 70 figures plus 27 versions/variations.

Note: The eight minor varieties are described in Louise Irvine's "Beatrix Potter Figures," 2nd edition, pp74-75. Three of the varieties (B1, B3 abd B4) are included in BP-3a; three (B2, B5 and B6) are included in BP-3b; and two (B7 and B8) are included in BP-3c. Similarly, there are two varieties (B9 and B10) included in BP-4."

BP-3b Potter's, date, issued 1974 to 1985
(copyright date)
Used on 63 figures, plus 16 versions/varieties

BP-3c Potter, date, issued 1985 to 1988
(no "s" on Potter)
Used on 63 figures, plus 16 versions/varieties

BP-4   **BESWICK SIGNATURE**
ISSUED 1988 TO 1989

BEATRIX POTTER
"Mr. Jeremy Fisher Digging"
© F.Warne & Co. 1988
Licensed by Copyrights
John Beswick
Studio of Royal Doulton
England

BP-4 Beswick Signature
Used on a total of 29 figures

This era saw the Beswick backstamp converted to the Royal Doulton backstamp. The connection with Beswick was kept by the addition of the John Beswick signature to the backstamp. In use for a year to a year and a half, this is one of the shortest time periods for a backstamp.

BP-5   **ROYAL ALBERT GOLD CROWN**
ISSUED 1989

BP-5 Royal Albert Gold Crown

The gold backstamp was reinstituted for 1989 to mark the change from the Doulton/Beswick backstamps to Royal Albert. It was used on only the following six figures:

Benjamin Bunny, third version, first variation
Flopsy, Mopsy and Cottontail, style one
Hunca Munca, style one
Jemima Puddleduck, first version, first variation
Mrs. Rabbit and Bunnies
Peter Rabbit, first version, second variation

BP-6   **ROYAL ALBERT BROWN CROWN**
ISSUED 1989 TO 1998

BP-6a Small brown crown   **BP-6b** Large brown crown

This backstamp was issued in two sizes. A small version was used on the standard figures with a larger size for the large size figures. The small size was issued in 1989 and was used on 90 figures. The large size was issued in 1993 and was used on 10 figures. A variation of the small size exists without the crown for small base figures.

BP-7   BESWICK BROWN OVAL
                    ISSUED 1993

BP-7 Brown Oval

Issued only on the large size Peter Rabbit to commemorate the 100th anniversary of Peter Rabbit 1893-1993.

BP-8   BESWICK WARE BROWN SCRIPT
                    ISSUED 1994 TO 1998

"Beswick Ware England" or the mark that followed, "Beswick Ware Made in England" is the earliest printed backstamp of the J. W. Beswick, Baltimore Works, Longton, and it was for the Beswick Centenary that the Beswick Ware logo was reinstated as the primary backstamp of the John Beswick Studio of Royal Doulton.

BP-8a   General Backstamp Issue 1998

BP-8a Beswick Ware Brown Script

Issued as a general backstamp for a very short period of time in 1998, the brown script may turn out to be the rarest of the Beatrix Potter backstamps. It is found on only 2 figures.

Jemima and her Ducklings
Mrs. Tiggy-Winkle Washing

BP-8b   50th Anniversary of Production of
         Beatrix Potter Figures at Beswick, Issued 1997

BP-8b Beswick 50th Anniversary

1997 was the 50th anniversary of production of Beatrix Potter figurines at the John Beswick Studios in Longton. This backstamp was in use only during 1997.

BP-8c   Limited Edition Backstamp

BP-8c Beswick Ware Brown Script
Limited Edition Backstamp

BP-8c is a modification of BP-8a and designed for a limited edition figurines.

The following is a list of figures that can be found with a BP-8c backstamp:

Hiding From the Cat
Mittens, Tom Kitten and Moppet
Peter and Benjamin Picking Up Onions

BP-9   **BESWICK WARE GOLD SCRIPT**
               ISSUED 1997 TO 1999

A gold Beswick Ware script backstamp was coupled with the anniversary, limited edition, gold or platinum highlighted figurines. There are three varieties of this backstamp.

BP-9a   **100th Anniversary of**
                  John Beswick Studios, Issued 1994

BP-9a Beswick Centenary

Issued to commemorate the 100th anniversary of the founding of the Beswick studios. This backstamp was available only on Jemima Puddle-Duck.

BP-9b   **General Backstamp**
                        1997-1998

BP-9b Beswick Gold Script

The following small size figures issued with gold accents are coupled with gold Beswick Ware backstamps:

Benjamin Bunny, third version, second variation
Hunca Munca Sweeping, first version, second variation
Jemima Puddle-Duck, first version, second variation
Mrs. Tiggy-Winkle, first version, third variation
Peter Rabbit, first version, third variation
Tom Kitten, first version, third variation

BP-9c   **Limited Edition Backstamp**

BP-9c Beswick Ware Gold Script
Limited Edition

This backstamp, a modification of BP-9b, appears on 12 large size figurines issued by Lawleys By Post between 1997-1999. They were issued in pairs except for "Mrs. Rabbit and Peter" (1999) and "Tabitha Twitchet and Miss Moppet" (2000).

Issued in pairs:
1. Benjamin Bunny, fourth version, second variation
   Peter Rabbit, second version, second variation
2. Jemima Puddle-Duck, second version, second var.
   Mrs. Tiggy-Winkle, second version, second variation
3. Mr. Jeremy Fisher, second version, second variation
   Tom Kitten, second version, second variation
4. Foxy Whiskered Gentleman, second version,
      second variation
   Mrs. Rabbit, third version, second variation
5. Peter and the Red Pocket Handkerchief, second
      version, second variation
   Tailor of Gloucester, second version, second var.
6. Hunca Munca Sweeping, second version
   Squirrel Nutkin, second version

Issued singly (double figures):
1. Mrs. Rabbit and Peter, second version
      (Single issue-double figure)
2. Tabitha Twitchit and Moppet, second version

BP-9d   **Peter Rabbit and Friends**
                     Limited Editions

BP-9d Peter Rabbit and Friends
Limited Editions

This backstamp is a modification of BP-9b and is found on limited edition figures with gold accents issued by Peter Rabbit and Friends.

Duchess and Ribby
Ginger and Pickles
Mrs. Tiggy-Winkle and Lucie
Peter and the Red Pocket Handkerchief, first version,
      second variation
This Pig Had a Bit of Meat

BP-10   **BESWICK BLACK CREST**
                   ISSUED 1998 TO DATE

In 1998 the Beswick backstamp was redesigned and the Beswick crest, first seen in 1968-1969, was re-introduced for the Beswick line of Storybook figurines. There are three varieties of this backstamp.

BP-10a   General Backstamp Issue

BP-10a Beswick Black Crest

This backstamp, now in general use, will be found on the following Beatrix Potter figurines:

Amiable Guinea-Pig, style two
And This Pig Had None
Appley Dapply, second version
Benjamin Ate a Lettuce Leaf
Farmer Potatoes
Foxy Whiskered Gentleman, first version, first variation
Hunca Munca Sweeping, first version, first variation
Jemima and her Ducklings
Jemima Puddle-Duck, first version, first variation
Jemima Puddle-Duck with Foxy Whiskered Gentleman
Jeremy Fisher Catches a Fish
Johnny Town-Mouse Eating Corn
Lady Mouse
Mr. Jeremy Fisher, first version, second variation
Mrs. Tiggy-Winkle Takes Tea
Mrs. Tiggy-Winkle Washing
Mrs. Tittlemouse, style two
Old Mr. Brown
Peter and the Red Pocket Handkerchief, first version, first variation
Peter in Bed
Peter in the Watering Can
Squirrel Nutkin, first version, second variation
The Old Woman Who Lived in a Shoe Knitting
Timmy Willie Fetching Milk
Tom Kitten in the Rockery
Tommy Brock, second version, second variation
Yock-Yock in the Tub

BP-10b   Beswick Black Arch

BP-10b A modification of backstamp BP-10a

This backstamp is a modification of BP-10a and can be found on the following figurines. The modification was necessary due to base restriction.

Hunca Munca, style one
Miss Moppet, second variation
Mr. Benjamin Bunny, second version
Mr. Drake Puddle-Duck
Mr. McGregor
Mrs. Flopsy Bunny
Mrs. Rabbit and Peter, first version
Mrs. Rabbit Cooking
Peter Ate a Raddish
Peter Rabbit, first version, second variation
Peter Rabbit Gardening
Peter with Daffodils
Peter with Postbag
Rebeccah Puddle-Duck

BP-10c   Beswick Black Circle

BP-10c A modification of backstamp BP-10a

This backstamp is a modification of BP-10a. Its modification is also due to base restriction. It can be found on the following figurines:

Benjamin Bunny, third version, first variation
Little Pig Robinson, second variation
Mrs. Rabbit, second version
Mrs. Tiggy-Winkle, first version, second variation
Pigling Bland, second variation
Ribby
Tailor of Gloucester, first version
Tom Kitten, first version, second variation

BP-10d   Peter Rabbit and Friends Limited Editions

BP-10d Beswick Gold Crest

At the time of publication BP-10d was found only on Sweet Peter Rabbit, a limited edition figurine commissioned by Peter Rabbit and Friends. This backstamp is a gold version of BP-10a

BP-11   JOHN BESWICK SIGNATURE
ISSUED 2001 TO 2002

Beginning in 2001 all standard range figures and limited/special edition figures carry a "John Beswick" signature in lieu of the word "Beswick". In addition, the Doulton "P" number for each figure is included for all limited/special edition figures beginning in 2001 and for the standard range figures beginning in 2002.

BP-11a   General Backstamp Issue

BP-11a John Beswick Signature

Standard range figures:

Head Gardener, The
Hunca Munca, style two
Hunca Munca Sweeping
Little Pig Robinson
Mr. Benjamin Bunny
Mrs. Tiggy-Winkle Buys Provisions
Peter Rabbit Digging
Rebeccah Puddle-duck
Two Gentlemen Rabbits

Satin glaze figures:

Benjamin Bunny, third version, third variation
Foxy Whiskered Gentleman, first version, second variation
Jemima Puddle-duck, first version, third variation
Mr. Jeremy Fisher, first version, third variation
Mrs. Tiggy-Winkle, first version, fourth variation
Peter Rabbit, first version, fourth variation

BP-11b   Limited/Special Edition Backstamp

BP-11b John Beswick Signature

Limited/special edition figures:

Flopsy and Benjamin Bunny
Flopsy, Mopsy and Cottontail, style two
Kep and Jemima
My Dear Son Thomas
Peter and Benjamin Picking Apples
Peter on his Book

BEATRIX POTTER

AMIABLE GUINEA-PIG
Style One

AND THIS PIG HAD NONE

ANNA MARIA

APPLEY DAPPLY
First Version

AUNT PETTITOES

BABBITTY BUMBLE

BENJAMIN ATE A
LETTTUCE LEAF

BENJAMIN BUNNY
First Version

BENJAMIN BUNNY SAT ON
A BANK, First Version

BENJAMIN WAKES UP

CECILY PARSLEY
First Version

CHIPPY HACKEE

BEATRIX POTTER

CHRISTMAS STOCKING

COTTONTAIL

COUSIN RIBBY

DIGGORY DIGGORY DELVET

DUCHESS (HOLDING FLOWERS)
Style One

DUCHESS AND RIBBY

DUCHESS (HOLDING A PIE)
Style Two

FLOPSY AND
BENJAMIN BUNNY

FARMER POTATOES

FLOPSY, MOPSY AND COTTONTAIL
Style One

BEATRIX POTTER

FIERCE BAD RABBIT
First Version

FOXY READING
COUNTRY NEWS

FOXY WHISKERED
GENTLEMAN, First Version

GENTLEMAN MOUSE
MADE A BOW

FLOPSY, MOPSY AND COTTONTAIL
Style Two

GINGER

GINGER AND PICKLES

GOODY TIPTOES

GOODY AND TIMMY TIPTOES

THE HEAD GARDENER

BEATRIX POTTER

HIDING FROM THE CAT

HUNCA MUNCA
Style One

HUNCA MUNCA
SPILLS THE BEADS

HUNCA MUNCA SWEEPING
First Version, First Variation

HUNCA MUNCA
Style Two

JEMIMA AND HER DUCKLINGS

JEMIMA PUDDLE-DUCK
First Version, First Variation

JEMIMA PUDDLE-DUCK
MADE A FEATHER NEST

JEMIMA PUDDLE-DUCK WITH
FOXY WHISKERED GENTLEMAN

JEREMY FISHER
CATCHES A FISH

BEATRIX POTTER

JOHN JOINER

JOHNNY TOWN-MOUSE

JOHNNY TOWN-MOUSE
EATING CORN

JOHNNY TOWN-MOUSE
WITH BAG

KEP AND JEMIMA

LADY MOUSE

LADY MOUSE MADE
A CURTSY

LITTLE BLACK RABBIT

LITTLE PIG ROBINSON
First Variation

LITTLE PIG ROBINSON
SPYING

MISS DORMOUSE

BEATRIX POTTER

MISS MOPPET
First Variation

MITTENS AND MOPPET

MITTENS, TOM KITTEN AND MOPPET

MOTHER LADYBIRD

MR. ALDERMAN PTOLEMY

MR. BENJAMIN BUNNY
First Version

MR. BENJAMIN BUNNY
AND PETER RABBIT

MR. DRAKE PUDDLE-DUCK

MR. JACKSON
First Variation

MR. JEREMY FISHER
First Version, First Variation

MR. JEREMY FISHER
DIGGING

BEATRIX POTTER

MR. McGREGOR

MR. TOD

MRS. FLOPSY BUNNY

MRS. RABBIT
First Version

MRS. RABBIT
AND BUNNIES

MRS. RABBIT COOKING

MRS. RABBIT AND THE FOUR BUNNIES

MRS. RABBIT AND PETER
Second Version

MRS. TIGGY-WINKLE
First Version, Second Variation

MRS. TIGGY-WINKLE
BUYS PROVISIONS

MRS. TIGGY-WINKLE
TAKES TEA

BEATRIX POTTER

MRS. TIGGY-WINKLE AND LUCIE

MRS. TIGGY-WINKLE
WASHING

MRS. TITTLEMOUSE
Style One

MRS. TITTLEMOUSE
STYLE TWO

MY DEAR SON THOMAS

NO MORE TWIST

OLD MR. BOUNCER

OLD MR. BROWN

OLD MR. PRICKLEPIN

PETER AND THE RED POCKET
HANDKERCHIEF, First Version

AMIABLE GUINEA-PIG™
Style One

Modeller:	Albert Hallam
Height:	3 ½", 8.9 cm
Colour:	Tan jacket, white waistcoat, yellow trousers
Issued:	1967 - 1983

Back Stamp	Beswick Number	Doulton Number	Price			
			U.S. $	Can. $	U.K. £	Aust. $
BP-2	2061	P2061	600.00	850.00	375.00	900.00
BP-3a			275.00	400.00	175.00	425.00
BP-3b			275.00	400.00	175.00	425.00

Note: The colour of the coat varies from tan to brown.

AMIABLE GUINEA-PIG™
Style Two

Modeller:	Warren Platt
Height:	4 ¼", 10.8 cm
Colour:	Brown jacket and waistcoat, beige trousers and hat, blue bowtie and book
Issued:	2000 - 2002

Back Stamp	Beswick Number	Doulton Number	Price			
			U.S. $	Can. $	U.K. £	Aust. $
BP-10a	4031	P4031	60.00	110.00	35.00	125.00

AND THIS PIG HAD NONE™

Modeller:	Martyn Alcock
Height:	4", 10.1 cm
Colour:	Mauve dress, mottled burgundy and green shawl, brown hat
Issued:	1992 - 1998

Back Stamp	Beswick Number	Doulton Number	Price			
			U.S. $	Can. $	U.K. £	Aust. $
BP-6a	3319	P3319	55.00	75.00	30.00	80.00
BP-10a			60.00	85.00	35.00	90.00

ANNA MARIA™

Modeller:	Albert Hallam
Height:	3", 7.6 cm
Colour:	Blue dress and white apron
Issued:	1963 - 1983

BEATRIX POTTER'S
Anna Maria
F. WARNE & CO. LTD.
COPYRIGHT
BESWICK
ENGLAND

Back Stamp	Beswick Number	Doulton Number	Price			
			U.S. $	Can. $	U.K. £	Aust. $
BP-2	1851	P1851	400.00	550.00	250.00	575.00
BP-3a			175.00	250.00	110.00	275.00
BP-3b			175.00	250.00	110.00	275.00

Note: Dress is bright blue in earlier versions and pale blue in later versions.

APPLEY DAPPLY™

Modeller:	Albert Hallam
Height:	3 ¼", 8.3 cm
Colour:	Brown mouse, white apron, blue trim, blue bow, yellow basket, tray of jam tarts

BEATRIX POTTER'S
APPLEY DAPPLY
F. WARNE & CO. LTD.
COPYRIGHT
BESWICK
ENGLAND

FIRST VERSION: BOTTLE OUT

Issued: 1971 - 1975

Back Stamp	Beswick Number	Doulton Number	Price			
			U.S. $	Can. $	U.K. £	Aust. $
BP-2	2333/1	P2333/1	400.00	600.00	250.00	675.00
BP-3a			250.00	350.00	160.00	375.00
BP-3b			250.00	350.00	160.00	375.00

First version: Bottle out

BEATRIX POTTER'S
"APPLEY DAPPLY"
F. Warne & Co. Ltd.
© Copyright 1971
BESWICK
ENGLAND

SECOND VERSION: BOTTLE IN

Issued: 1975 - 2002

Back Stamp	Beswick Number	Doulton Number	Price			
			U.S. $	Can. $	U.K. £	Aust. $
BP-3b	2333/2	P2333/2	80.00	110.00	45.00	115.00
BP-3c			90.00	125.00	50.00	130.00
BP-6a			50.00	65.00	25.00	70.00
BP-10a			35.00	50.00	20.00	55.00

AUNT PETTITOES™

Modeller:	Albert Hallam
Height:	3 ¾", 9.5 cm
Colour:	Blue dress and white cap with blue polka dots
Issued:	1970 - 1993

Back Stamp	Beswick Number	Doulton Number	Price			
			U.S. $	Can. $	U.K. £	Aust. $
BP-2	2276	P2276	400.00	600.00	250.00	675.00
BP-3a			95.00	135.00	65.00	150.00
BP-3b			90.00	130.00	60.00	135.00
BP-3c			85.00	120.00	55.00	125.00
BP-6a			85.00	120.00	55.00	125.00

Note: The dress is light blue in earlier versions and bright blue in later versions.

BABBITTY BUMBLE™

Modeller:	Warren Platt
Height:	2 ¾", 7.0 cm
Colour:	Black and gold
Issued:	1989 - 1993

Back Stamp	Beswick Number	Doulton Number	Price			
			U.S. $	Can. $	U.K. £	Aust. $
BP-6a	2971	P2971	275.00	375.00	175.00	400.00

BENJAMIN ATE A LETTUCE LEAF™

Modeller:	Martyn Alcock
Height:	4 ¾", 11.9 cm
Colour:	Brown, white and yellow
Issued:	1992 - 1998

Back Stamp	Beswick Number	Doulton Number	Price			
			U.S. $	Can. $	U.K. £	Aust. $
BP-6a	3317	P3317	55.00	75.00	30.00	80.00
BP-10a			60.00	85.00	35.00	90.00

First version: Ears out, shoes out

Second version: Ears out, shoes in

Third version: Ears in, shoes in

BENJAMIN BUNNY™

Modeller: Arthur Gredington
Height: 4", 10.1 cm
Size: Small

FIRST VERSION: EARS OUT, SHOES OUT

Colour: Variation No. 1 Pale green jacket
             Variation No. 2 Brown jacket
Issued: 1948 - 1974

Back Stamp	Beswick Number	Colour Variation	U.S. $	Can. $	U.K. £	Aust. $
BP-1a	1105/1	Pale green	450.00	600.00	275.00	650.00
BP-1b		Pale green			Rare	
BP-2		Pale green	400.00	550.00	250.00	575.00
BP-2		Brown	400.00	550.00	250.00	575.00
BP-3a		Pale green	350.00	500.00	225.00	525.00
BP-3b		Brown	325.00	450.00	200.00	475.00

SECOND VERSION: EARS OUT, SHOES IN

Colour: Variation No. 1 Pale green jacket
             Variation No. 2 Brown jacket
Issued: 1972 - c.1980

Back Stamp	Beswick Number	Colour Variation	U.S. $	Can. $	U.K. £	Aust. $
BP-2	1105/2	Pale green	1,000.00	1,400.00	625.00	1,500.00
BP-3a		Pale green	325.00	450.00	200.00	475.00
BP-3a		Brown	325.00	450.00	200.00	475.00
BP-3b		Pale green	275.00	400.00	175.00	425.00
BP-3b		Brown	275.00	400.00	175.00	425.00

THIRD VERSION: EARS IN, SHOES IN
FIRST VARIATION: BROWN SHOES

Colour: Brown jacket, green beret with orange pompon, brown shoes
Issued: c.1980 - 2000

Back Stamp	Beswick Number	Doulton Number	U.S. $	Can. $	U.K. £	Aust. $
BP-3b	1105/3	P1105/3	80.00	110.00	50.00	115.00
BP-3c			95.00	135.00	60.00	150.00
BP-4			115.00	150.00	70.00	165.00
BP-5			150.00	200.00	90.00	225.00
BP-6a			40.00	55.00	25.00	60.00
BP-10c			30.00	45.00	20.00	50.00

THIRD VERSION: EARS IN, SHOES IN
SECOND VARIATION: GOLD SHOES

Colour: Brown jacket, green beret with orange pompon, gold shoes
Issued: 1998 - 1998

Back Stamp	Beswick Number	Doulton Number	U.S. $	Can. $	U.K. £	Aust. $
BP-9b	1105/4	PG1105	65.00	90.00	40.00	95.00

THIRD VERSION: EARS IN, SHOES IN
THIRD VARIATION: BROWN SHOES, SATIN FINISH

Colour: Brown jacket, green beret with orange pompon, brown shoes
Issued: 2001 - 2002

Back Stamp	Beswick Number	Doulton Number	U.S. $	Can. $	U.K. £	Aust. $
BP-11a	1105/5	PS1105	40.00	60.00	25.00	65.00

BENJAMIN BUNNY™

Modeller:	Martyn Alcock
Height:	6 ¼", 15.9 cm
Size:	Large

FOURTH VERSION: LARGE SIZE, EARS IN, SHOES IN
FIRST VARIATION: BROWN SHOES

Colour:	Tan jacket, green beret with orange pompon
Issued:	1994 - 1997

Back Stamp	Beswick Number	Doulton Number	Price U.S. $	Can. $	U.K. £	Aust. $
BP-6b	3403/1	P3403	70.00	100.00	45.00	110.00

FOURTH VERSION: LARGE SIZE, EARS IN, SHOES IN
SECOND VARIATION, GOLD SHOES

Issued:	1997 in a limited edition of 1,947
Series:	Gold edition

Back Stamp	Beswick Number	Doulton Number	Price U.S. $	Can. $	U.K. £	Aust. $
BP-9c	3403/2	PG3403	95.00	135.00	60.00	150.00

Note: Issued, numbered and sold as a pair with Peter Rabbit, second version, second variation.

Benjamin Bunny, large size, gold shoes

BENJAMIN BUNNY SAT ON A BANK™

Modeller:	David Lyttleton
Height:	3 ¾", 9.5 cm

FIRST VERSION: HEAD LOOKS DOWN

Colour:	Brown jacket
Issued:	1983 - 1985

Back Stamp	Beswick Number	Doulton Number	Price U.S. $	Can. $	U.K. £	Aust. $
BP-3b	2803/1	P2803/1	125.00	175.00	80.00	200.00
BP-3c			150.00	200.00	100.00	225.00

First version: Head looks down

SECOND VERSION: HEAD LOOKS UP

Colour:	Golden brown jacket
Issued:	1983 - 1997

Back Stamp	Beswick Number	Doulton Number	Price U.S. $	Can. $	U.K. £	Aust. $
BP-3b	2803/2	P2803/2	125.00	175.00	80.00	200.00
BP-3c			150.00	200.00	100.00	225.00
BP-6a			60.00	85.00	35.00	90.00

Second version: Head looks up

BENJAMIN WAKES UP™

Modeller:	Amanda Hughes-Lubeck
Height:	2 ¼", 5.7 cm
Colour:	Green, white and orange
Issued:	1991 - 1997

Back Stamp	Beswick Number	Doulton Number	Price U.S. $	Can. $	U.K. £	Aust. $
BP-6a	3234	P3234	75.00	100.00	50.00	110.00

CECILY PARSLEY™

Modeller:	Arthur Gredington
Height:	4", 10.1 cm

FIRST VERSION: HEAD DOWN, BRIGHT BLUE DRESS

Colour:	Bright blue dress, white apron, brown pail
Issued:	1965 - 1985

Back Stamp	Beswick Number	Doulton Number	Price U.S. $	Can. $	U.K. £	Aust. $
BP-2	1941/1	P1941/1	250.00	375.00	150.00	400.00
BP-3a			120.00	175.00	75.00	185.00
BP-3b			100.00	150.00	65.00	160.00
BP-3c			120.00	175.00	75.00	185.00

First version: Head down

SECOND VERSION: HEAD UP, PALE BLUE DRESS

Colour:	Pale blue dress, white apron
Issued:	1985 - 1993

Back Stamp	Beswick Number	Doulton Number	Price U.S. $	Can. $	U.K. £	Aust. $
BP-3c	1941/2	P1941/2	125.00	175.00	75.00	185.00
BP-6a			100.00	150.00	65.00	160.00

Note: Cecily Parsley was issued with both a dark and a light blue dress.

Second version: Head up

CHIPPY HACKEE™

Modeller: David Lyttleton
Height: 3 ¾", 9.5 cm
Colour: Pale green blanket, white
             handkerchief, green foot bath
Issued: 1979 - 1993

BEATRIX POTTER'S
Chippy Hackee
F. Warne & Co. Ltd.
© Copyright 1979
BESWICK ENGLAND

Back Stamp	Beswick Number	Doulton Number	Price			
			U.S. $	Can. $	U.K. £	Aust. $
BP-3b	2627	P2627	90.00	135.00	60.00	150.00
BP-3c			110.00	150.00	70.00	160.00
BP-6a			100.00	140.00	65.00	155.00

Note: The colour of the blanket may range from pale green to pale yellow.

CHRISTMAS STOCKING™

Modeller: Martyn Alcock
Height: 3 ¼", 8.3 cm
Colour: Brown mice, red and
             white striped stocking
Issued: 1991 - 1994

ROYAL ALBERT ®
ENGLAND
The Christmas Stocking
Beatrix Potter
© F. Warne & Co. 1991
© 1991 ROYAL ALBERT LTD

Back Stamp	Beswick Number	Doulton Number	Price			
			U.S. $	Can. $	U.K. £	Aust. $
BP-6a	3257	P3257	400.00	600.00	250.00	650.00

COTTONTAIL™

Modeller: David Lyttleton
Height: 3 ¾", 9.5 cm
Colour: Blue dress, brown chair
Issued: 1985 - 1996

BEATRIX POTTER'S
"Cottontail"
© Frederick Warne P.L.C. 1985
BESWICK ENGLAND

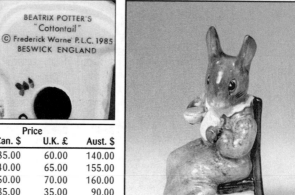

Back Stamp	Beswick Number	Doulton Number	Price			
			U.S. $	Can. $	U.K. £	Aust. $
BP-3b	2878	P2878	95.00	135.00	60.00	140.00
BP-3c			100.00	140.00	65.00	155.00
BP-4			110.00	150.00	70.00	160.00
BP-6a			60.00	85.00	35.00	90.00

COUSIN RIBBY™

Modeller:	Albert Hallam
Height:	3 ½", 8.9 cm
Colour:	Pink skirt and hat, green apron, blue shawl, yellow basket
Issued:	1970 - 1993

Back Stamp	Beswick Number	Doulton Number	Price			
			U.S. $	Can. $	U.K. £	Aust. $
BP-2	2284	P2284	450.00	600.00	275.00	625.00
BP-3a			80.00	120.00	50.00	125.00
BP-3b			80.00	120.00	50.00	125.00
BP-3c			80.00	120.00	50.00	125.00
BP-6a			125.00	175.00	75.00	185.00

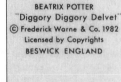

DIGGORY DIGGORY DELVET™

Modeller:	David Lyttleton
Height:	2 ¾", 7.0 cm
Colour:	Grey mole
Issued:	1982 - 1997

Back Stamp	Beswick Number	Doulton Number	Price			
			U.S. $	Can. $	U.K. £	Aust. $
BP-3b	2713	P2713	80.00	120.00	50.00	125.00
BP-3c			95.00	135.00	60.00	145.00
BP-6a			65.00	90.00	40.00	95.00

DUCHESS™
Style One (Holding Flowers)

Modeller:	Graham Orwell
Height:	3 ¾", 9.5 cm
Colour:	Black dog, multicoloured flowers
Issued:	1955 - 1967

Back Stamp	Beswick Number	Doulton Number	Price			
			U.S. $	Can. $	U.K. £	Aust. $
BP-1a	1355	P1355			Extremely Rare	
BP-2			2,500.00	4,250.00	1,600.00	4,500.00

DUCHESS™
Style Two (Holding a Pie)

Modeller: Graham Tongue
Height: 4", 10.1 cm
Colour: Black dog, blue bow, light brown pie
Issued: 1979 - 1982

Back Stamp	Beswick Number	Doulton Number	Price			
			U.S. $	Can. $	U.K. £	Aust. $
BP-3b	2601	P2601	575.00	800.00	350.00	850.00

For **Duchess and Ribby** see the Tableaux Section, page 84.

FARMER POTATOES™

Modeller: Shane Ridge
Height: 5", 12.7 cm
Colour: Tan jacket, brown trousers, yellow shirt, blue hat and lantern
Issued: 2000 - 2002

Back Stamp	Beswick Number	Doulton Number	Price			
			U.S. $	Can. $	U.K. £	Aust. $
BP-10a	4014	P4014	60.00	125.00	35.00	135.00

First version: Feet out

FIERCE BAD RABBIT™

Modeller: David Lyttleton
Height: 4 ¾", 12.1 cm

FIRST VERSION: FEET OUT

Colour: Dark brown and white rabbit,
              red-brown carrot, green seat
Issued: 1977 - 1980

Back Stamp	Beswick Number	Doulton Number	Price U.S. $	Can. $	U.K. £	Aust. $
BP-3b	2586/1	P2586/1	200.00	275.00	125.00	300.00

BEATRIX POTTER'S
"Fierce Bad Rabbit"
F. Warne & Co.Ltd.
© Copyright 1977
BESWICK ENGLAND

SECOND VERSION: FEET IN

Colour: Light brown and white rabbit,
              red-brown carrot, green seat
Issued: 1980 - 1997

BEATRIX POTTER
"Fierce Bad Rabbit"
© Frederick Warne & Co. 1977
Licensed by Copyrights
BESWICK ENGLAND

Back Stamp	Beswick Number	Doulton Number	Price U.S. $	Can. $	U.K. £	Aust. $
BP-3b	2586/2	P2586/2	100.00	150.00	65.00	160.00
BP-3c			95.00	135.00	60.00	145.00
BP-4			100.00	150.00	65.00	160.00
BP-6a			65.00	90.00	40.00	95.00

Second version: Feet in

For **Flopsy and Benjamin Bunny** see the Tableaux Section, page 84.

FLOPSY, MOPSY AND COTTONTAIL™
Style One

Modeller:	Arthur Gredington
Height:	2 ½", 6.4 cm
Colour:	Brown/white rabbits wearing rose-pink cloaks
Issued:	1954 - 1997

Back Stamp	Beswick Number	Doulton Number	Price			
			U.S. $	Can. $	U.K. £	Aust. $
BP-1a	1274	P1274	800.00	1,150.00	500.00	1,20000
BP-2			250.00	350.00	150.00	375.00
BP-3a			95.00	135.00	60.00	145.00
BP-3b			95.00	135.00	60.00	145.00
BP-3c			100.00	150.00	65.00	160.00
BP-4			100.00	150.00	65.00	160.00
BP-5			200.00	275.00	125.00	300.00
BP-6a			65.00	90.00	40.00	95.00

Note: Colour variations of the cloaks exist. Angle of bunnies heads may vary.

For **Flopsy, Mopsy and Cottontail**, Style Two, see the Tableaux Section, page 84.

FOXY READING COUNTRY NEWS™

Modeller:	Amanda Hughes-Lubeck
Height:	4 ¼", 10.8 cm
Colour:	Brown and green
Issued:	1990 - 1997

Back Stamp	Beswick Number	Doulton Number	Price			
			U.S. $	Can. $	U.K. £	Aust. $
BP-6a	3219	P3219	75.00	100.00	45.00	110.00

FOXY WHISKERED GENTLEMAN™

Modeller: Arthur Gredington

FIRST VERSION: SMALL
FIRST VARIATION: GLOSS FINISH

Height: 4 ¾", 12.1 cm
Size: Small
Colour: Pale green jacket and trousers, pink waistcoat
Issued: 1954 - 2002

Back Stamp	Beswick Number	Doulton Number	Price			
			U.S. $	Can. $	U.K. £	Aust. $
BP-1a	1277/1	P1277	800.00	1,150.00	500.00	1,200.00
BP-2			150.00	200.00	100.00	225.00
BP-3a			95.00	135.00	60.00	150.00
BP-3b			80.00	110.00	50.00	120.00
BP-3c			90.00	125.00	55.00	135.00
BP-4			95.00	135.00	60.00	150.00
BP-6a			40.00	60.00	25.00	65.00
BP-10a			30.00	45.00	20.00	50.00

Note: Variations occur with the head looking either right or left.

Small size, gloss glaze

FIRST VERSION: SMALL
SECOND VARIATION: SATIN FINISH

Height: 4 ¾", 12.1 cm
Size: Small
Colour: Pale green jacket and trousers,
          pink waistcoat
Issued: 2001 - 2002

Back Stamp	Beswick Number	Doulton Number	Price			
			U.S. $	Can. $	U.K. £	Aust. $
BP-11a	1277/2	PS1277	40.00	60.00	25.00	65.00

SECOND VERSION: LARGE
FIRST VARIATION: GREEN BUTTONS

Height: 7 ½", 19.1 cm
Size: Large
Colour: Pale green jacket and trousers, pink waistcoat
Issued: 1995 - 1997

Back Stamp	Beswick Number	Doulton Number	Price			
			U.S. $	Can. $	U.K. £	Aust. $
BP-6b	3450/1	P3450	70.00	100.00	45.00	110.00

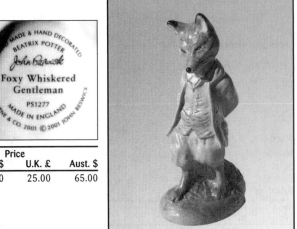

Small size, satin glaze

SECOND VERSION: LARGE
SECOND VARIATION: GOLD BUTTONS

Height: 7 ½", 19.1 cm
Size: Large
Colour: Pale green jacket and trousers, pink waistcoat, gold buttons
Issued: 1998 in a limited edition of 1,947
Series: Gold edition

Back Stamp	Beswick Number	Doulton Number	Price			
			U.S. $	Can. $	U.K. £	Aust. $
BP-9c	3450/2	PG3450	95.00	135.00	60.00	150.00

Note: The gold edition was issued, numbered and sold as a pair with Mrs. Rabbit, third version, first variation.

Large size

GENTLEMAN MOUSE MADE A BOW™

Modeller: Ted Chawner
Height: 3", 7.6 cm
Colour: Brown, blue and white
Issued: 1990 - 1996

Back Stamp	Beswick Number	Doulton Number	Price			
			U.S. $	Can. $	U.K. £	Aust. $
BP-6a	3200	P3200	65.00	90.00	40.00	95.00

GINGER™

Modeller: David Lyttleton
Height: 3 ¾", 9.5 cm
Colour: Green, white and brown
Issued: 1976 - 1982

Back Stamp	Beswick Number	Doulton Number	Price			
			U.S. $	Can. $	U.K. £	Aust. $
BP-3b	2559	P2559	500.00	675.00	300.00	700.00

Note: The jacket colour varies from light to dark green.

For **Ginger and Pickles** see the Tableaux Section, page 85.

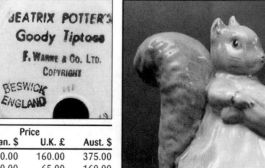

GOODY TIPTOES™

Modeller: Arthur Gredington
Height: 3 ½", 8.9 cm
Colour: Grey squirrel wearing pink dress and white apron, brown sack with yellow nuts
Issued: 1961 - 1997

Back Stamp	Beswick Number	Doulton Number	Price			
			U.S. $	Can. $	U.K. £	Aust. $
BP-2	1675	P1675	250.00	350.00	160.00	375.00
BP-3a			100.00	150.00	65.00	160.00
BP-3b			80.00	110.00	50.00	115.00
BP-3c			100.00	150.00	65.00	160.00
BP-6a			50.00	70.00	30.00	75.00

Note: This model has two different bases and the dress comes in various shades of pink.

GOODY AND TIMMY TIPTOES™

Modeller:	David Lyttleton
Height:	4", 10.1 cm
Colour:	Timmy - rose coat
	Goody - pink overdress with green and biege underskirt, green umbrella
Issued:	1986 - 1996

Back Stamp	Beswick Number	Doulton Number	Price			
			U.S. $	Can. $	U.K. £	Aust. $
BP-3c	2957	P2957	325.00	450.00	200.00	475.00
BP-6a			95.00	135.00	60.00	145.00

HEAD GARDENER™

Modeller:	Shane Ridge
Height:	3 ½", 8.9 cm
Colour:	Brown and green
Issued:	2002 - 2002

Back Stamp	Beswick Number	Doulton Number	Price			
			U.S. $	Can. $	U.K. £	Aust. $
BP-11a	P4236	P4236	250.00	350.00	150.00	375.00

For **Hiding From the Cat** see the Tableaux Section, page 85.

HUNCA MUNCA™
Style One

Modeller:	Arthur Gredington
Height:	2 ¾", 7.0 cm
Colour:	Blue dress, white apron, pink blanket and straw cradle
Issued:	1951 - 2000

Back Stamp	Beswick Number	Doulton Number	Price			
			U.S. $	Can. $	U.K. £	Aust. $
BP-1a	1198	P1198	325.00	450.00	200.00	475.00
BP-2			200.00	275.00	130.00	300.00
BP-3a			80.00	110.00	50.00	115.00
BP-3b			65.00	90.00	40.00	95.00
BP-3c			70.00	100.00	45.00	110.00
BP-4			120.00	170.00	75.00	180.00
BP-5			115.00	160.00	70.00	170.00
BP-6a			55.00	80.00	35.00	85.00
BP-10b			65.00	90.00	40.00	95.00

HUNCA MUNCA™
Style Two

Modeller: Shane Ridge
Height: 4 ¼", 10.8 cm
Colour: Mauve dress, white apron, grey pans
Issued: 2001 - 2002

Back Stamp	Beswick Number	Doulton Number	Price			
			U.S. $	Can. $	U.K. £	Aust. $
BP-11a	P4074	P4074	60.00	90.00	30.00	100.00

HUNCA MUNCA SPILLS THE BEADS™

Modeller: Martyn Alcock
Height: 3 ¼", 8.3 cm
Colour: Brown mouse, blue and white rice jar
Issued: 1992 - 1996

Back Stamp	Beswick Number	Doulton Number	Price			
			U.S. $	Can. $	U.K. £	Aust. $
BP-6a	3288	P3288	65.00	90.00	40.00	95.00

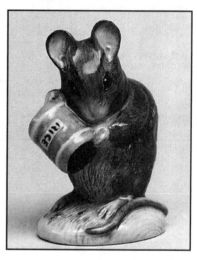

HUNCA MUNCA SWEEPING™

Modeller:	David Lyttleton
Height:	3 ½", 8.9 cm
Size:	Small

FIRST VERSION: SMALL SIZE
FIRST VARIATION: LIGHT BROWN DUSTPAN

Colour:	Mauve patterned dress with white apron, green broom handle
Issued:	1977 - 2002

BEATRIX POTTER'S
"Hunca Munca Sweeping"
F. Warne & Co.Ltd.
© Copyright 1977
BESWICK ENGLAND

Back Stamp	Beswick Number	Doulton Number	Price			
			U.S. $	Can. $	U.K. £	Aust. $
BP-3b	2584/1	P2584	90.00	125.00	55.00	135.00
BP-3c			95.00	135.00	60.00	150.00
BP-4			95.00	135.00	60.00	150.00
BP-6a			40.00	55.00	25.00	60.00
BP-10a			35.00	45.00	20.00	50.00
BP-11a			40.00	55.00	25.00	60.00

Green broom handle

FIRST VERSION: SMALL SIZE
SECOND VARIATION: GOLD DUSTPAN

Colour:	Mauve patterned dress, white apron, green broom handle, gold dustpan
Issued:	1998 - 1998

Back Stamp	Beswick Number	Doulton Number	Price			
			U.S. $	Can. $	U.K. £	Aust. $
BP-9b	2584/2	PG2584	55.00	80.00	35.00	85.00

Gold dustpan

SECOND VERSION: LARGE SIZE, GOLD DUSTPAN AND BROOM HANDLE

Modeller:	Amanda Hughes-Lubeck
Height:	5 ¼", 13.3 cm
Size:	Large
Colour:	Mauve patterned dress, white apron, gold dustpan and broom handle
Issued:	1999 in a limited edition of 1,947
Series:	Gold edition

Back Stamp	Beswick Number	Doulton Number	Price			
			U.S. $	Can. $	U.K. £	Aust. $
BP-9c	3894	PG3894	95.00	135.00	60.00	150.00

Note: Issued, numbered and sold as a pair with Squirrel Nutkin, large size.

Gold dustpan and broom handle

JEMIMA AND HER DUCKLINGS™

Modeller: Martyn Alcock
Height: 4 ¼", 10.5 cm
Colour: Mauve shawl
Issued: 1998 - 2002

Back Stamp	Beswick Number	Doulton Number	Price			
			U.S. $	Can. $	U.K. £	Aust. $
BP-8a	3786	P3786	Very Rare			
BP-10a			60.00	110.00	30.00	120.00

Note: Very few examples of BP-8a are known

JEMIMA PUDDLE-DUCK™

Modeller: Arthur Gredington
Height: 4 ¾", 12.1 cm
Size: Small

FIRST VERSION: SMALL SIZE
FIRST VARIATION: GLOSS FINISH, YELLOW SCARF CLIP

Colour: Mauve or pink shawl, light blue
bonnet, yellow scarf clip
Issued: 1948 - 2002

Back Stamp	Beswick Number	Doulton Number	Price			
			U.S. $	Can. $	U.K. £	Aust. $
BP-1a	1092/1	P1092	275.00	400.00	175.00	425.00
BP-2			160.00	225.00	100.00	250.00
BP-3a			80.00	110.00	50.00	115.00
BP-3b			80.00	110.00	50.00	115.00
BP-3c			95.00	135.00	60.00	145.00
BP-4			100.00	150.00	65.00	160.00
BP-5			160.00	225.00	100.00	250.00
BP-6a			55.00	80.00	35.00	85.00
BP-10a			35.00	50.00	20.00	55.00

Small size, yellow scarf clip

FIRST VERSION: SMALL SIZE
SECOND VARIATION: GLOSS FINISH, GOLD SCARF CLIP

Colour: Mauve or pink shawl, light blue bonnet, gold scarf clip
Issued: 1997 - 1997

Back Stamp	Beswick Number	Doulton Number	Price			
			U.S. $	Can. $	U.K. £	Aust. $
BP-9b	1092/2	PG1092	65.00	90.00	40.00	95.00

FIRST VERSION: SMALL SIZE
THIRD VARIATION: SATIN FINISH

Colour: Pink shawl with blue design, light blue bonnet, yellow scarf clip
Issued: 2001 - 2002

Back Stamp	Beswick Number	Doulton Number	Price			
			U.S. $	Can. $	U.K. £	Aust. $
BP-11a	1092/3	PS1092	40.00	60.00	25.00	65.00

Small size, gold scarf clip

Large size, yellow scarf clip

JEMIMA PUDDLE-DUCK™

Modeller:	Martyn Alcock
Height:	6", 15.0 cm
Size:	Large

SECOND VERSION: LARGE SIZE
FIRST VARIATION: YELLOW SCARF CLIP

Colour:	White duck, mauve shawl, light blue bonnet, yellow scarf clip
Issued:	1993 - 1997

Back Stamp	Beswick Number	Doulton Number	Price			
			U.S. $	Can. $	U.K. £	Aust. $
BP-6b	3373/1	P3373	70.00	100.00	45.00	110.00
BP-9a	Beswick Centenary		90.00	125.00	55.00	135.00

Large size, gold scarf clip

SECOND VERSION: LARGE SIZE
SECOND VARIATION: GOLD SCARF CLIP

Colour:	White duck, mauve shawl, light blue bonnet, gold scarf clip
Issued:	1998 in a limited edition of 1,947
Series:	Gold edition

Back Stamp	Beswick Number	Doulton Number	Price			
			U.S. $	Can. $	U.K. £	Aust. $
BP-9c	3373/2	PG3373	95.00	135.00	60.00	145.00

Note: The second variation was issued, numbered and sold as a pair with Mrs. Tiggy-Winkle, second version, second variation.

JEMIMA PUDDLE-DUCK MADE A FEATHER NEST™

Modeller:	David Lyttleton
Height:	2 ¼", 5.7 cm
Colour:	White duck, mauve or pink shawl, blue hat
Issued:	1983 - 1997

Back Stamp	Beswick Number	Doulton Number	Price			
			U.S. $	Can. $	U.K. £	Aust. $
BP-3b	2823	P2823	80.00	110.00	50.00	115.00
BP-3c			90.00	125.00	55.00	135.00
BP-4			95.00	135.00	60.00	145.00
BP-6a			50.00	70.00	30.00	75.00

Note: This model was issued with either a mauve or pink shawl.

JEMIMA PUDDLE-DUCK WITH FOXY WHISKERED GENTLEMAN™

Modeller:	Ted Chawner
Height:	4 ¾", 12.1 cm
Colour:	Brown, green, white and blue
Issued:	1990 - 1999

Back Stamp	Beswick Number	Doulton Number	Price			
			U.S. $	Can. $	U.K. £	Aust. $
BP-6a	3193	P3193	70.00	100.00	45.00	110.00
BP-10a			65.00	90.00	40.00	95.00

JEREMY FISHER CATCHES A FISH™

Modeller:	Martyn Alcock
Height:	3", 7.6 cm
Colour:	Green frog with brown spots, lilac coat, green, yellow and red fish
Issued:	1999 - 2002

Back Stamp	Beswick Number	Doulton Number	Price			
			U.S. $	Can. $	U.K. £	Aust. $
BP-10a	3919	P3919	75.00	135.00	40.00	150.00

Note: There are two variations of P3919: the base can be found with a cut-out "v" through both the lilypad and the water, and with a half-way "v" through the lilypad but not through the water (as illustrated).

JOHN JOINER™

Modeller:	Graham Tongue
Height:	2 ½", 6.4 cm
Colour:	Brown dog wearing green jacket
Issued:	1990 - 1997

Back Stamp	Beswick Number	Doulton Number	Price			
			U.S. $	Can. $	U.K. £	Aust. $
BP-6a	2965	P2965	65.00	90.00	40.00	95.00

Note: John Joiner will vary in shade from black to blue-black.

JOHNNY TOWN-MOUSE™

Modeller:	Arthur Gredington
Height:	3 ½", 8.9 cm
Colour:	Pale blue jacket, white and brown waistcoat
Issued:	1954 - 1993

Back Stamp	Beswick Number	Doulton Number	Price			
			U.S. $	Can. $	U.K. £	Aust. $
BP-1a	1276	P1276		Very rare		
BP-2			160.00	220.00	100.00	230.00
BP-3a			90.00	125.00	55.00	135.00
BP-3b			90.00	125.00	55.00	135.00
BP-3c			95.00	135.00	60.00	145.00
BP-6a			55.00	80.00	35.00	85.00

Note: 1. Jacket colouring varies from pale to deep blue.
2. Because of it's small base very few figures have the BP-1a backstamp.

JOHNNY TOWN-MOUSE EATING CORN™

Modeller:	Martyn Alcock
Height:	3 ¾", 9.5 cm
Colour:	Blue jacket, green and white waistcoat, pink trousers
Issued:	2000 - 2002

Back Stamp	Beswick Number	Doulton Number	Price			
			U.S. $	Can. $	U.K. £	Aust. $
BP-10a	3931	P3931	50.00	90.00	30.00	100.00

JOHNNY TOWN-MOUSE WITH BAG™

Modeller:	Ted Chawner
Height:	3 ½", 8.9 cm
Colour:	Light brown coat and hat, yellow-cream waistcoat
Issued:	1988 - 1994

Back Stamp	Beswick Number	Doulton Number	Price			
			U.S. $	Can. $	U.K. £	Aust. $
BP-4	3094	P3094	300.00	450.00	200.00	475.00
BP-6a			200.00	300.00	125.00	325.00

For **Kep and Jemima** see the Tableaux Section, page 85.

LADY MOUSE™

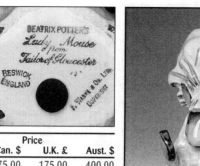

			Price			
Modeller:	Arthur Gredington					
Height:	4", 10.1 cm					
Colour:	White dress with yellow trim and blue polka-dot sleeves, white hat with purple and blue highlights					
Issued:	1950 - 2000					

Back Stamp	Beswick Number	Doulton Number	U.S. $	Can. $	U.K. £	Aust. $
BP-1a	1183	P1183	275.00	375.00	175.00	400.00
BP-2			160.00	220.00	100.00	230.00
BP-3a			95.00	135.00	60.00	145.00
BP-3b			70.00	100.00	45.00	110.00
BP-3c			80.00	115.00	50.00	125.00
BP-6a			50.00	70.00	30.00	75.00
BP-10a			70.00	100.00	45.00	110.00

LADY MOUSE MADE A CURTSY™

Modeller:	Amanda Hughes-Lubeck
Height:	3 ¼", 8.3 cm
Colour:	Purple-pink and white
Issued:	1990 - 1997

Back Stamp	Beswick Number	Doulton Number	U.S. $	Can. $	U.K. £	Aust. $
BP-6a	3220	P3220	50.00	70.00	30.00	75.00

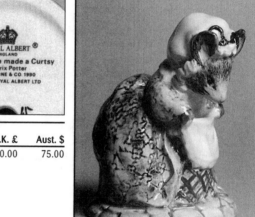

LITTLE BLACK RABBIT™

Modeller:	David Lyttleton
Height:	4 ½", 11.4 cm
Colour:	Black rabbit wearing green waistcoat
Issued:	1977 - 1997

Back Stamp	Beswick Number	Doulton Number	U.S. $	Can. $	U.K. £	Aust. $
BP-3b	2585	P2585	80.00	115.00	50.00	125.00
BP-3c			80.00	115.00	50.00	125.00
BP-4				Very Rare		
BP-6a			80.00	115.00	50.00	125.00

Note: 1. The jacket colouring varies from light to dark green.
2. The BP-4 version is very rare.

First version: Blue striped outfit

LITTLE PIG ROBINSON™

Modeller: Arthur Gredington

FIRST VARIATION: BLUE STRIPED OUTFIT

Height: 4", 10.2 cm
Colour: White and blue striped outfit,
           brown basket with yellow
           cauliflowers
Issued: 1948 - 1974

Back Stamp	Beswick Number	Doulton Number	Price U.S. $	Can. $	U.K. £	Aust. $
BP-1a	1104/1	P1104/1	475.00	675.00	300.00	700.00
BP-1b					Rare	
BP-2			250.00	350.00	160.00	375.00
BP-3a			240.00	325.00	150.00	350.00
BP-3b			240.00	325.00	150.00	350.00

Second version: Blue checked outfit

SECOND VARIATION: BLUE CHECKED OUTFIT

Height: 3 ½", 8.9 cm
Colour: Blue outfit, brown basket
           with cream cauliflowers
Issued: c.1974 - 1999
Re-issued: 2002

Back Stamp	Beswick Number	Doulton Number	Price U.S. $	Can. $	U.K. £	Aust. $
BP-3b	1104/2	P1104/2	90.00	125.00	55.00	135.00
BP-3c			80.00	115.00	50.00	125.00
BP-6a			50.00	70.00	30.00	75.00
BP-10c			30.00	45.00	20.00	50.00
BP-11a			40.00	60.00	25.00	65.00

LITTLE PIG ROBINSON SPYING™

Modeller: Ted Chawner
Height: 3 ½", 8.9 cm
Colour: Blue and white striped
             outfit, rose-pink chair
Issued: 1987 - 1993

Back Stamp	Beswick Number	Doulton Number	Price U.S. $	Can. $	U.K. £	Aust. $
BP-3c	3031	P3031	275.00	400.00	175.00	425.00
BP-6a			160.00	225.00	100.00	250.00

MISS DORMOUSE™

Modeller:	Martyn Alcock
Height:	4", 10.1 cm
Colour:	Blue, white and pink
Issued:	1991 - 1995

Back Stamp	Beswick Number	Doulton Number	Price U.S. $	Can. $	U.K. £	Aust. $
BP-6a	3251	P3251	120.00	170.00	75.00	180.00

MISS MOPPET™

Modeller:	Arthur Gredington
Height:	3", 7.6 cm

FIRST VARIATION: MOTTLED BROWN CAT

Colour:	Mottled brown cat, blue checkered kerchief
Issued:	1954 - c.1978

Back Stamp	Beswick Number	Doulton Number	Price U.S. $	Can. $	U.K. £	Aust. $
BP-1a	1275/1	P1275/1	800.00	1,150.00	500.00	1,200.00
BP-2			150.00	200.00	100.00	225.00
BP-3a			120.00	170.00	75.00	180.00
BP-3b			95.00	135.00	60.00	145.00

First version: Mottled brown cat

SECOND VARIATION: BROWN STRIPED CAT

Colour:	Striped brown cat, blue checkered kerchief
Issued:	1978 - 2002

Back Stamp	Beswick Number	Doulton Number	Price U.S. $	Can. $	U.K. £	Aust. $
BP-1a	1275/2	P1275/2	800.00	1,150.00	500.00	1,200.00
BP-2			150.00	200.00	100.00	225.00
BP-3a			80.00	115.00	50.00	125.00
BP-3b			80.00	115.00	50.00	125.00
BP-3c			70.00	100.00	45.00	110.00
BP-6a			50.00	70.00	30.00	75.00
BP-10b			35.00	50.00	20.00	55.00

Second version: Brown striped cat

MITTENS AND MOPPET™

Modeller:	Ted Chawner
Height:	3 ¾", 9.5 cm
Colour:	Blue, brown and grey
Issued:	1990 - 1994

ROYAL ALBERT
ENGLAND
Mittens and Moppet
Beatrix Potter
© F. WARNE & CO. 1989
© 1989 ROYAL ALBERT LTD

Back Stamp	Beswick Number	Doulton Number	Price			
			U.S. $	Can. $	U.K. £	Aust. $
BP-6a	3197	P3197	200.00	275.00	125.00	300.00

For **Mittens, Tom Kitten and Moppet** see the Tableaux Section, page 86.

MOTHER LADYBIRD™

Modeller:	Warren Platt
Height:	2 ½", 6.4 cm
Colour:	Red and black
Issued:	1989 - 1996

ROYAL ALBERT ®
ENGLAND
Mother Ladybird
Beatrix Potter
© F. WARNE & CO. 1989
© 1989 ROYAL ALBERT LTD

Back Stamp	Beswick Number	Doulton Number	Price			
			U.S. $	Can. $	U.K. £	Aust. $
BP-6a	2966	P2966	200.00	275.00	125.00	300.00

MR. ALDERMAN PTOLEMY™

Modeller:	Graham Tongue
Height:	3 ½", 8.9 cm
Colour:	Brown, grey and green
Issued:	1973 - 1997

BEATRIX POTTER'S
"Mr. Alderman Ptolemy"
F. Warne & Co. Ltd.
© Copyright 1973
BESWICK
MADE IN ENGLAND

Back Stamp	Beswick Number	Doulton Number	Price			
			U.S. $	Can. $	U.K. £	Aust. $
BP-3a	2424	P2424	200.00	275.00	125.00	300.00
BP-3b			150.00	200.00	100.00	210.00
BP-3c			200.00	275.00	125.00	300.00
BP-6a			55.00	75.00	35.00	80.00

Note: Mr. Alderman Ptolemy and Sir Isaac Newton are the only figures with backstamps using the words "Made in England" vice "England."

MR. BENJAMIN BUNNY™

Modeller: Arthur Gredington
Height: 4 ¼", 10.8 cm

FIRST VERSION: PIPE OUT

Colour: Variation No. 1 Dark maroon jacket
Variation No. 2 Lilac jacket
Issued: 1965 - 1974

Back Stamp	Beswick Number	Colour Variation	Price			
			U.S. $	Can. $	U.K. £	Aust. $
BP-2	1940/1	Dark maroon	475.00	675.00	300.00	700.00
BP-3a		Dark maroon	400.00	550.00	250.00	575.00
BP-3a		Lilac		Very Rare		

First version: Pipe out

SECOND VERSION: PIPE IN

Colour: Variation No. 1 Dark maroon jacket
Variation No. 2 Lilac jacket
Issued: 1. c.1970 - c.1974
2. 1975 - 2000
Re-issued: 2. 2002

Back Stamp	Beswick Number	Colour Variation	Price			
			U.S. $	Can. $	U.K. £	Aust. $
BP-3a	1940/2	Dark maroon	400.00	575.00	250.00	600.00
BP-3a		Lilac	500.00	700.00	325.00	725.00
BP-3b		Dark maroon	400.00	575.00	250.00	600.00
BP-3b		Lilac	110.00	150.00	70.00	160.00
BP-3c		Lilac	110.00	150.00	70.00	160.00
BP-4		Lilac	95.00	135.00	60.00	150.00
BP-6a		Lilac	40.00	55.00	25.00	60.00
BP-10b		Lilac	30.00	45.00	20.00	50.00
BP-11a		Lilac	40.00	55.00	25.00	60.00

Second version: Pipe in

MR. BENJAMIN BUNNY AND PETER RABBIT™

Modeller: Alan Maslankowski
Height: 4", 10.1 cm
Colour: Benjamin Bunny: lilac jacket,
yellow waistcoat
Peter Rabbit: blue jacket
Issued: 1975 - 1995

Back Stamp	Beswick Number	Doulton Number	Price			
			U.S. $	Can. $	U.K. £	Aust. $
BP-3b	2509	P2509	200.00	275.00	135.00	300.00
BP-3c			175.00	250.00	110.00	275.00
BP-6a			80.00	110.00	50.00	115.00

MR. DRAKE PUDDLE-DUCK™

Modeller: David Lyttleton
Height: 4", 10.1 cm
Colour: White duck, blue
waistcoat and trousers
Issued: 1979 - 2000

BEATRIX POTTER
"Mr. Drake Puddle-Duck"
© Frederick Warne & Co. 1979
Licensed by Copyrights
BESWICK ENGLAND

Back Stamp	Beswick Number	Doulton Number	Price			
			U.S. $	Can. $	U.K. £	Aust. $
BP-3b	2628	P2628	65.00	90.00	40.00	95.00
BP-3c			80.00	110.00	50.00	115.00
BP-4			80.00	110.00	50.00	115.00
BP-6a			50.00	70.00	30.00	75.00
BP-10b			55.00	80.00	35.00	85.00

First version: Green toad

MR. JACKSON™

Modeller: Albert Hallam
Height: 2 ¾", 7.0 cm

FIRST VARIATION: GREEN TOAD

Colour: Green toad wearing
mauve jacket
Issued: 1974 - c.1974

BEATRIX POTTER'S
"Mr Jackson"
F. Warne & Co. Ltd.
Copyright
BESWICK ENGLAND

Back Stamp	Beswick Number	Doulton Number	Price			
			U.S. $	Can. $	U.K. £	Aust. $
BP-3a	2453/1	P2453/1	600.00	850.00	375.00	875.00

Second version: Brown toad

SECOND VARIATION: BROWN TOAD

Colour: Brown toad wearing mauve jacket
Issued: 1975 - 1997

BEATRIX POTTER'S
"Mr Jackson"
F. Warne & Co. Ltd.
© Copyright 1974
BESWICK ENGLAND

Back Stamp	Beswick Number	Doulton Number	Price			
			U.S. $	Can. $	U.K. £	Aust. $
BP-3b	2453/2	P2453/2	100.00	150.00	65.00	160.00
BP-3c			110.00	160.00	70.00	170.00
BP-6a			55.00	75.00	35.00	80.00

MR. JEREMY FISHER™

Modeller:	Arthur Gredington
Height:	3", 7.6 cm
Size:	Small

FIRST VERSION: SMALL SIZE
FIRST VARIATION: SPOTTED LEGS

Colour:	Lilac coat, green frog with small brown spots on head and legs
Issued:	1950 - c.1974

Back Stamp	Beswick Number	Doulton Number	U.S. $	Can. $	Price U.K. £	Aust. $
BP-1a	1157/1	P1157/1	400.00	550.00	250.00	575.00
BP-2			250.00	335.00	150.00	360.00
BP-3a			150.00	200.00	90.00	225.00
BP-3b			115.00	160.00	70.00	175.00

FIRST VERSION: SMALL SIZE
SECOND VARIATION: STRIPED LEGS

Colour:	Lilac coat, green frog with large spots on head and stripes on legs
Issued:	c.1950 - 2002

Back Stamp	Beswick Number	Doulton Number	U.S. $	Can. $	Price U.K. £	Aust. $
BP-1a	1157/2	P1157/2	400.00	550.00	250.00	575.00
BP-3b			70.00	100.00	45.00	110.00
BP-3c			95.00	135.00	60.00	150.00
BP-6a			50.00	70.00	30.00	75.00
BP-10a			30.00	45.00	20.00	50.00

Note: BP-3c backstamp name exists with and without "Mr."

FIRST VERSION: SMALL SIZE
THIRD VARIATION: SATIN FINISH

Colour:	Lilac coat, beige frog with large spots on head and stripes on legs
Issued:	2001 - 2002

Back Stamp	Beswick Number	Doulton Number	U.S. $	Can. $	Price U.K. £	Aust. $
BP-11a	1157/3	PS1157	40.00	60.00	25.00	65.00

SECOND VERSION: LARGE SIZE
FIRST VARIATION: LILAC BUTTONS

Modeller:	Martyn Alcock
Height:	5", 12.7 cm
Size:	Large
Colour:	Lilac coat, green frog with stripes on legs
Issued:	1994 - 1997

Back Stamp	Beswick Number	Doulton Number	U.S. $	Can. $	Price U.K. £	Aust. $
BP-6b	3372/1	P3372	70.00	100.00	45.00	110.00

SECOND VERSION: LARGE SIZE
SECOND VARIATION: GOLD BUTTONS

Colour:	Green frog with stripes on legs, lilac coat with gold buttons
Issued:	1998 in a limited edition of 1,947
Series:	Gold edition

Back Stamp	Beswick Number	Doulton Number	U.S. $	Can. $	Price U.K. £	Aust. $
BP-9c	3372/2	PG3372	95.00	135.00	60.00	150.00

Note: Issued, numbered and sold as a pair with Tom Kitten, second version, second variation.

Small size, spotted legs

Small size, striped legs

Large size, striped legs

MR. JEREMY FISHER DIGGING™

Modeller:	Ted Chawner
Height:	3 ¾", 9.5 cm
Colour:	Mauve coat, pink waistcoat, white cravat, green frog with brown highlights
Issued:	1988 - 1994

BEATRIX POTTER
"Mr. Jeremy Fisher Digging"
© F. Warne & Co. 1988
Licensed by Copyrights
John Baswick
Studio of Royal Doulton
England

Back Stamp	Beswick Number	Doulton Number	Price			
			U.S. $	Can. $	U.K. £	Aust. $
BP-4	3090	P3090	275.00	400.00	175.00	425.00
BP-6a			125.00	175.00	75.00	200.00

Note: Jeremy Fisher's skin may have dark or light spots.

MR. McGREGOR™

Modeller:	Martyn Alcock
Height:	5 ¼", 13.5 cm
Colour:	Brown hat and trousers, tan vest and pale blue shirt
Issued:	1995 - 2002

ROYAL ALBERT ®
ENGLAND
Mr McGregor
Beatrix Potter
© F. WARNE & CO. 1995
© 1995 ROYAL ALBERT LTD

Back Stamp	Beswick Number	Doulton Number	Price			
			U.S. $	Can. $	U.K. £	Aust. $
BP-6a	3506/1	P3506/1	75.00	100.00	45.00	110.00
BP-10b			60.00	85.00	25.00	95.00

Note: A variation of this figure exists with the right arm at chest height.

MR. TOD™

Modeller:	Ted Chawner
Height:	4 ¾", 12.1 cm
Colour:	Green suit, red waistcoat, dark brown walking stick
Issued:	1988 - 1993

BEATRIX POTTER
"Mr. Tod"
© F. Warne & Co. 1988
Licensed by Copyrights
John Baswick
Studio of Royal Doulton
England

Back Stamp	Beswick Number	Doulton Number	Price			
			U.S. $	Can. $	U.K. £	Aust. $
BP-4	3091/1	P3091/1	275.00	400.00	175.00	425.00
BP-6a			200.00	300.00	135.00	135.00

Note: Variations occur with the head facing right or left, and the base in either green or brown.

MRS. FLOPSY BUNNY™

Modeller: Arthur Gredington
Height: 4", 10.1 cm
Colour: 1. Dark blue dress, pink bag
2. Light blue dress, pink bag
Issued: 1965 - 1998

Back Stamp	Beswick Number	Colour Variation	Price			
			U.S. $	Can. $	U.K. £	Aust. $
BP-2	1942	Dark blue	200.00	275.00	125.00	300.00
BP-3a		Dark blue	80.00	110.00	50.00	115.00
BP-3b		Dark blue	65.00	90.00	40.00	95.00
BP-3b		Light blue	80.00	110.00	50.00	115.00
BP-3c		Light blue	90.00	125.00	55.00	135.00
BP-4		Light blue	95.00	135.00	60.00	150.00
BP-6a		Light blue	50.00	70.00	30.00	75.00
BP-10b		Light blue	50.00	70.00	30.00	75.00

MRS. RABBIT™

Modeller: Arthur Gredington
Height: 4 ¼", 10.8 cm
Size: Small

FIRST VERSION: SMALL SIZE, UMBRELLA OUT

Colour: 1. Pink and yellow striped dress
2. Lilac and yellow striped dress
Issued: 1951 - c.1974

Back Stamp	Beswick Number	Colour Variation	Price			
			U.S. $	Can. $	U.K. £	Aust. $
BP-1a	1200/1	Pink		Very Rare		
BP-2		Pink	325.00	450.00	200.00	475.00
BP-2		Lilac	325.00	450.00	200.00	475.00
BP-3a		Lilac	200.00	275.00	125.00	300.00
BP-3b		Lilac	200.00	275.00	125.00	300.00

Note: Due to its small base a gold oval backstamp was used for the bulk of pre-1955 production; the gold circle backstamp is very rare.

First version: Umbrella out

SECOND VERSION: SMALL SIZE UMBRELLA MOULDED TO DRESS

Colour: Lilac and yellow striped dress, red collar and cap, light straw coloured basket
Issued: c.1975 - 2002

Back Stamp	Beswick Number	Doulton Number	Price			
			U.S. $	Can. $	U.K. £	Aust. $
BP-3b	1200/2	P1200/2	80.00	110.00	50.00	115.00
BP-3c			95.00	135.00	60.00	150.00
BP-4			100.00	150.00	65.00	165.00
BP-6a			50.00	70.00	30.00	75.00
BP-10c			30.00	45.00	20.00	50.00

Second version: Umbrella moulded to dress

Brown umbrella point and handle

MRS. RABBIT™

Modeller:	Martyn Alcock
Height:	6 ¼", 15.9 cm
Size:	Large

THIRD VERSION: LARGE SIZE
FIRST VARIATION: BROWN UMBRELLA POINT AND HANDLE

Colour:	White, pink, yellow and green
Issued:	1994 - 1997

ROYAL ALBERT ®
ENGLAND
Mrs Rabbit
Beatrix Potter
© F. WARNE & CO. 1993
© 1993 ROYAL ALBERT LTD.

Back Stamp	Beswick Number	Doulton Number	Price			
			U.S. $	Can. $	U.K. £	Aust. $
BP-6b	3398/1	P3398	70.00	100.00	45.00	110.00

Gold umbrella point and handle

THIRD VERSION: LARGE SIZE
SECOND VARIATION: GOLD UMBRELLA POINT AND HANDLE

Colour:	White, pink, yellow and green, gold umbrella point and handle
Issued:	1998 in a limited edition of 1,947
Series:	Gold edition

Back Stamp	Beswick Number	Doulton Number	Price			
			U.S. $	Can. $	U.K. £	Aust. $
BP-9c	3398/2	PG3398	95.00	135.00	60.00	150.00

Note: Issued, numbered and sold as a pair with Foxy Whiskered Gentleman, second version, second variation.

MRS. RABBIT AND BUNNIES™

Modeller:	David Lyttleton
Height:	3 ¾", 9.5 cm
Colour:	Blue dress with white apron, dark blue chair
Issued:	1976 - 1997

BEATRIX POTTER'S
Mrs. Rabbit and Bunnies
F. Warne & Co. Ltd.
© Copyright 1976
BESWICK ENGLAND

Back Stamp	Beswick Number	Doulton Number	Price			
			U.S. $	Can. $	U.K. £	Aust. $
BP-3b	2543	P2543	80.00	110.00	50.00	125.00
BP-3c			100.00	150.00	65.00	165.00
BP-4			115.00	160.00	70.00	175.00
BP-5			140.00	190.00	85.00	200.00
BP-6a			55.00	80.00	35.00	85.00

MRS. RABBIT AND PETER™
FIRST VERSION: SMALL SIZE

Modeller: Warren Platt
Height: 3 ½", 8.9 cm
Size: Small
Colour: Mrs. Rabbit: Pale blue dress, white apron
Peter: Pale blue coat, yellow buttons
Issued: 1997 - 2002

Back Stamp	Beswick Number	Doulton Number	Price			
			U.S. $	Can. $	U.K. £	Aust. $
BP-6a	3646	P3646	65.00	90.00	40.00	95.00
BP-10b			75.00	100.00	35.00	110.00

First version: Small size

SECOND VERSION: LARGE SIZE

Modeller: Amanda Hughes-Lubeck
Height: 5 ¼", 13.3 cm
Size: Large
Colour: Mrs. Rabbit: Pale blue dress; white apron
Peter: Pale blue coat with gold buttons
Issued: 1999 in a limited edition of 2,500

Back Stamp	Beswick Number	Doulton Number	Price			
			U.S. $	Can. $	U.K. £	Aust. $
BP-9c	3978	PG3978	130.00	180.00	80.00	200.00

Second version: Large size, gold buttons

MRS. RABBIT COOKING™

Modeller: Martyn Alcock
Height: 4", 10.1 cm
Colour: Blue dress, white apron
Issued: 1992 - 1999

Back Stamp	Beswick Number	Doulton Number	Price			
			U.S. $	Can. $	U.K. £	Aust. $
BP-6a	3278	P3278	50.00	70.00	30.00	75.00
BP-10b			65.00	90.00	40.00	95.00

For **Mrs. Rabbit and the Four Bunnies** see the Tableaux Section, page 86.

Small size, diagonal stripes

Small size, plaid

Small size, platinum iron

MRS. TIGGY-WINKLE™

Modeller:	Arthur Gredington
Height:	3 ¼", 8.3 cm
Size:	Small

FIRST VERSION: SMALL SIZE
FIRST VARIATION: GLOSS FINISH, DIAGONAL STRIPES

Colour: Diagonal striped red-brown and white dress, green and blue striped skirt, white apron

Issued: 1948 - 1974

Back Stamp	Beswick Number	Doulton Number	Price U.S. $	Can. $	U.K. £	Aust. $
BP-1a	1107/1	P1107/1	275.00	400.00	175.00	425.00
BP-2			200.00	275.00	125.00	300.00
BP-3a			100.00	150.00	65.00	165.00

Note: This figurine is also recognizable by the heavily patterned bustle.

FIRST VERSION: SMALL SIZE
SECOND VARIATION: GLOSS FINISH, PLAID

Colour: Red-brown and white plaid dress, green and blue striped skirt, white apron

Issued: 1972 - 2000

Back Stamp	Beswick Number	Doulton Number	Price U.S. $	Can. $	U.K. £	Aust. $
BP-2	1107/2	P1107/2	200.00	275.00	125.00	300.00
BP-3a			100.00	150.00	65.00	165.00
BP-3b			80.00	110.00	50.00	125.00
BP-3c			100.00	150.00	65.00	165.00
BP-4			110.00	160.00	70.00	175.00
BP-6a			50.00	70.00	30.00	75.00
BP-10c			35.00	45.00	20.00	55.00

FIRST VERSION: SMALL SIZE
THIRD VARIATION: GLOSS FINISH, PLATINUM IRON

Colour: Red-brown and white dress, green and blue striped skirt, white apron, platinum iron

Issued: 1998 - 1998

Back Stamp	Beswick Number	Doulton Number	Price U.S. $	Can. $	U.K. £	Aust. $
BP-9b	1107/3	PG1107	55.00	80.00	35.00	90.00

FIRST VERSION: SMALL SIZE
FOURTH VARIATION: SATIN FINISH

Colour: Red-brown and white dress, tan and blue striped skirt, white apron; satin glaze

Issued: 2001 - 2002

Back Stamp	Beswick Number	Doulton Number	Price U.S. $	Can. $	U.K. £	Aust. $
BP-11a	1107/4	PS1107	40.00	60.00	25.00	65.00

MRS. TIGGY-WINKLE™

Modeller: Amanda Hughes-Lubeck
Height: 4 ½", 11.9 cm
Size: Large

SECOND VERSION: LARGE SIZE
FIRST VARIATION: CREAMY-BROWN IRON

Colour: Brown and white striped dress, white apron, creamy-brown iron
Issued: 1996 - 1997

Back Stamp	Beswick Number	Doulton Number	Price			
			U.S. $	Can. $	U.K. £	Aust. $
BP-6b	3437/1	P3437	70.00	100.00	45.00	110.00

Large size, creamy-brown iron

SECOND VERSION: LARGE SIZE
SECOND VARIATION: PLATINUM IRON

Colour: Brown and white striped dress, white apron, platinum iron
Issued: 1998 in a limited edition of 1,947
Series Gold edition

Back Stamp	Beswick Number	Doulton Number	Price			
			U.S. $	Can. $	U.K. £	Aust. $
BP-9c	3437/2	PG3437	95.00	135.00	60.00	150.00

Note: Issued, numbered and sold as a pair with Jemima Puddle-Duck, second version, second variation.

For **Mrs. Tiggy-Winkle and Lucie** see the Tableaux Section, page 86.

Large size, platinum iron

MRS. TIGGY-WINKLE BUYS PROVISIONS™

Modeller: Martin Alcock
Height: 3 ¼", 8.3 cm
Colour: Pink and white dress, white and brown mob cap
Issued: 2002 - 2002

Back Stamp	Beswick Number	Doulton Number	Price			
			U.S. $	Can. $	U.K. £	Aust. $
BP-11a	4234	P4234	250.00	350.00	150.00	375.00

MRS. TIGGY WINKLE TAKES TEA™

Modeller:	David Lyttleton
Height:	3 ¼", 8.3 cm
Colour:	Pink and white dress, white and brown mob cap
Issued:	1985 - 2002

Back Stamp	Beswick Number	Doulton Number	Price			
			U.S. $	Can. $	U.K. £	Aust. $
BP-3b	2877	P2877	100.00	150.00	65.00	165.00
BP-3c			100.00	150.00	65.00	165.00
BP-4			125.00	175.00	80.00	185.00
BP-6a			40.00	55.00	25.00	60.00
BP-10a			35.00	45.00	20.00	50.00

MRS. TIGGY-WINKLE WASHING™

Modeller:	David Lyttleton
Height:	2 ½", 6.4 cm
Colour:	Brown and white
Issued:	1998 - 2000

Back Stamp	Beswick Number	Doulton Number	Price			
			U.S. $	Can. $	U.K. £	Aust. $
BP-8a	3789	P3789	200.00	300.00	125.00	325.00
BP-10a			40.00	55.00	25.00	60.00

Note: Approximately 1,800 pieces were issued with the BP-8a backstamp.

MRS. TITTLEMOUSE™
STYLE ONE

Modeller: Arthur Gredington
Height: 3 ½", 8.9 cm
Colour: White and red striped blouse, blue and white striped skirt
Issued: 1948 - 1993

Back Stamp	Beswick Number	Doulton Number	Price			
			U.S. $	Can. $	U.K. £	Aust. $
BP-1a	1103	P1103	275.00	400.00	175.00	425.00
BP-2			160.00	225.00	100.00	250.00
BP-3a			90.00	125.00	55.00	135.00
BP-3b			80.00	115.00	50.00	125.00
BP-3c			90.00	125.00	55.00	135.00
BP-6a			65.00	90.00	40.00	100.00

MRS. TITTLEMOUSE™
STYLE TWO

Modeller: Shane Ridge
Height: 3 ½", 8.9 cm
Colour: White and red striped blouse, blue and white striped skirt, white apron
Issued: 2000 - 2002

Back Stamp	Beswick Number	Doulton Number	Price			
			U.S. $	Can. $	U.K. £	Aust. $
BP-10a	4015	P4015	60.00	110.00	35.00	125.00

For **My Dear Son Thomas** see the Tableaux Section, page 87.

NO MORE TWIST™

Modeller: Martyn Alcock
Height: 3 ½", 9.2 cm
Colour: Brown and white mouse
Issued: 1992 - 1997

Back Stamp	Beswick Number	Doulton Number	Price			
			U.S. $	Can. $	U.K. £	Aust. $
BP-6a	3325	P3325	60.00	85.00	35.00	90.00

OLD MR. BOUNCER™

Modeller:	David Lyttleton
Height:	3", 7.6 cm
Colour:	Brown jacket and trousers, blue scarf
Issued:	1986 - 1995

BEATRIX POTTER
"Old Mr. Bouncer"
© Frederick Warne & Co. 1986
Licensed by Copyrights
BESWICK ENGLAND

Back Stamp	Beswick Number	Doulton Number	Price			
			U.S. $	Can. $	U.K. £	Aust. $
BP-3c	2956	P2956	95.00	135.00	60.00	150.00
BP-6a			115.00	160.00	70.00	175.00

OLD MR. BROWN™

Modeller:	Albert Hallam
Height:	3 ¼", 8.3 cm
Colour:	1. Brown owl, red squirrel
	2. Orange owl, red squirrel
Issued:	1963 - 1999

BEATRIX POTTER'S
Old Mr. Brown
F. WARNE & CO. LTD
COPYRIGHT
BESWICK
ENGLAND

Back Stamp	Beswick Number	Colour Variation	Price			
			U.S. $	Can. $	U.K. £	Aust. $
BP-2	1796	Brown	160.00	225.00	100.00	250.00
BP-3a		Brown	85.00	125.00	55.00	135.00
BP-3b		Brown	80.00	110.00	50.00	115.00
BP-3b		Orange	95.00	135.00	60.00	150.00
BP-3c		Orange	95.00	135.00	60.00	150.00
BP-6a		Orange	50.00	70.00	30.00	75.00
BP-10a		Orange	35.00	45.00	20.00	50.00

OLD MR. PRICKLEPIN™

Modeller:	David Lyttleton
Height:	2 ½", 6.4 cm
Colour:	Brown
Issued:	1983 - 1989

BEATRIX POTTER'S
"Old Mr Pricklepin"
© Frederick Warne P.L.C. 1983
BESWICK ENGLAND

Back Stamp	Beswick Number	Doulton Number	Price			
			U.S. $	Can. $	U.K. £	Aust. $
BP-3b	2767	P2767	150.00	200.00	95.00	225.00
BP-3c			150.00	200.00	95.00	225.00
BP-6a				Very Rare		

For **Peter and Benjamin Picking Apples** and **Peter and Benjamin Picking Up Onions** see the Tableaux Section, page 87

PETER AND THE RED POCKET HANDKERCHIEF™

Modeller: Martyn Alcock
Height: 4 ¾", 12.3 cm
Size: Small

ROYAL ALBERT ®
ENGLAND
Peter and the
Red Pocket Handkerchief
Beatrix Potter
© F. WARNE & CO. 1990
© 1990 ROYAL ALBERT LTD

FIRST VERSION: SMALL SIZE
FIRST VARIATION: YELLOW BUTTONS

Colour: Light blue jacket with yellow
buttons, red handkerchief
Issued: 1991 - 1999

Back Stamp	Beswick Number	Doulton Number	Price			
			U.S. $	Can. $	U.K. £	Aust. $
BP-6a	3242	P3242	50.00	70.00	30.00	75.00
BP-10a			40.00	55.00	25.00	60.00

First version: Small size

FIRST VERSION: SMALL SIZE
SECOND VARIATION: GOLD BUTTONS

Colour: Dark blue jacket with gold buttons,
red handkerchief
Issued: 1997 - 1997

Back Stamp	Beswick Number	Doulton Number	Price			
			U.S. $	Can. $	U.K. £	Aust. $
BP-9d	5190	PG5190	80.00	110.00	50.00	125.00

Note: Peter Rabbit, first version, second variation was commissioned by Petter Rabbit and Friends.

Second version: Small size, gold buttons

Second version: Large size

PETER AND THE RED POCKET HANDKERCHIEF™

Modeller: Amanda Hughes-Lubeck
Height: 7 ¼", 18.4 cm
Size: Large

SECOND VERSION: LARGE SIZE
FIRST VARIATION: YELLOW BUTTONS

Colour: Light blue coat with yellow
             buttons, red handkerchief
Issued: 1996 - 1997

Back Stamp	Beswick Number	Doulton Number	Price			
			U.S. $	Can. $	U.K. £	Aust. $
BP-6b	3592/1	P3592	70.00	110.00	45.00	110.00

Note: The backstamp on this version reads Peter "with" the Red Pocket Handkerchief.

Second version: Large size, gold buttons

SECOND VERSION: LARGE SIZE
SECOND VARIATION: GOLD BUTTONS

Colour: Light blue coat with gold buttons,
             red handkerchief
Issued: 1998 in a limited edition of 1,947
Series: Gold edition

Back Stamp	Beswick Number	Doulton Number	Price			
			U.S. $	Can. $	U.K. £	Aust. $
BP-9c	3592/2	PG3592	95.00	135.00	60.00	150.00

Note: Issued, numbered and sold as a pair with The Tailor of Gloucester, second version, second variation.

PETER ATE A RADISH™

Modeller: Warren Platt
Height: 4", 10.1 cm
Colour: Blue jacket, brown and
             white rabbit, red radishes
Issued: 1995 - 1998

Back Stamp	Beswick Number	Doulton Number	Price			
			U.S. $	Can. $	U.K. £	Aust. $
BP-6a	3533	P3533	50.00	75.00	30.00	85.00

Note: BP-10b backstamp was reported by Royal Doulton in the backstamp changeover in 1998. We need confirmation that this backstamp was used on an actual issued figure. If it does exist, it is very rare.

PETER IN BED™

Modeller:	Martyn Alcock
Height:	2 ¾", 7.0 cm
Colour:	Blue, white, pink and green
Issued:	1995 - 2002

Back Stamp	Beswick Number	Doulton Number	Price			
			U.S. $	Can. $	U.K. £	Aust. $
BP-6a	3473	P3473	55.00	75.00	35.00	85.00
BP-10a			60.00	80.00	25.00	90.00

PETER IN THE GOOSEBERRY NET™

Modeller:	David Lyttleton
Height:	2", 4.6 cm
Colour:	Brown and white rabbit wearing blue jacket, green netting
Issued:	1989 - 1995

Back Stamp	Beswick Number	Doulton Number	Price			
			U.S. $	Can. $	U.K. £	Aust. $
BP-6a	3157	P3157	80.00	125.00	55.00	135.00

PETER IN THE WATERING CAN™

Modeller:	Warren Platt
Height:	5", 12.7 cm
Colour:	Brown rabbit in a green watering can
Issued:	1999 - 2002

Back Stamp	Beswick Number	Doulton Number	Price			
			U.S. $	Can. $	U.K. £	Aust. $
BP-10a	3940	P3940	60.00	95.00	30.00	100.00

PETER ON HIS BOOK™

Modeller:	Martyn Alcock
Height:	5", 12.7 cm
Colour:	Pale blue jacket, gold buttons, white book
Issued:	2002 - 2002

Back Stamp	Beswick Number	Doulton Number	Price			
			U.S. $	Can. $	U.K. £	Aust. $
BP-11b	P4217	P4217	100.00	150.00	50.00	165.00

Note: Issued to commemorate the 100th anniversary of the book The Tales of Peter Rabbit.

PETER RABBIT™

Modeller:	Arthur Gredington
Height:	4 ½", 11.4 cm
Size:	Small

FIRST VERSION: SMALL SIZE
FIRST VARIATION: DEEP BLUE JACKET

Colour:	Dark blue jacket with yellow buttons
Issued:	1948 - c.1980

Back Stamp	Beswick Number	Doulton Number	Price			
			U.S. $	Can. $	U.K. £	Aust. $
BP-1a	1098/1	P1098/1	275.00	400.00	175.00	425.00
BP-1b					Rare	
BP-2			200.00	275.00	120.00	300.00
BP-3a			110.00	150.00	70.00	160.00
BP-3b			90.00	125.00	55.00	135.00

FIRST VERSION: SMALL SIZE; SECOND VARIATION: LIGHT BLUE JACKET

Colour:	Light blue jacket with yellow buttons
Issued:	c.1980 - 2002

Back Stamp	Beswick Number	Base Variation	Price			
			U.S. $	Can. $	U.K. £	Aust. $
BP-3b	1098/2	Short base	65.00	90.00	40.00	100.00
BP-3b		Long base	65.00	90.00	40.00	100.00
BP-3c		Long base	75.00	100.00	45.00	110.00
BP-4		Long base	85.00	125.00	50.00	135.00
BP-5		Long base	125.00	175.00	75.00	190.00
BP-6a		Long base	40.00	60.00	25.00	70.00
BP-10b		Long base	36.00	50.00	20.00	60.00

FIRST VERSION: SMALL SIZE; THIRD VARIATION: LIGHT BLUE JACKET, GOLD BUTTONS

Colour:	Light blue jacket with gold buttons
Issued:	1997 - 1997

Back Stamp	Beswick Number	Doulton Number	Price			
			U.S. $	Can. $	U.K. £	Aust. $
BP-9b	1098/3	PG1098	65.00	90.00	40.00	100.00

FIRST VERSION: SMALL SIZE; FOURTH VARIATION: SATIN FINISH

Colour:	Blue jacket with yellow buttons
Issued:	2001 - 2002

Back Stamp	Beswick Number	Doulton Number	Price			
			U.S. $	Can. $	U.K. £	Aust. $
BP-11a	1098/4	PS1098	40.00	60.00	25.00	65.00

Small size, deep blue jacket

Small size, gold buttons

PETER RABBIT™

Modeller: Martyn Alcock
Height: 6 ¾", 17.1 cm
Size: Large

SECOND VERSION: LARGE SIZE
FIRST VARIATION: YELLOW BUTTONS

Colour: Light blue jacket, yellow buttons
Issued: 1993 - 1997

Back Stamp	Beswick Number	Doulton Number	Price			
			U.S. $	Can. $	U.K. £	Aust. $
BP-6b	3356/1	P3356	70.00	100.00	45.00	110.00
BP-7	100th Anniversary		95.00	135.00	60.00	150.00

Note: The BP-7 backstamp was used only in 1993.

Large size, yellow buttons

SECOND VERSION: LARGE SIZE
SECOND VARIATION: GOLD BUTTONS

Colour: Blue jacket with gold buttons
Issued: 1997 in a limited edtion of 1,947
Series: Gold edition

Back Stamp	Beswick Number	Doulton Number	Price			
			U.S. $	Can. $	U.K. £	Aust. $
BP-9c	3356/2	PG3356	95.00	135.00	60.00	150.00

Note: The second variation of this model was issued, numbered and sold as a pair with Benjamin Bunny, fourth version, fourth variation.

Large size, gold buttons

PETER RABBIT DIGGING™

Modeller: Martyn Alcock
Height: 5", 12.7 cm
Colour: Pale blue jacket
Issued: 2001 - 2002

Back Stamp	Beswick Number	Doulton Number	Price			
			U.S. $	Can. $	U.K. £	Aust. $
BP-11a	P4075	P4075	60.00	90.00	30.00	100.00

PETER RABBIT GARDENING™

Modeller:	Warren Platt
Height:	5", 12.7 cm
Colour:	Blue jacket, brown shovel, basket of carrots
Issued:	1998 - 1999

Back Stamp	Beswick Number	Doulton Number	Price			
			U.S. $	Can. $	U.K. £	Aust. $
BP-10b	3739	P3739	55.00	80.00	35.00	90.00

PETER WITH DAFFODILS™

Modeller:	Warren Platt
Height:	4 ¾", 12.1 cm
Colour:	Light blue coat, yellow daffodils
Issued:	1996 - 1999

Back Stamp	Beswick Number	Doulton Number	Price			
			U.S. $	Can. $	U.K. £	Aust. $
BP-6a	3597	P3597	50.00	70.00	30.00	75.00
BP-10b			50.00	70.00	30.00	75.00

ROYAL ALBERT ®
ENGLAND
Peter with Postbag
Beatrix Potter
© F. WARNE & CO 1996
© 1996 ROYAL ALBERT LTD

PETER WITH POSTBAG™

Modeller:	Amanda Hughes-Lubeck
Height:	4 ¾", 12.1 cm
Colour:	Light brown rabbit and postbag, lilac jacket trimmed in red
Issued:	1996 - 2002

Back Stamp	Beswick Number	Doulton Number	Price			
			U.S. $	Can. $	U.K. £	Aust. $
BP-6a	3591	P3591	50.00	70.00	30.00	75.00
BP-10b			40.00	60.00	25.00	65.00

PICKLES™

Modeller:	Albert Hallam
Height:	4 ½", 11.4 cm
Colour:	Black face dog with brown jacket and white apron, pink book
Issued:	1971 - 1982

Back Stamp	Beswick Number	Doulton Number	Price			
			U.S. $	Can. $	U.K. £	Aust. $
BP-2	2334	P2334	450.00	625.00	285.00	650.00
BP-3a			375.00	525.00	250.00	550.00
BP-3b			350.00	500.00	225.00	525.00

PIGLING BLAND™

Modeller:	Graham Orwell
Height:	4 ¼", 10.8 cm

FIRST VARIATION: DEEP MAROON JACKET

Colour:	Purple jacket, blue waistcoat, yellow trousers
Issued:	1955 - 1974

Back Stamp	Beswick Number	Doulton Number	Price			
			U.S. $	Can. $	U.K. £	Aust. $
BP-1a	1365/1	P1365/1		Very rare		
BP-2			400.00	550.00	250.00	575.00
BP-3a			275.00	375.00	175.00	400.00
BP-3b			250.00	350.00	150.00	375.00

First variation: Purple jacket

SECOND VARIATION: LILAC JACKET

Colour:	Lilac jacket, blue waistcoat, yellow trousers
Issued:	c.1975 - 1998

Back Stamp	Beswick Number	Doulton Number	Price			
			U.S. $	Can. $	U.K. £	Aust. $
BP-3b	1365/2	P1365/2	65.00	95.00	40.00	100.00
BP-3c			95.00	125.00	60.00	135.00
BP-6a			50.00	70.00	30.00	75.00
BP-10c			55.00	80.00	35.00	85.00

Note: An example is known to exist with a grey jacket, light blue waistcoat, white trousers and tie. (BP-6a).

Second variation: Lilac jacket

PIGLING EATS HIS PORRIDGE™

Modeller:	Martyn Alcock
Height:	4", 10.1 cm
Colour:	Brown coat, blue waistcoat and yellow trousers
Issued:	1991 - 1994

Back Stamp	Beswick Number	Doulton Number	U.S. $	Can. $	U.K. £	Aust. $
					Price	
BP-6a	3252	P3252	200.00	275.00	125.00	300.00

PIG-WIG™

Modeller:	Albert Hallam
Height:	4", 10.1 cm
Colour:	1. Grey pig, pale blue dress
	2. Black pig, deep blue dress
Issued:	1972 - 1982

Back Stamp	Beswick Number	Colour Variation	U.S. $	Can. $	U.K. £	Aust. $
					Price	
BP-2	2381	Grey pig			Extremely Rare	
BP-3a		Black pig	475.00	675.00	300.00	700.00
BP-3b		Black pig	450.00	625.00	285.00	650.00

POORLY PETER RABBIT™

Modeller:	David Lyttleton
Height:	3 ¾", 9.5 cm
Colour:	Brown-red and white blanket
Issued:	1976 - 1997

Back Stamp	Beswick Number	Doulton Number	U.S. $	Can. $	U.K. £	Aust. $
					Price	
BP-3b	2560	P2560	100.00	150.00	65.00	165.00
BP-3c			95.00	135.00	60.00	150.00
BP-4			125.00	175.00	75.00	200.00
BP-6a			70.00	100.00	45.00	110.00

Note: Later models have a lighter brown blanket.

REBECCAH PUDDLE-DUCK™

Modeller:	David Lyttleton
Height:	3 ¼", 8.3 cm
Colour:	White goose, pale blue coat and hat
Issued:	1981 - 2000
Re-Issued:	2002

Back Stamp	Beswick Number	Doulton Number	Price			
			U.S. $	Can. $	U.K. £	Aust. $
BP-3b	2647	P2647	65.00	90.00	40.00	95.00
BP-3c			90.00	125.00	55.00	135.00
BP-4			90.00	125.00	55.00	135.00
BP-6a			40.00	55.00	25.00	60.00
BP-10b			30.00	45.00	20.00	50.00
BP-11a			40.00	55.00	25.00	60.00

RIBBY™

Modeller:	Arthur Gredington
Height:	3 ¼", 8.3 cm
Colour:	White dress with blue rings, white apron, pink and white striped shawl
Issued:	1951 - 2000

Back Stamp	Beswick Number	Doulton Number	Price			
			U.S. $	Can. $	U.K. £	Aust. $
BP-1a	1199	P1199	325.00	450.00	200.00	475.00
BP-2			160.00	225.00	100.00	235.00
BP-3a			90.00	125.00	55.00	135.00
BP-3b			90.00	125.00	55.00	135.00
BP-3c			90.00	125.00	50.00	135.00
BP-6a			50.00	70.00	30.00	75.00
BP-10c			35.00	50.00	20.00	55.00

Note: The name shown on BP-6a and BP-10c is Mrs Ribby.

RIBBY AND THE PATTY PAN™

Modeller:	Martyn Alcock
Height:	3 ½", 8.9 cm
Colour:	Blue dress, white apron
Issued:	1992 - 1998

Back Stamp	Beswick Number	Doulton Number	Price			
			U.S. $	Can. $	U.K. £	Aust. $
BP-6a	3280	P3280	50.00	70.00	30.00	75.00

SALLY HENNY PENNY™

Modeller:	Albert Hallam
Height:	4", 10.1 cm
Colour:	Brown and gold chicken, black hat and cloak, two yellow chicks
Issued:	1974 - 1993

BEATRIX POTTER'S
"Sally Henny Penny"
F. Warne & Co. Ltd.
© Copyright 1974
BESWICK ENGLAND

Back Stamp	Beswick Number	Doulton Number	Price			
			U.S. $	Can. $	U.K. £	Aust. $
BP-3a	2452	P2452	150.00	250.00	100.00	275.00
BP-3b			90.00	125.00	50.00	135.00
BP-3c			100.00	150.00	65.00	165.00
BP-6a			55.00	80.00	35.00	85.00

SAMUEL WHISKERS™

Modeller:	Arthur Gredington
Height:	3 ¼", 8.3 cm
Colour:	Light green coat, yellow waistcoat and trousers
Issued:	1948 - 1995

BEATRIX POTTER'S
Samuel Whiskers
COPYRIGHT
F. WARNE & Co. Ltd.
BESWICK · ENGLAND
> 8

Correct

ROYAL ALBERT ®
ENGLAND
Samuel Whiskers
Beatrix Potter
© F. WARNE & CO. 1948
1989 ROYAL ALBERT LTD

Error

Backstamp Variations

Back Stamp	Beswick Number	Doulton Number	Price			
			U.S. $	Can. $	U.K. £	Aust. $
BP-1a	1106	P1106	275.00	400.00	175.00	425.00
BP-2			200.00	275.00	125.00	300.00
BP-3a			95.00	125.00	50.00	135.00
BP-3b			60.00	85.00	35.00	100.00
BP-3c			95.00	125.00	50.00	135.00
BP-4			95.00	125.00	50.00	135.00
BP-6a			95.00	125.00	50.00	135.00

SIMPKIN™

Modeller:	Alan Maslankowski
Height:	4", 10.1 cm
Colour:	Green coat
Issued:	1975 - 1983

BEATRIX POTTER'S
"Simpkin"
F. Warne & Co. Ltd.
© Copyright 1975
BESWICK ENGLAND

Back Stamp	Beswick Number	Doulton Number	Price			
			U.S. $	Can. $	U.K. £	Aust. $
BP-3b	2508	P2508	500.00	700.00	300.00	750.00

SIR ISAAC NEWTON™

Modeller:	Graham Tongue
Height:	3 ¾", 9.5 cm
Colour:	Pale green jacket, yellow waistcoat with tan markings
Issued:	1973 - 1984

BEATRIX POTTER'S
"Sir Isaac Newton"
F. Warne & Co. Ltd.
© Copyright 1973
BESWICK
MADE IN ENGLAND

Back Stamp	Beswick Number	Doulton Number	Price			
			U.S. $	Can. $	U.K. £	Aust. $
BP-3a	2425	P2425	475.00	675.00	300.00	700.00
BP-3b			450.00	625.00	275.00	650.00

Note: 1.   The colour and size of Sir Isaac Newton may vary.
2.   Sir Isaac Newton and Mr. Alderman Ptolemy are the only figures with backstamps using the words "Made in England" vice "England."

SQUIRREL NUTKIN™

Modeller:	Arthur Gredington
Height:	3 ¾", 9.5 cm
Size:	Small

FIRST VERSION: SMALL SIZE
FIRST VARIATION: RED-BROWN SQUIRREL

Colour:	Red-brown squirrel, green-brown apple
Issued:	1948 - c.1980

BEATRIX POTTER'S
Squirrel Nutkin
copyright
BESWICK. ENGLAND

Back Stamp	Beswick Number	Doulton Number	Price			
			U.S. $	Can. $	U.K. £	Aust. $
BP-1a	1102/1	P1102/1	325.00	450.00	200.00	475.00
BP-2			250.00	350.00	150.00	375.00
BP-3a			135.00	200.00	85.00	225.00
BP-3b			100.00	150.00	60.00	175.00

FIRST VERSION: SMALL SIZE
SECOND VARIATION: GOLDEN BROWN SQUIRREL

Colour:	Golden brown squirrel, green apple
Issued:	c.1980 - 2000

Small size, red-brown squirrel

Back Stamp	Beswick Number	Doulton Number	Price			
			U.S. $	Can. $	U.K. £	Aust. $
BP-3b	1102/2	P1102/2	65.00	90.00	40.00	95.00
BP-3c			100.00	150.00	60.00	175.00
BP-6a			40.00	55.00	25.00	65.00
BP-10a			35.00	45.00	20.00	50.00

SECOND VERSION: LARGE SIZE
RED CRAB APPLE, GOLD CORE

Modeller:	Amanda Hughes-Lubeck
Height:	5 ¼", 13.3 cm
Size:	Large
Colour:	Golden brown squirrel, red crab-apple, gold core
Issued:	1999 in a limited edition of 1,947
Series:	Gold edition

Back Stamp	Beswick Number	Doulton Number	Price			
			U.S. $	Can. $	U.K. £	Aust. $
BP-9c	3893	PG3893	95.00	135.00	60.00	150.00

Note: The second version of Squirrel Nutkin was issued, numbered and sold as a pair with Hunca Munca Sweeping, second version.

Large size, gold core

SUSAN™

Modeller:	David Lyttleton
Height:	4", 10.1 cm
Colour:	Blue dress, green, pink and black shawl and hat
Issued:	1983 - 1989

BEATRIX POTTER
"Susan"
© F. Warne & Co. 1983
Licensed by Copyrights
BESWICK ENGLAND

Back Stamp	Beswick Number	Doulton Number	Price			
			U.S. $	Can. $	U.K. £	Aust. $
BP-3b	2716	P2716	275.00	375.00	175.00	400.00
BP-3c			275.00	375.00	175.00	400.00
BP-6a			2,000.00	2,750.00	1,250.00	3,000.00

Note: The colour and size of Susan may vary.

SWEET PETER RABBIT™

Modeller:	Shane Ridge
Height:	4 ¾", 12.1 cm
Colour:	Beige and cream rabbit, blue jacket, green and beige base
Issued:	1999 in a special edition of 2,950

BESWICK
MADE IN ENGLAND   TM
Sweet Peter Rabbit
Beatrix Potter
© F. WARNE & CO. 1999
© 1999 ROYAL DOULTON
SPECIAL GOLD EDITION OF 2,950
FOR
PETER RABBIT AND FRIENDS

Back Stamp	Beswick Number	Doulton Number	Price			
			U.S. $	Can. $	U.K. £	Aust. $
BP-10d	3888	P3888	80.00	120.00	50.00	140.00

Note: This figure was commissioned by Peter Rabbit and Friends to commemorate the Year of the Rabbit, 1999.

First variation: Blue striped top

Second variation: White top

TABITHA TWITCHIT™

Modeller: Arthur Gredington
Height: 3 ½", 8.9 cm

FIRST VARIATION: BLUE STRIPED TOP

Colour: Blue and white striped dress, white apron
Issued: 1961 - 1974

Back Stamp	Beswick Number	Doulton Number	Price			
			U.S. $	Can. $	U.K. £	Aust. $
BP-2	1676/1	P1676/1	250.00	350.00	150.00	375.00
BP-3a			200.00	275.00	125.00	300.00
BP-3b			200.00	275.00	125.00	300.00

SECOND VARIATION: WHITE TOP

Colour: Blue and white striped dress, white apron
Issued: c.1975 - 1995

Back Stamp	Beswick Number	Doulton Number	Price			
			U.S. $	Can. $	U.K. £	Aust. $
BP-3b	1676/2	P1676/2	95.00	135.00	60.00	150.00
BP-3c			90.00	125.00	55.00	135.00
BP-6a			100.00	150.00	65.00	165.00

Note: 1. BP-3b and forward has Twitchit spelled "Twitchett."
2. The white face became very dark/mottled shortly after the second variation was introduced.

First version: Small size

TABITHA TWITCHIT AND MISS MOPPET™
FIRST VERSION: SMALL SIZE

Modeller:	David Lyttleton
Height:	3 ½", 8.9 cm
Size:	Small
Colour:	Lilac dress, white apron, yellow sponge and hassock
Issued:	1976 - 1993

BEATRIX POTTER'S
Tabitha Twitchit and Miss Moppet
F. Warne & Co. Ltd.
© Copyright 1976
BESWICK ENGLAND

Back Stamp	Beswick Number	Doulton Number	Price			
			U.S. $	Can. $	U.K. £	Aust. $
BP-3b	2544	P2544	190.00	265.00	120.00	290.00
BP-3c			200.00	275.00	125.00	300.00
BP-4			250.00	325.00	150.00	350.00
BP-6a			150.00	200.00	90.00	225.00

Second version: Large size

TABITHA TWITCHIT AND MOPPET™
SECOND VERSION: LARGE SIZE

Modeller:	Martyn Alcock
Height:	5 ½", 14.0 cm
Size:	Large
Colour:	Tabitha Twitchit: Lilac dress and white apron
	Moppet: Grey striped kitten
	Stool: Yellow with gold legs
Issued:	2000 in a limited edition of 2,000
Series:	Gold edition

Back Stamp	Beswick Number	Doulton Number	Price			
			U.S. $	Can. $	U.K. £	Aust. $
BP-9c	4020	PG4020	125.00	175.00	80.00	185.00

First version, Small size

Second version: Large size

Second version: Large size, gold accents

TAILOR OF GLOUCESTER™
FIRST VERSION: SMALL SIZE

Modeller:	Arthur Gredington
Height:	3 ½", 8.9 cm
Size:	Small
Colour:	Brown mouse, yellow bobbin of red thread
Issued:	1949 - 2002

Back Stamp	Beswick Number	Doulton Number	Price U.S. $	Price Can. $	Price U.K. £	Price Aust. $
BP-1a	1108	P1108	600.00	850.00	375.00	875.00
BP-1b				Very rare		
BP-2			150.00	250.00	100.00	275.00
BP-3a			65.00	90.00	40.00	95.00
BP-3b			65.00	90.00	40.00	95.00
BP-3c			65.00	90.00	40.00	95.00
BP-4			80.00	110.00	50.00	115.00
BP-6a			40.00	55.00	25.00	60.00
BP-10c			30.00	45.00	20.00	50.00

Note: Only a very small quantity with the BP-1a backstamp are known to exist.

SECOND VERSION: LARGE SIZE
FIRST VARIATION: STANDARD COLOURS

Modeller:	Arthur Gredington
Height:	6", 15.0 cm
Size:	Large
Colour:	Brown mouse, yellow bobbin of red thread
Issued:	1995 - 1997

Back Stamp	Beswick Number	Doulton Number	Price U.S. $	Price Can. $	Price U.K. £	Price Aust. $
BP-6b	3449/1	P3449	70.00	100.00	45.00	110.00

SECOND VERSION: LARGE SIZE
SECOND VARIATION: GOLD ACCENTS

Colour:	Brown mouse, yellow bobbin of red thread, gold accents
Issued:	1998 in a limited edition of 1,947
Series:	Gold edition

Back Stamp	Beswick Number	Doulton Number	Price U.S. $	Price Can. $	Price U.K. £	Price Aust. $
BP-9c	3449/2	PG3449	95.00	130.00	60.00	140.00

Note: The second version, second variation of this model was issued, numbered and sold as a pair with Peter Rabbit and the Red Pocket Handkerchief, second version, second variation.

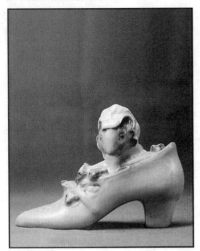

THE OLD WOMAN WHO LIVED IN A SHOE™

Modeller:	Colin Melbourne
Size:	2 ¾" x 3 ¾", 7.0 cm x 9.5 cm
Colour:	Blue shoe
Issued:	1959 - 1998

Back Stamp	Beswick Number	Doulton Number	Price			
			U.S. $	Can. $	U.K. £	Aust. $
BP-2	1545	P1545	225.00	300.00	135.00	325.00
BP-3a			95.00	135.00	60.00	150.00
BP-3b			80.00	110.00	50.00	115.00
BP-3c			95.00	135.00	60.00	150.00
BP-6a			50.00	65.00	30.00	70.00

Note: The lettering of the BP-2 backstanp, which is gold, is frequently not very bright.

THE OLD WOMAN WHO LIVED IN A SHOE KNITTING™

Modeller:	David Lyttleton
Height:	3", 7.5 cm
Colour:	Purple dress, white apron, pale blue shawl and mob cap, yellow chair
Issued:	1983 - 2002

Back Stamp	Beswick Number	Doulton Number	Price			
			U.S. $	Can. $	U.K. £	Aust. $
BP-3b	2804	P2804	200.00	275.00	125.00	300.00
BP-3c			200.00	275.00	125.00	300.00
BP-6a			50.00	65.00	30.00	70.00
BP-10a			30.00	45.00	20.00	50.00

THIS PIG HAD A BIT OF MEAT™

Modeller:	Martyn Alcock
Height:	4", 10.1 cm
Colour:	Lilac dress, grey shawl, white apron and cap, gold-framed spectacles
Issued:	2000 in a special edition of 1,500

Back Stamp	Beswick Number	Doulton Number	Price			
			U.S. $	Can. $	U.K. £	Aust. $
BP-9d	4030	P4030	125.00	175.00	80.00	200.00

Note: Commissioned by Peter Rabbit and Friends.

THOMASINA TITTLEMOUSE™

Modeller: David Lyttleton
Height: 3 ¼", 8.3 cm
Colour: Brown and pink highlights
Issued: 1981 - 1989

			Correct		Incorrect	

Backstamp Variations

Back Stamp	Beswick Number	Doulton Number	Price U.S. $	Can. $	U.K. £	Aust. $
BP-3b	2668	P2668	135.00	190.00	85.00	210.00
BP-3c	Error		150.00	225.00	100.00	250.00
BP-6a			400.00	550.00	250.00	575.00

TIMMY TIPTOES™

Modeller: Arthur Gredington
Height: 3 ¾", 9.5 cm

FIRST VARIATION: RED JACKET

Colour: 1. Brown-grey squirrel, red jacket
2. Grey squirrel, red jacket
Issued: 1948 - c.1980

Back Stamp	Beswick Number	Colour Variation	Price U.S. $	Can. $	U.K. £	Aust. $
BP-1a	1101/1	Brown-grey	250.00	325.00	150.00	350.00
BP-1a		Grey	250.00	325.00	150.00	350.00
BP-2		Brown-grey	150.00	225.00	100.00	225.00
BP-2		Grey	150.00	225.00	100.00	225.00
BP-3a		Brown-grey	135.00	200.00	85.00	210.00
BP-3a		Grey	135.00	200.00	85.00	210.00
BP-3b		Brown-grey	120.00	165.00	75.00	175.00
BP-3b		Grey	120.00	165.00	75.00	175.00

First variation: Red jacket

SECOND VARIATION: LIGHT PINK JACKET

Colour: Grey squirrel, pink jacket
Issued: c.1970 - 1997

Back Stamp	Beswick Number	Doulton Number	Price U.S. $	Can. $	U.K. £	Aust. $
BP-2	1101/2	P1101/2	190.00	270.00	120.00	285.00
BP-3b			80.00	110.00	50.00	115.00
BP-3c			95.00	135.00	60.00	145.00
BP-6a			55.00	80.00	35.00	85.00

Note: Second variations will vary in colour in a similar manner as the first.

Second variation: Pink jacket

TIMMY WILLIE FETCHING MILK™

Modeller: Warren Platt
Height: 3 ¼", 8.3 cm
Colour: Brown and white mouse,
             blue milk jug
Issued: 2000 - 2002

Back Stamp	Beswick Number	Doulton Number	Price			
			U.S. $	Can. $	U.K. £	Aust. $
BP-10a	3976	P3976	48.00	100.00	25.00	110.00

TIMMY WILLIE FROM JOHNNY TOWN-MOUSE™

Modeller: Arthur Gredington
Height: 2 ½", 6.4 cm
Colour: Brown and white mouse, green
             or multicoloured base
Issued: 1949 - 1993

Back Stamp	Beswick Number	Doulton Number	Price			
			U.S. $	Can. $	U.K. £	Aust. $
BP-1a	1109	P1109	250.00	325.00	150.00	350.00
BP-2			150.00	200.00	100.00	225.00
BP-3a			65.00	95.00	45.00	100.00
BP-3b			55.00	80.00	35.00	85.00
BP-3c			65.00	95.00	45.00	100.00
BP-4			75.00	110.00	50.00	110.00
BP-6a			90.00	125.00	55.00	135.00

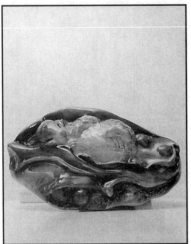

TIMMY WILLIE SLEEPING™

Modeller: Graham Tongue
Size: 1 ¼" x 3 ¾",
             3.2 cm x 9.5 cm
Colour: Green, white and brown
Issued: 1986 - 1996

Back Stamp	Beswick Number	Doulton Number	Price			
			U.S. $	Can. $	U.K. £	Aust. $
BP-3c	2996	P2996	200.00	275.00	125.00	300.00
BP-6a			65.00	90.00	40.00	100.00

TOM KITTEN™

Modeller:	Arthur Gredington
Height:	3 ½", 8.9 cm
Size:	Small

FIRST VERSION: SMALL SIZE
FIRST VARIATION: DEEP BLUE OUTFIT

Colour:	Tabby kitten wearing deep blue jacket and trousers, dark green base
Issued:	1948 - c.1980

Back Stamp	Beswick Number	Doulton Number	Price			
			U.S. $	Can. $	U.K. £	Aust. $
BP-1a	1100/1	P1100/1	225.00	325.00	140.00	350.00
BP-2			150.00	200.00	100.00	225.00
BP-3a			95.00	135.00	60.00	150.00
BP-3b			75.00	110.00	50.00	110.00

Small size, deep blue colourway

FIRST VERSION: SMALL SIZE
SECOND VARIATION: LIGHT BLUE OUTFIT

Colour:	Tabby kitten wearing light blue jacket and trousers, light green base
Issued:	c.1980 - 1999

Back Stamp	Beswick Number	Doulton Number	Price			
			U.S. $	Can. $	U.K. £	Aust. $
BP-3b	1100/2	P1100/2	80.00	110.00	50.00	115.00
BP-3c			75.00	100.00	45.00	110.00
BP-4			80.00	110.00	50.00	115.00
BP-6a			40.00	55.00	25.00	60.00
BP-10c			50.00	65.00	30.00	70.00

Small size, light blue colourway

FIRST VERSION: SMALL SIZE
THIRD VARIATION: GOLD BUTTONS

Colour:	Tabby kitten wearing light blue jacket and trousers; gold buttons
Issued:	1997 - 1997

Back Stamp	Beswick Number	Doulton Number	Price			
			U.S. $	Can. $	U.K. £	Aust. $
BP-9b	1100/3	PG1100	65.00	90.00	40.00	100.00

Note: The small version of Tom Kitten was issued with two different style bases.

Small size, gold buttons

TOM KITTEN™
SECOND VERSION: LARGE SIZE
FIRST VARIATION: YELLOW BUTTONS

Modeller:	Martyn Alcock
Height:	5 ¼", 13.3 cm
Size:	Large
Colour:	Tabby kitten wearing light blue jacket and trousers; light green base
Issued:	1994 - 1997

Back Stamp	Beswick Number	Doulton Number	Price U.S. $	Can. $	U.K. £	Aust. $
BP-8	3405/1	P3405	70.00	100.00	45.00	110.00

Large size, yellow buttons

SECOND VERSION: LARGE SIZE
SECOND VARIATION: GOLD BUTTONS

Colour:	Light blue jacket and trousers; gold buttons
Issued:	1994 - 1997
Series:	Gold edition

Back Stamp	Beswick Number	Doulton Number	Price U.S. $	Can. $	U.K. £	Aust. $
BP-9c	3405/2	PG3405	95.00	135.00	60.00	150.00

Note: The second variation was issued, numbered and sold as a pair with Mr. Jeremy Fisher, second version, second variation.

TOM KITTEN AND BUTTERFLY™

Modeller:	Ted Chawner
Height:	3 ½", 8.9 cm
Colour:	Blue outfit, yellow hat
Issued:	1987 - 1994

Back Stamp	Beswick Number	Doulton Number	Price U.S. $	Can. $	U.K. £	Aust. $
BP-3c	3030	P3030	325.00	450.00	200.00	475.00
BP-6a			200.00	300.00	150.00	325.00

TOM KITTEN IN THE ROCKERY™

Modeller:	Warren Platt
Height:	3 ½", 8.9 cm
Colour:	Pale blue jacket and trousers, yellow hat
Issued:	1998 - 2002

Back Stamp	Beswick Number	Doulton Number	Price			
			U.S. $	Can. $	U.K. £	Aust. $
BP-10a	3719	P3719	40.00	55.00	25.00	60.00

TOM THUMB™

Modeller:	Warren Platt
Height:	3 ¼", 8.3 cm
Colour:	Rose-pink and yellow chimney
Issued:	1987 - 1997

Back Stamp	Beswick Number	Doulton Number	Price			
			U.S. $	Can. $	U.K. £	Aust. $
BP-3c	2989	P2989	185.00	250.00	115.00	275.00
BP-6a			55.00	80.00	35.00	90.00

TOMMY BROCK™

Modeller: Graham Orwell
Height: 3 ½", 8.9 cm

FIRST VERSION: SPADE HANDLE OUT
FIRST VARIATION: SMALL EYE PATCH

Colour: Blue jacket, pink waistcoat,
           yellow-green trousers
Issued: 1955 - 1974

Back Stamp	Beswick Number	Doulton Number	Price			
			U.S. $	Can. $	U.K. £	Aust. $
BP-1a	1348/1	P1348/1	Extremely rare			
BP-2	1348/1	P1348/1	450.00	600.00	275.00	650.00
BP-3a			375.00	500.00	225.00	525.00

Note: Until the 1972-1974 time period the eye patches curved inward towards the centre of the forehead; they also tended to have a feathery appearance.

Handle out, small eye patch

FIRST VERSION: SPADE HANDLE OUT
SECOND VARIATION: LARGE EYE PATCH

Colour: Blue jacket, pink waistcoat,
           yellow trousers
Issued: c.1970 - c.1974

Back Stamp	Beswick Number	Doulton Number	Price			
			U.S. $	Can. $	U.K. £	Aust. $
BP-2	1348/2	P1348/2	Rare			
BP-3a			375.00	500.00	225.00	525.00

Note: Beginning in 1972-1974 the eye patches, large and small, tended to run straight up towards the ears; also, they were a solid black.

Handle out, large eye patch

TOMMY BROCK™

Modeller:	Graham Orwell
Height:	3 ½", 8.9 cm
Colour:	Blue-grey jacket, pink waistcoat, yellow trousers
Issued:	c.1974 - 1976

SECOND VERSION: HANDLE IN
FIRST VARIATION: SMALL EYE PATCH

Back Stamp	Beswick Number	Doulton Number	Price			
			U.S. $	Can. $	U.K. £	Aust. $
BP-3a	1348/3	P1348/3	140.00	200.00	85.00	225.00
BP-3b			125.00	175.00	75.00	200.00

Handle in, small eye patch

SECOND VERSION: HANDLE IN
SECOND VARIATION: LARGE EYE PATCH

Colour:	Blue-grey jacket, red waistcoat, yellow trousers
Issued:	c.1975 - 2002

Back Stamp	Beswick Number	Doulton Number	Price			
			U.S. $	Can. $	U.K. £	Aust. $
BP-3b	1348/4	P1348/4	65.00	90.00	40.00	100.00
BP-3c			80.00	115.00	50.00	120.00
BP-4			80.00	115.00	50.00	125.00
BP-6a			40.00	55.00	25.00	60.00
BP-10a			35.00	50.00	20.00	60.00

Note: The jacket colour varies from pale to dark blue in BP-3b.

Handle in, large eye patch

TWO GENTLEMEN RABBITS™

Modeller:	Shane Ridge
Height:	5", 12.5 cm
Colour:	Brown, green and red
Issued:	2002 - 2002

Back Stamp	Beswick Number	Doulton Number	Price U.S. $	Can. $	U.K. £	Aust. $
BP-11a	P4210	P4210	175.00	250.00	110.00	275.00

YOCK-YOCK IN THE TUB™

Modeller:	Warren Platt
Height:	3", 7.6 cm
Colour:	Pink pig, brown tub
Issued:	2000 to the present

Back Stamp	Beswick Number	Doulton Number	Price U.S. $	Can. $	U.K. £	Aust. $
BP-10a	3946	P3946	60.00	100.00	30.00	115.00

BEATRIX POTTER

TABLEAUX

TABLEAUX

DUCHESS AND RIBBY™

Modeller:	Martyn Alcock
Length:	7 ¾", 19.7 cm
Colour:	Black, lilac, grey and gold
Issued:	2000 in a limited edition of 1,500
Series:	Tableau

Back Stamp	Beswick Number	Doulton Number	U.S. $	Can. $	U.K. £	Aust. $
				Price		
BP-9d	3983	P3983	325.00	450.00	200.00	475.00

Note: This figure was commissioned by Peter Rabbit and Friends.

FLOPSY AND BENJAMIN BUNNY™

Modeller:	Shane Ridge
Height:	5", 12.7 cm
Colour:	Benjamin: Pink jacket
	Flopsy: Blue dress
Issued:	2001 - 2002

Back Stamp	Beswick Number	Doulton Number	U.S. $	Can. $	U.K. £	Aust. $
				Price		
BP-11b	P4155	P4155	125.00	185.00	70.00	200.00

FLOPSY, MOPSY AND COTTONTAIL™
Style Two

Modeller:	Shane Ridge
Height:	3 ¾", 9.5 cm
Colour:	Brown, pink and white
Issued:	2002 in a limited edition of 1,500 (C of A)
Comm. by:	Doulton-Direct

Back Stamp	Beswick Number	Doulton Number	U.S. $	Can. $	U.K. £	Aust. $
				Price		
BP-11b	—	P4161	150.00	225.00	100.00	250.00

Note: Final piece in the series.

GINGER AND PICKLES™

Modeller:	David Lyttleton
Height:	3 ¾", 9.5 cm
Colour:	Green, white and brown
Issued:	1998 in a limited edition of 2,750
Series:	Tableau

Back Stamp	Beswick Number	Doulton Number	Price			
			U.S. $	Can. $	U.K. £	Aust. $
BP-9d	3790	P3790	350.00	500.00	225.00	525.00

Note: This figure was commissioned by Peter Rabbit and Friends.

HIDING FROM THE CAT™

Modeller:	Graham Tongue
Height:	5", 12.7 cm
Colour:	Brown, blue and grey
Issued:	1998 in a limited edition of 3,500
Series:	Tableau of the Year

Back Stamp	Beswick Number	Doulton Number	Price			
			U.S. $	Can. $	U.K. £	Aust. $
BP-8c	3672	P3672	250.00	350.00	150.00	375.00

KEP AND JEMIMIA™

Modeller:	Martyn Alcock
Length:	4 ½", 11.4 cm
Colour:	Jemima: Pink and blue shawl
	Kep: Brown and white collie
Issued:	2002 in a limited edition of 2,000 (C of A)
Series:	Tableau

Back Stamp	Beswick Number	Doulton Number	Price			
			U.S. $	Can. $	U.K. £	Aust. $
BP-11b	P4901	P4901	200.00	300.00	130.00	325.00

MITTENS, TOM KITTEN AND MOPPET™

Modeller:	Amanda Hughes-Lubeck
Length:	7", 17.8 cm
Colour:	Pale blue and beige
Issued:	1999 - 1999
Series:	Tableau of the Year

Back Stamp	Beswick Number	Doulton Number	Price			
			U.S. $	Can. $	U.K. £	Aust. $
BP-8c	3792	P3792	200.00	275.00	125.00	300.00

MRS. RABBIT AND THE FOUR BUNNIES™

Modeller:	Shane Ridge
Height:	4 ½", 11.9 cm
Colour:	Mrs Rabbit: Pale blue dress, white apron
	Bunnies: Rose cloaks
	Peter: Pale blue jacket
Issued:	1997 in a limited edition of 1,997
Series:	Tableau of the Year

Back Stamp	Beswick Number	Doulton Number	Price			
			U.S. $	Can. $	U.K. £	Aust. $
BP-8b	3672	P3672	725.00	1,000.00	450.00	1,100.00

MRS. TIGGY-WINKLE AND LUCIE™

Modeller:	Martyn Alcock
Height:	4", 10.1 cm
Colour:	Mrs. Tiggy-Winkle: Brown, pink and cream dress, yellow and blue striped skirt, white apron, red handkerchief, platinum iron and horseshoe,
	Lucie: Pink dress, white pinafore
Issued:	1999 in a limited edition of 2,950
Series:	Tableau

Back Stamp	Beswick Number	Doulton Number	Price			
			U.S. $	Can. $	U.K. £	Aust. $
BP-9d	3867	P3867	250.00	350.00	150.00	375.00

Note: Commissioned by Peter Rabbit and Friends.

MY DEAR SON THOMAS™

Modeller:	Martyn Alcock
Height:	3 ½", 8.9 cm
Colour:	Blue, white, pink, grey and tan
Issued:	2001 in a limited edition of 3,000

Back Stamp	Beswick Number	Doulton Number	Price			
			U.S. $	Can. $	U.K. £	Aust. $
BP-11b	P4169	P4169	195.00	325.00	110.00	350.00

PETER AND BENJAMIN PICKING APPLES™

Modeller:	Martyn Alcock
Height:	4 ¾", 11.4 cm
Colour:	Blue, brown, tan, red and green
Issued:	2002 in a limited edition of 3,000
Series:	Tabluea

Back Stamp	Beswick Number	Doulton Number	Price			
			U.S. $	Can. $	U.K. £	Aust. $
BP-11b	P4160	P4160	175.00	250.00	110.00	275.00

PETER AND BENJAMIN PICKING UP ONIONS™

Modeller:	Martyn Alcock
Height:	5", 12.7 cm
Colour:	Peter: Pale blue jacket
	Benjamin: Brown jacket
Issued:	2000 in a limited edition of 3,000
Series:	Tableau of the Year

Back Stamp	Beswick Number	Doulton Number	Price			
			U.S. $	Can. $	U.K. £	Aust. $
BP-8c	3930	P3930	250.00	350.00	150.00	375.00

Mittens, Tom Kitten and Moppet Tableau of the Year 1999

BEATRIX POTTER MISCELLANEOUS

CHARACTER JUGS
PLAQUES
STANDS

CHARACTER JUGS

JEMIMA PUDDLE-DUCK
CHARACTER JUG™

Modeller:	Ted Chawner
Height:	4", 10.1 cm
Colour:	Blue, pink and white
Issued:	1989 - 1992

Back Stamp	Beswick Number	Doulton Number	Price			
			U.S. $	Can. $	U.K. £	Aust. $
BP-4	3088	P3088	150.00	225.00	100.00	250.00
BP-6a			125.00	175.00	80.00	200.00

MR. JEREMY FISHER
CHARACTER JUG™

Modeller:	Graham Tongue
Height:	3", 7.6 cm
Colour:	Mauve
Issued:	1987 - 1992

Back Stamp	Beswick Number	Doulton Number	Price			
			U.S. $	Can. $	U.K. £	Aust. $
BP-4	2960	P2960	150.00	225.00	100.00	250.00
BP-6a			125.00	175.00	80.00	200.00

MRS. TIGGY-WINKLE
CHARACTER JUG™

Modeller:	Ted Chawner
Height:	3", 7.6 cm
Colour:	White dress with brown stripes
Issued:	1988 - 1992

Back Stamp	Beswick Number	Doulton Number	Price			
			U.S. $	Can. $	U.K. £	Aust. $
BP-4	3102	P3102	150.00	225.00	100.00	250.00
BP-6a			125.00	175.00	80.00	200.00

OLD MR. BROWN
CHARACTER JUG™

Modeller: Graham Tongue
Height: 3", 7.6 cm
Colour: Brown and cream
Issued: 1987 - 1992

Back Stamp	Beswick Number	Doulton Number	Price			
			U.S. $	Can. $	U.K. £	Aust. $
BP-4	2959	P2959	150.00	225.00	100.00	250.00
BP-6a			125.00	175.00	80.00	200.00

PETER RABBIT
CHARACTER JUG™

Modeller: Graham Tongue
Height: 3", 7.6 cm
Colour: Brown, blue and white
Issued: 1987 - 1992

Back Stamp	Beswick Number	Doulton Number	Price			
			U.S. $	Can. $	U.K. £	Aust. $
BP-4	3006	P3006	150.00	225.00	100.00	250.00
BP-6a			125.00	175.00	80.00	200.00

TOM KITTEN
CHARACTER JUG™

Modeller: Ted Chawner
Height: 3", 7.6 cm
Colour: Brown, blue and white
Issued: 1989 - 1992

Back Stamp	Beswick Number	Doulton Number	Price			
			U.S. $	Can. $	U.K. £	Aust. $
BP-4	3103	P3103	150.00	225.00	100.00	250.00
BP-6a			125.00	175.00	80.00	200.00

PLAQUES

JEMIMA PUDDLE-DUCK PLAQUE™

Modeller: Albert Hallam
Height: 6", 15.2 cm
Colour: White duck, mauve shawl, pale blue bonnet
Issued: 1967 - 1969

Back Stamp	Beswick Number	Doulton Number	Price			
			U.S. $	Can. $	U.K. £	Aust. $
BP-2	2082	P2082		Extremely rare		

JEMIMA PUDDLE-DUCK WITH FOXY WHISKERED GENTLEMAN PLAQUE™

Modeller: Harry Sales and
             David Lyttleton
Size: 7 ½" x 7 ½",
             19.1 cm x 19.1 cm
Colour: Brown, green, white and blue
Issued: 1977 - 1982

Back Stamp	Beswick Number	Doulton Number	Price			
			U.S. $	Can. $	U.K. £	Aust. $
BP-3	2594	P2594	125.00	165.00	75.00	180.00

MRS. TITTLEMOUSE PLAQUE™

Modeller: Harry Sales
Height: 7 ½" x 7 ½",
             19.1 cm x 19.1 cm
Colour: Blue, pink and green
Issued: 1982 - 1984

Back Stamp	Beswick Number	Doulton Number	Price			
			U.S. $	Can. $	U.K. £	Aust. $
BP-3	2685	P2685	125.00	165.00	75.00	180.00

PETER RABBIT PLAQUE™
First Version

Modeller:	Graham Tongue
Height:	6", 15.2 cm
Colour:	Brown rabbit wearing a blue coat
Issued:	1967 - 1969

Back Stamp	Beswick Number	Doulton Number	U.S. $	Can. $	U.K. £	Aust. $
				Price		
BP-2	2083	P2083		Extremely rare		

PETER RABBIT PLAQUE™
Second Version

Modeller:	Harry Sales and David Lyttleton
Size:	7 ½" x 7 ½", 19.1 cm x 19.1 cm
Colour:	Blue, green, brown and orange
Issued:	1979 - 1983

Back Stamp	Beswick Number	Doulton Number	U.S. $	Can. $	U.K. £	Aust. $
				Price		
BP-3	2650	P2650	125.00	165.00	75.00	180.00

TOM KITTEN PLAQUE™

Modeller:	Graham Tongue
Height:	6", 15.2 cm
Colour:	Brown, blue and white
Issued:	1967 - 1969

Back Stamp	Beswick Number	Doulton Number	U.S. $	Can. $	U.K. £	Aust. $
				Price		
BP-2	2085	P2085		Extremely rare		

STANDS

TREE STUMP STAND

Modeller:	Andrew Brindley
Size:	12 ½" x 12 ½",
	31.7 cm x 31.7 cm
Colour:	Brown, light brown
Issued:	1970 - 1997

Back Stamp	Beswick Number	Doulton Number	Price			
			U.S. $	Can. $	U.K. £	Aust. $
Beswick	2295	P2295	80.00	115.00	50.00	125.00
Doulton			80.00	115.00	50.00	125.00

TREE LAMP BASE™

Modeller:	Albert Hallam and
	James Hayward
Height:	7", 17.8 cm
Colour:	Brown and green
Issued:	1958 - 1982

Back Stamp	Beswick Number	Doulton Number	Price			
			U.S. $	Can. $	U.K. £	Aust. $
BP-2	1531	P1531	125.00	175.00	75.00	185.00
BP-3			80.00	115.00	50.00	125.00

Note: 1. The above prices are for figureless lamp bases. Those with figures will vary in accordance with the figurine found attached to the base.
   2. Lamp bases are known with the black circle backstamp.

BEATRIX POTTER

RESIN STUDIO SCULPTURES

SS1
TIMMY WILLIE™

Designer:	Harry Sales
Modeller:	Graham Tongue
Height:	4 ¼", 10.8 cm
Colour:	Green and brown
Issued:	1985 - 1985
U.S.	**$ 95.00**
Can.	**$125.00**
U.K.	**£ 60.00**
Aust.	**$135.00**

SS2
FLOPSY BUNNIES™

Designer:	Harry Sales
Modeller:	Graham Tongue
Height:	5", 12.7 cm
Colour:	Browns and green
Issued:	1985 - 1985
U.S.	**$ 95.00**
Can.	**$125.00**
U.K.	**£ 60.00**
Aust.	**$135.00**

SS3
MR. JEREMY FISHER™

Designer:	Harry Sales
Modeller:	David Lyttleton
Height:	4", 10.1 cm
Colour:	Beige, green and cream
Issued:	1985 - 1985
U.S.	**$ 95.00**
Can.	**$125.00**
U.K.	**£ 60.00**
Aust.	**$135.00**

SS4
PETER RABBIT™

Designer:	Harry Sales
Modeller:	Graham Tongue
Height:	7", 17.8 cm
Colour:	Browns, blue and green
Issued:	1985 - 1985
U.S.	**$ 95.00**
Can.	**$125.00**
U.K.	**£ 60.00**
Aust.	**$135.00**

SS11
MRS. TIGGY-WINKLE™

Designer:	Harry Sales
Modeller:	Graham Tongue
Height:	5", 12.7 cm
Colour:	Browns, green, white and blue
Issued:	1985 - 1985
U.S.	**$ 95.00**
Can.	**$125.00**
U.K.	**£ 60.00**
Aust.	**$135.00**

SS26
YOCK YOCK™
(In The Tub)

Designer:	Harry Sales
Modeller:	David Lyttleton
Height:	2", 5.0 cm
Colour:	Pink and brown
Issued:	1986 - 1986
U.S.	**$275.00**
Can.	**$400.00**
U.K.	**£175.00**
Aust.	**$425.00**

SS27
PETER RABBIT™
(In The Watering Can)

Designer:	Harry Sales
Modeller:	David Lyttleton
Height:	3 ¼", 8.3 cm
Colour:	Browns and blue
Issued:	1986 - 1986
U.S.	**$350.00**
Can.	**$500.00**
U.K.	**£225.00**
Aust.	**$525.00**

BEDTIME CHORUS

1801
PIANIST™

Designer:	Albert Hallam
Height:	3", 7.6 cm
Colour:	Pale blue and yellow
Issued:	1962 - 1969
U.S.	**$150.00**
Can.	**$225.00**
U.K.	**£100.00**
Aust.	**$225.00**

1802
PIANO™

Designer:	Albert Hallam
Height:	3", 7.6 cm
Colour:	Brown and white
Issued:	1962 - 1969
U.S.	**$100.00**
Can.	**$135.00**
U.K.	**£ 60.00**
Aust.	**$135.00**

1803
CAT - SINGING™

Designer:	Albert Hallam
Height:	1 ¼", 3.2 cm
Colour:	Ginger stripe
Issued:	1962 - 1971
U.S.	**$ 65.00**
Can.	**$100.00**
U.K.	**£ 40.00**
Aust.	**$100.00**

1804
BOY WITHOUT SPECTACLES™

Designer:	Albert Hallam
Height:	3 ½", 8.9 cm
Colour:	Yellow, white and blue
Issued:	1962 - 1969
U.S.	**$200.00**
Can.	**$275.00**
U.K.	**£125.00**
Aust.	**$275.00**

1805
BOY WITH SPECTACLES™

Designer:	Albert Hallam
Height:	3", 7.6 cm
Colour:	Green, white and blue
Issued:	1962 - 1969
U.S.	**$200.00**
Can.	**$275.00**
U.K.	**£125.00**
Aust.	**$275.00**

1824
DOG - SINGING™

Designer:	Albert Hallam
Height:	1 ½", 3.8 cm
Colour:	Tan
Issued:	1962 - 1971
U.S.	**$ 85.00**
Can.	**$135.00**
U.K.	**£ 50.00**
Aust.	**$135.00**

1825
BOY WITH GUITAR™

Designer:	Albert Hallam
Height:	3", 7.6 cm
Colour:	Blue-grey, brown and blue
Issued:	1962 - 1969
U.S.	**$200.00**
Can.	**$275.00**
U.K.	**£125.00**
Aust.	**$275.00**

1826
GIRL WITH HARP™

Designer:	Albert Hallam
Height:	3 ½", 8.9 cm
Colour:	Purple, red and brown
Issued:	1962 - 1969
U.S.	**$200.00**
Can.	**$275.00**
U.K.	**£125.00**
Aust.	**$275.00**

BESWICK BEARS

Beswick Bears

WILLIAM

BB001

BILLY
kicked his ball up high
and it landed "SPLAT"
in the apple pie.
Beswick Bears
BB002

HARRY
slipped – he'd made a mistake.
He dropped the plates,
but saved his cake.
Beswick Bears
BB003

BOBBY
hits his ball in the air,
It comes to land,
he knows not where.
Beswick Bears
BB004

BB001
WILLIAM™

Designer:	Unknown
Height:	2 ¼", 5.7 cm
Colour:	Brown bear, blue apron, white and rose book
Issued:	1993 - 1993
U.S.	**$100.00**
Can.	**$150.00**
U.K.	**£ 65.00**
Aust.	**$150.00**

BB002
BILLY™

Designer:	Unknown
Height:	4", 10.1 cm
Colour:	Brown bear, green waistcoat, blue hat, yellow, red and blue ball
Issued:	1993 - 1993
U.S.	**$ 85.00**
Can.	**$125.00**
U.K.	**£ 50.00**
Aust.	**$125.00**

BB003
HARRY™

Designer:	Unknown
Height:	3 ¼", 8.3 cm
Colour:	Brown bear, blue waistcoat, brown hat, white plates
Issued:	1993 - 1993
U.S.	**$ 85.00**
Can.	**$125.00**
U.K.	**£ 50.00**
Aust.	**$125.00**

BB004
BOBBY™

Designer:	Unknown
Height:	4", 10.1 cm
Colour:	Brown bear, blue waistcoat, brown hat, yellow ball, black and red bat
Issued:	1993 - 1993
U.S.	**$ 85.00**
Can.	**$125.00**
U.K.	**£ 50.00**
Aust.	**$125.00**

JAMES
has a gift wrapped up in a bow –
It's a nice little "thank you",
un petit cadeau.

Beswick Bears

BB005

SUSIE
is playing her new recorder
Any time she'll play to order.

Beswick Bears

BB006

ANGELA
kneels to pick some flowers
Happily dreaming for
hours and hours.

Beswick Bears

BB007

CHARLOTTE
tries to keep in the shade,
Twirling her parasol,
a pretty young maid.

Beswick Bears

BB008

BB005
JAMES™

Designer:	Unknown
Height:	3 ¾", 9.5 cm
Colour:	Brown bear, yellow waistcoat, blue hat, blue gift box with pink ribbon
Issued:	1993 - 1993
U.S.	**$ 85.00**
Can.	**$125.00**
U.K.	**£ 50.00**
Aust.	**$125.00**

BB006
SUSIE™

Designer:	Unknown
Height:	3 ½", 8.9 cm
Colour:	Brown bear, blue dress, brown recorder
Issued:	1993 - 1993
U.S.	**$ 85.00**
Can.	**$125.00**
U.K.	**£ 50.00**
Aust.	**$125.00**

BB007
ANGELA™

Designer:	Unknown
Height:	3 ¼", 8.3 cm
Colour:	Brown bear, yellow dress, white flowers
Issued:	1993 - 1993
U.S.	**$ 85.00**
Can.	**$125.00**
U.K.	**£ 50.00**
Aust.	**$125.00**

BB008
CHARLOTTE™

Designer:	Unknown
Height:	4", 10.1 cm
Colour:	Brown bear, pink dress, blue and yellow parasol
Issued:	1993 - 1993
U.S.	**$ 85.00**
Can.	**$125.00**
U.K.	**£ 50.00**
Aust.	**$125.00**

SAM
plays his banjo all day long.
Amusing friends
with a tune and a song.
Beswick Bears
BB009

LIZZY
paints pictures of places and scenes,
Using yellows and blues,
pinks and greens.
Beswick Bears
BB010

EMILY
is in charge of the afternoon tea –
Perhaps she has buns
for you and for me.
Beswick Bears
BB011

SARAH
is sipping her afternoon tea
Perched on the stump
of an old oak tree.
Beswick Bears
BB012

BB009
SAM™

Designer:	Unknown
Height:	3 ½", 8.9 cm
Colour:	Brown bear, rose waistcoat, yellow banjo
Issued:	1993 - 1993
U.S.	**$ 85.00**
Can.	**$125.00**
U.K.	**£ 50.00**
Aust.	**$125.00**

BB010
LIZZY™

Designer:	Unknown
Height:	2 ¼", 5.7 cm
Colour:	Brown bear, pink dress, paint box
Issued:	1993 - 1993
U.S.	**$ 85.00**
Can.	**$125.00**
U.K.	**£ 50.00**
Aust.	**$125.00**

BB011
EMILY™

Designer:	Unknown
Height:	3 ½", 8.9 cm
Colour:	Brown bear, pale blue dress, brown picnic hamper
Issued:	1993 - 1993
U.S.	**$ 85.00**
Can.	**$125.00**
U.K.	**£ 50.00**
Aust.	**$125.00**

BB012
SARAH™

Designer:	Unknown
Height:	3 ¼", 8.3 cm
Colour:	Brown bear, green dress, white cup and saucer
Issued:	1993 - 1993
U.S.	**$ 85.00**
Can.	**$125.00**
U.K.	**£ 50.00**
Aust.	**$125.00**

BEATRIX POTTER

PETER AND BENJAMIN PICKING APPLES

PETER ATE A RADISH

PETER AND BENJAMIN PICKING UP ONIONS

PETER IN BED

PETER IN THE
GOOSEBERRY NET

PETER IN THE
WATERING CAN

PETER ON HIS BOOK

PETER RABBIT
First Version, First Variation

PETER RABBIT DIGGING

PETER RABBIT GARDENING

PETER WITH DAFFODILS

BEATRIX POTTER

PETER WITH POSTBAG

PICKLES

PIGLING BLAND
Second Variation

PIGLING EATS HIS
PORRIDGE

PIG-WIG

POORLY PETER RABBIT

REBECCAH PUDDLE-DUCK

RIBBY

RIBBY AND
THE PATTY PAN

SALLY HENNY PENNY

SAMUEL WHISKERS

SIMPKIN

BEATRIX POTTER

SIR ISAAC NEWTON

SQUIRREL NUTKIN
First Version, First Variation

SUSAN

SWEET PETER RABBIT

TABITHA TWITCHIT
First Variation

TABITHA TWITCHIT AND MISS
MOPPET, First Version

TAILOR OF GLOUCESTER
First Version

THE OLD WOMAN WHO
LIVED IN A SHOE KNITTING

THE OLD WOMAN WHO
LIVED IN A SHOE

THIS PIG HAD A BIT
OF MEAT

THOMASINA
TITTLEMOUSE

BEATRIX POTTER

TIMMY TIPTOES
First Variation

**TIMMY WILLIE
FETCHING MILK**

**TIMMY WILLIE FROM
JOHNNY TOWN-MOUSE**

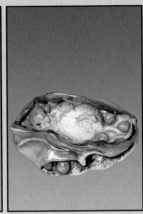

TIMMY WILLIE SLEEPING

TOM KITTEN
First Version, First Variation

**TOM KITTEN AND
BUTTERFLY**

**TOM KITTEN IN
THE ROCKERY**

TOM THUMB

TOMMY BROCK
First Version, First Variation

TWO GENTLEMEN RABBITS

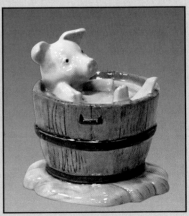

YOCK-YOCK IN THE TUB

JILL BARKLEM'S BRAMBLY HEDGE

POPPY EYEBRIGHT
Style One

MR. APPLE
Style One

MRS. APPLE
Style One

LORD WOODMOUSE
Style One

LADY WOODMOUSE
Style One

DUSTY DOGWOOD
Style One

WILFRED TOADFLAX
Style One

PRIMROSE WOODMOUSE

OLD MRS. EYEBRIGHT

MR. TOADFLAX
Style One, Second Version

MRS. TOADFLAX

CATKIN

JILL BARKLEM'S BRAMBLY HEDGE

OLD VOLE

BASIL
Style One

MRS. CRUSTYBREAD

CLOVER

TEASEL

STORE STUMP MONEY BOX

LILY WEAVER
Style One

FLAX WEAVER
Style One

CONKER

PRIMROSE ENTERTAINS

WILFRED ENTERTAINS

MR. SALTAPPLE
Style One

JILL BARKLEM'S BRAMBLY HEDGE

MRS. SALTAPPLE
Style One

DUSTY AND BABY

THE ICE BALL

LORD WOODMOUSE
Style Two

LADY WOODMOUSE
Style Two

PRIMROSE PICKING
BERRIES

WILFRED CARRIES
THE PICNIC

WILFRED AND THE TOY CHEST (MONEY BOX)

HAPPY BIRTHDAY WILFRED

JILL BARKLEM'S BRAMBLY HEDGE

TEA AT HORNBEAM TREE

A CHEERFUL BLAZE

ON THE LEDGE

SHOOTING THE RAPIDS

LILY WEAVER SPINNING

LILY WEAVER
Style Two

WILFRED TOADFLAX
Style Two

MR. APPLE
Style Two

FLAX WEAVER
Style Two

JILL BARKLEM'S
BRAMBLY HEDGE

DBH 1
POPPY EYEBRIGHT™
Style One

Designer:	Harry Sales
Modeller:	David Lyttleton
Height:	3 ¼", 8.3 cm
Colour:	Grey-white and pink dress, white apron trimmed with blue flowers
Issued:	1983 - 1997

Doulton Number	Price			
	U.S. $	Can. $	U.K. £	Aust. $
DBH 1	65.00	100.00	40.00	100.00

DBH 2
MR. APPLE™
Style One

Designer:	Harry Sales
Modeller:	David Lyttleton
Height:	3 ¼", 8.3 cm
Colour:	Black trousers, white and blue striped shirt, white apron
Issued:	1983 - 1997

Doulton Number	Price			
	U.S. $	Can. $	U.K. £	Aust. $
DBH 2	65.00	100.00	40.00	100.00

DBH 3
MRS. APPLE™
Style One

Designer:	Harry Sales
Modeller:	David Lyttleton
Height:	3 ¼", 8.3 cm
Colour:	White and blue striped dress, white apron
Issued:	1983 - 1997

Doulton Number	Price			
	U.S. $	Can. $	U.K. £	Aust. $
DBH 3	65.00	100.00	40.00	100.00

DBH 4
LORD WOODMOUSE™
Style One

Designer:	Harry Sales
Modeller:	David Lyttleton
Height:	3 ¼", 8.3 cm
Colour:	Green trousers, brown coat and burgundy waistcoat
Issued:	1983 - 1997

Doulton Number	Price			
	U.S. $	Can. $	U.K. £	Aust. $
DBH 4	85.00	125.00	50.00	135.00

DBH 5
LADY WOODMOUSE™
Style One

Designer:	Harry Sales
Modeller:	David Lyttleton
Height:	3 ¼", 8.3 cm
Colour:	Red and white striped dress, white apron
Issued:	1983 - 1997

Doulton Number	Price			
	U.S. $	Can. $	U.K. £	Aust. $
DBH 5	65.00	100.00	40.00	100.00

DBH 6
DUSTY DOGWOOD™
Style One

Designer:	Harry Sales
Modeller:	David Lyttleton
Height:	3 ¼", 8.3 cm
Colour:	Dark grey suit, rose-pink waistcoat
Issued:	1984 - 1995

Doulton Number	Price			
	U.S. $	Can. $	U.K. £	Aust. $
DBH 6	85.00	125.00	50.00	135.00

DBH 7
WILFRED TOADFLAX™
Style One

Designer:	Harry Sales
Modeller:	David Lyttleton
Height:	3 ¼", 8.3 cm
Colour:	Grey overalls, red and white striped shirt
Issued:	1983 - 1997

Doulton Number	Price			
	U.S. $	Can. $	U.K. £	Aust. $
DBH 7	85.00	125.00	50.00	135.00

DBH 8
PRIMROSE WOODMOUSE™

Designer:	Harry Sales
Modeller:	David Lyttleton
Height:	3 ¼", 8.3 cm
Colour:	Yellow dress with white apron
Issued:	1983 - 1997

Doulton Number	Price			
	U.S. $	Can. $	U.K. £	Aust. $
DBH 8	85.00	125.00	50.00	135.00

DBH 9
OLD MRS. EYEBRIGHT™

Designer:	Harry Sales
Modeller:	David Lyttleton
Height:	3 ¼", 8.3 cm
Colour:	Mauve skirt, white and pink striped shawl, white apron
Issued:	1984 - 1995

Doulton Number	Price			
	U.S. $	Can. $	U.K. £	Aust. $
DBH 9	200.00	275.00	125.00	300.00

DBH 10A
MR. TOADFLAX™
Style One, First Version (Tail at front, with cushion)

Designer:	Harry Sales
Modeller:	David Lyttleton
Height:	3 ¼", 8.3 cm
Colour:	Blue and white striped shirt, pink trousers, burgundy braces, multicoloured patchwork quilt
Issued:	1984 - 1984

Doulton Number	Price			
	U.S. $	Can. $	U.K. £	Aust. $
DBH 10A	1,850.00	2,500.00	1,200.00	2,750.00

DBH 10B
MR. TOADFLAX™
Style One, Second Version (Tail at back, without cushion)

Designer:	Harry Sales
Modeller:	David Lyttleton
Height:	3 ¼", 8.3 cm
Colour:	Blue and white striped shirt, pink trousers, burgundy braces
Issued:	1984 - 1985

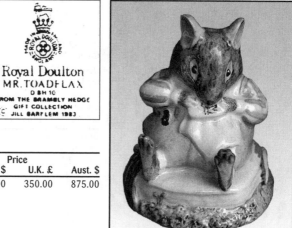

Doulton Number	Price			
	U.S. $	Can. $	U.K. £	Aust. $
DBH 10B	600.00	850.00	350.00	875.00

DBH 10C
MR. TOADFLAX™
Style One, Third Version (Tail at back, with cushion)

Designer:	Harry Sales
Modeller:	David Lyttleton
Height:	3 ¼", 8.3 cm
Colour:	Blue and white striped shirt, lilac trousers, burgundy braces, multicoloured patchwork cushion
Issued:	1985 - 1997

Doulton Number	Price			
	U.S. $	Can. $	U.K. £	Aust. $
DBH 10C	85.00	125.00	50.00	135.00

Note: For further illustrations see page 124.

DBH 11
MRS. TOADFLAX™

Designer:	Harry Sales
Modeller:	David Lyttleton
Height:	3 ¼", 8.3 cm
Colour:	Green and white striped dress, white apron
Issued:	1985 - 1995

Doulton Number	Price			
	U.S. $	Can. $	U.K. £	Aust. $
DBH 11	150.00	225.00	85.00	250.00

Note: The contents of the bowl may vary in colour.

DBH 12
CATKIN™

Designer:	Harry Sales
Modeller:	David Lyttleton
Height:	3 ¼", 8.3 cm
Colour:	Yellow dress and white apron
Issued:	1985 - 1994

Doulton Number	Price			
	U.S. $	Can. $	U.K. £	Aust. $
DBH 12	250.00	350.00	150.00	375.00

DBH 13
OLD VOLE™

Designer:	Harry Sales
Modeller:	David Lyttleton
Height:	3 ¼", 8.3 cm
Colour:	Green jacket, blue trousers, yellow waistcoat
Issued:	1985 - 1992

Doulton Number	Price			
	U.S. $	Can. $	U.K. £	Aust. $
DBH 13	500.00	700.00	300.00	750.00

DBH 14
BASIL™
Style One

Designer:	Harry Sales
Modeller:	David Lyttleton
Height:	3 ¼", 8.3 cm
Colour:	Brown waistcoat, green and white striped trousers
Issued:	1985 - 1992

Doulton Number	Price			
	U.S. $	Can. $	U.K. £	Aust. $
DBH 14	450.00	650.00	250.00	675.00

DBH 15
MRS. CRUSTYBREAD™

Designer:	Graham Tongue
Modeller:	Ted Chawner
Height:	3 ¼", 8.3 cm
Colour:	Yellow dress, white apron and cap
Issued:	1987 - 1994

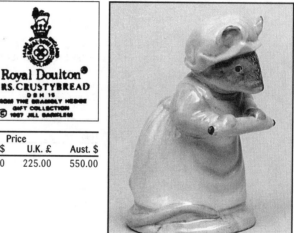

Doulton Number	Price			
	U.S. $	Can. $	U.K. £	Aust. $
DBH 15	375.00	525.00	225.00	550.00

DBH 16
CLOVER™

Designer:	Graham Tongue
Modeller:	Graham Tongue
Height:	3 ¼", 8.3 cm
Colour:	Burgundy dress, white apron
Issued:	1987 - 1997

Doulton Number	Price			
	U.S. $	Can. $	U.K. £	Aust. $
DBH 16	65.00	100.00	40.00	100.00

DBH 17
TEASEL™

Designer:	Graham Tongue
Modeller:	Ted Chawner
Height:	3 ¼", 8.3 cm
Colour:	Blue-grey dungarees, blue and white striped shirt
Issued:	1987 - 1992

Doulton Number	Price			
	U.S. $	Can. $	U.K. £	Aust. $
DBH 17	450.00	625.00	275.00	650.00

DBH 18
STORE STUMP MONEY BOX™

Designer:	Martyn Alcock
Height:	3 ¼", 8.3 cm
Colour:	Browns
Issued:	1987 - 1989

Doulton Number	Price			
	U.S. $	Can. $	U.K. £	Aust. $
DBH 18	375.00	500.00	225.00	525.00

DBH 19
LILY WEAVER™
Style One

Designer:	Graham Tongue
Modeller:	Ted Chawner
Height:	3 ¼", 8.3 cm
Colour:	White, green and mauve
Issued:	1988 - 1993

Doulton Number	Price			
	U.S. $	Can. $	U.K. £	Aust. $
DBH 19	375.00	500.00	225.00	525.00

DBH 20
FLAX WEAVER™
Style One

Designer:	Graham Tongue
Modeller:	Ted Chawner
Height:	3 ¼", 8.3 cm
Colour:	Grey trousers, grey and white striped shirt
Issued:	1988 - 1993

Doulton Number	Price			
	U.S. $	Can. $	U.K. £	Aust. $
DBH 20	375.00	500.00	225.00	525.00

DBH 21
CONKER™

Designer:	Graham Tongue
Modeller:	Ted Chawner
Height:	3 ¼", 8.3 cm
Colour:	Green jacket, yellow waistcoat, green striped trousers
Issued:	1988 - 1994

Doulton Number	Price			
	U.S. $	Can. $	U.K. £	Aust. $
DBH 21	375.00	500.00	225.00	525.00

DBH 22
PRIMROSE ENTERTAINS™

Designer:	Graham Tongue
Modeller:	Alan Maslankowski
Height:	3 ¼", 8.3 cm
Colour:	Green and yellow dress
Issued:	1990 - 1995

Doulton Number	Price			
	U.S. $	Can. $	U.K. £	Aust. $
DBH 22	165.00	225.00	85.00	250.00

DBH 23
WILFRED ENTERTAINS™

Designer:	Graham Tongue
Modeller:	Alan Maslankowski
Height:	3 ¼", 8.3 cm
Colour:	Burgundy and yellow outfit, black hat
Issued:	1990 - 1995

Doulton		Price		
Number	U.S. $	Can. $	U.K. £	Aust $
DBH 23	165.00	225.00	100.00	250.00

DBH 24
MR. SALTAPPLE™
Style One

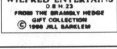

Designer:	Graham Tongue
Modeller:	Warren Platt
Height:	3 ¼", 8.3 cm
Colour:	Blue and white striped outfit, beige base
Issued:	1993 - 1997

Doulton		Price		
Number	U.S. $	Can. $	U.K. £	Aust. $
DBH 24	95.00	135.00	60.00	150.00

DBH 25
MRS. SALTAPPLE™
Style One

Designer:	Graham Tongue
Modeller:	Warren Platt
Height:	3 ¼", 8.3 cm
Colour:	Rose and cream dress, beige hat and base
Issued:	1993 - 1997

Doulton		Price		
Number	U.S. $	Can. $	U.K. £	Aust. $
DBH 25	85.00	125.00	50.00	135.00

DBH 26
DUSTY AND BABY™

Designer:	Graham Tongue
Modeller:	Martyn Alcock
Height:	3 ¾", 9.5 cm
Colour:	Dusty: Blue striped shirt, beige dungarees
	Baby: White gown
Issued:	1995 - 1997

Doulton Number	Price			
	U.S. $	Can. $	U.K. £	Aust. $
DBH 26	85.00	125.00	50.00	135.00

DBH 30
THE ICE BALL™

Designer:	Shane Ridge
Modeller:	Shane Ridge
Height:	4 ¼", 10.8 cm
Colour:	Green, yellow, pink and white
Issued:	2000 in a limited edition of 3,000 (C of A)
Series:	Tableau

Doulton Number	Price			
	U.S. $	Can. $	U.K. £	Aust. $
DBH 30	240.00	380.00	120.00	400.00

DBH 31
LORD WOODMOUSE™
Style Two

Designer:	Shane Ridge
Modeller:	Shane Ridge
Height:	4 ¼", 10.8 cm
Colour:	Brown, salmon, black, red and yellow
Issued:	2000 - 2002

Doulton Number	Price			
	U.S. $	Can. $	U.K. £	Aust. $
DBH 31	80.00	130.00	40.00	150.00

DBH 32
LADY WOODMOUSE™
Style Two

Designer:	Warren Platt
Modeller:	Warren Platt
Height:	4 ¼", 10.8 cm
Colour:	White, pale blue, red and yellow
Issued:	2000 - 2002

Doulton Number	Price			
	U.S. $	Can. $	U.K. £	Aust. $
DBH 32	80.00	130.00	40.00	150.00

DBH 33
PRIMROSE PICKING BERRIES™

Designer:	Shane Ridge
Modeller:	Shane Ridge
Height:	3 ½", 8.9 cm
Colour:	Yellow, white and purple
Issued:	2000 - 2002

Doulton Number	Price			
	U.S. $	Can. $	U.K. £	Aust. $
DBH 33	60.00	100.00	30.00	120.00

DBH 34
WILFRED CARRIES THE PICNIC™

Designer:	Shane Ridge
Modeller:	Shane Ridge
Height:	3 ½", 8.9 cm
Colour:	Blue, brown and red
Issued:	2000 - 2002

Doulton Number	Price			
	U.S. $	Can. $	U.K. £	Aust. $
DBH 34	60.00	100.00	30.00	120.00

DBH 35
WILFRED AND THE TOY CHEST (Money Box)™

Designer:	Martyn Alcock
Modeller:	Martyn Alcock
Height:	3 ¾", 9.5 cm
Colour:	Green, yellow, red and black
Issued:	2000 - 2002

Doulton Number	Price			
	U.S. $	Can. $	U.K. £	Aust. $
DBH 35	145.00	275.00	80.00	300.00

DBH 36
POPPY EYEBRIGHT™
Style Two

Designer:	Warren Platt
Modeller:	Warren Platt
Height:	4", 10.1 cm
Colour:	White skirt with red polka-dot; blue blouse; white apron
Issued:	2001 - 2002

Doulton Number	Price			
	U.S. $	Can. $	U.K. £	Aust. $
DBH 36	75.00	130.00	40.00	150.00

DBH 37
DUSTY DOGWOOD™
Style Two

Designer:	Martyn Alcock
Modeller:	Martyn Alcock
Height:	4", 10.1 cm
Colour:	Blue and white striped shirt; white, yellow and orange pants; white apron and neckerchief, tan sack
Issued:	2001 - 2002

Doulton Nunber	Price			
	U.S. $	Can. $	U.K. £	Aust. $
DBH 37	75.00	130.00	40.00	150.00

DBH 38
BASIL™
Style Two

Designer:	Shane Ridge
Modeller:	Shane Ridge
Height:	3 ½", 8.9 cm
Colour:	Red waistcoat, green and white striped trousers
Issued:	2001 - 2002

Doulton Number	Price			
	U.S. $	Can. $	U.K. £	Aust. $
DBH 38	80.00	130.00	40.00	150.00

DBH 39
MR. SALTAPPLE™
Style Two

Designer:	Shane Ridge
Modeller:	Shane Ridge
Height:	4", 10.1 cm
Colour:	Blue shirt, brown overalls and basket, green neckerchief
Issued:	2001 - 2002
Series:	Sea Story

Doulton Number	Price			
	U.S. $	Can. $	U.K. £	Aust. $
DBH 39	80.00	130.00	40.00	150.00

DBH 40
MRS. SALTAPPLE™
Style Two

Designer:	Martyn Alcock
Modeller:	Martyn Alcock
Height:	3 ½", 8.9 cm
Colour:	Lilac and white dress; pale yellow bonnet with purple ribbon; brown basket
Issued:	2001 - 2002
Series:	Sea Story

Doulton Number	Price			
	U.S. $	Can. $	U.K. £	Aust. $
DBH 40	80.00	130.00	40.00	150.00

DBH 41
PEBBLE™

Designer:	Martyn Alcock
Modeller:	Martyn Alcock
Height:	3 ¼", 8.3 cm
Colour:	Blue and white striped sailor suit; red boat
Issued:	2001 - 2002
Series:	Sea Story

Doulton Number	Price			
	U.S. $	Can. $	U.K. £	Aust. $
DBH 41	60.00	100.00	30.00	120.00

DBH 42
SHELL™

Designer:	Warren Platt
Modeller:	Warren Platt
Height:	3 ½", 8.9 cm
Colour:	Pink and white dress; pale yellow bonnet
Issued:	2001 - 2002
Series:	Sea Story

Doulton Number	Price			
	U.S. $	Can. $	U.K. £	Aust. $
DBH 42	60.00	100.00	30.00	120.00

DBH 43
SHRIMP™

Designer:	Warren Platt
Modeller:	Warren Platt
Height:	3", 7.6 cm
Colour:	White dress and hat, pink ribbons
Issued:	2001 - 2002
Series:	Sea Story

Doulton Number	Price			
	U.S. $	Can. $	U.K. £	Aust. $
DBH 43	60.00	100.00	30.00	120.00

DBH 44
THE BRIDE AND GROOM™

Designer:	Martyn Alcock
Modeller:	Martyn Alcock
Height:	4 ¼", 10.8 cm
Colour:	Bride: (Poppy Eyebright) White skirt, pink and white striped sleeves, white apron trimmed with flowers; multicoloured bouquet
	Groom: (Dusty Dogwood) Dark grey suit, lavender waistcoat
Issued:	2001 - 2002

Doulton Number	Price			
	U.S. $	Can. $	U.K. £	Aust. $
DBH 44	150.00	250.00	80.00	275.00

DBH 45
HAPPY BIRTHDAY WILFRED™

Designer:	Martyn Alcock
Modeller:	Martyn Alcock
Height:	3", 7.6 cm
Colour:	Multicoloured quilt, brown bed; brown mouse wearing red and white striped sweater; pink and white table cloth
Issued:	2001 in a limited edition of 3,000 (C of A)
Series:	Tableau

Doulton Number	Price			
	U.S. $	Can. $	U.K. £	Aust. $
DBH 45	235.00	380.00	120.00	400.00

DBH 46
MR. TOADFLAX™
Style Two

Designer:	Warren Platt
Modeller:	Warren Platt
Height:	3 ¼", 8.3 cm
Colour:	Mauve trousers, blue and white striped shirt; red suspenders
Issued:	2002 to the present

Doulton Number	Price			
	U.S. $	Can. $	U.K. £	Aust. $
DBH 46	N/I	130.00	40.00	N/I

DBH 47
MRS. APPLE™
Style Two

Designer:	Martyn Alcock
Modeller:	Martyn Alcock
Height:	4", 10.1 cm
Colour:	Blue and white striped dress; white apron; green tea set
Issued:	2002 to the present

Doulton Number	Price			
	U.S. $	Can. $	U.K. £	Aust. $
DBH 47	N/I	130.00	40.00	N/I

DBH 48
HEADING HOME™

Designer:	Martyn Alcock
Modeller:	Martyn Alcock
Height:	3 ½", 8.9 cm
Colour:	Blue and white striped dress; white apron; yellow straw hat; brown wheel barrow
Issued:	2003 to the present
Series:	Spring Story

Doulton Number	Price			
	U.S. $	Can. $	U.K. £	Aust. $
DBH 48	N/I	130.00	35.00	N/I

DBH 49
WILFRED'S BIRTHDAY CAKE™

Designer:	Warren Platt
Modeller:	Warren Platt
Height:	3 ¼", 8.3 cm
Colour:	Red and white striped shirt; blue overalls; pink and white cake
Issued:	2003 to the present
Series:	Spring Story

Doulton Number	Price			
	U.S. $	Can. $	U.K. £	Aust. $
DBH 49	N/I	95.00	25.00	N/I

DBH 50
WHERE ARE BASIL'S TROUSERS?™

Designer:	Unknown
Modeller:	Unknown
Height:	3 ¼", 8.3 cm
Colour:	Multicoloured quilt and cushion; pink sofa; brown table
Issued:	2003 to the present
Series:	Spring Story

Doulton Number	Price			
	U.S. $	Can. $	U.K. £	Aust. $
DBH 50	N/I	130.00	35.00	N/I

DBH 51
DUSTY'S BUNS™

Designer:	Unknown
Modeller:	Unknown
Height:	3 ½", 8.9 cm
Colour:	Blue and white striped shirt; yellow trousers, white apron and neckerchief
Issued:	2003 to the present
Series:	Spring Story

Doulton Number	Price			
	U.S. $	Can. $	U.K. £	Aust. $
DBH 51	N/I	95.00	25.00	N/I

DBH 52
MRS. TOADFLAX DECORATES CAKE™

Designer:	Unknown
Modeller:	Unknown
Height:	3 ¾", 9.5 cm
Colour:	Cream dress with orange and yellow stars; cream apron; pink and white cake; tan table
Issued:	2003 to the present
Series:	Spring Story

Doulton Number	Price			
	U.S. $	Can. $	U.K. £	Aust. $
DBH 52	N/I	130.00	40.00	N/I

DBH 53
MR. APPLE™
Style Two

Designer:	Unknown
Modeller:	Unknown
Height:	3 ½", 8.9 cm
Colour:	Black trousers and waistcoat; blue and white striped shirt; red neckerchief; brown jacket; yellow knapsack
Issued:	2003 to the present
Series:	High Hills Collection

Doulton Number	Price			
	U.S. $	Can. $	U.K. £	Aust. $
DBH 53	N/I	95.00	25.00	N/I

DBH 54
LILY WEAVER™
Style Two

Designer:	Unknown
Modeller:	Unknown
Height:	3 ¾", 9.5 cm
Colour:	Brown coat, yellow dress and knapsack, straw hat, brown basket
Issued:	2003 to the present
Series:	High Hills Collection

Doulton Number	Price			
	U.S. $	Can. $	U.K. £	Aust. $
DBH 54	N/I	95.00	25.00	N/I

DBH 55
FLAX WEAVER™
Style Two

Designer:	Unknown
Modeller:	unknown
Height:	4 ¼", 10.8 cm
Colour:	Blue jacket and trousers; orange and red striped shirt; red neckerchief
Issued:	2003 to the present
Series:	High Hills Collection

Doulton Number	Price			
	U.S. $	Can. $	U.K. £	Aust. $
DBH 55	N/I	95.00	25.00	N/I

DBH 56
WILFRED TOADFLAX™
Style Two

Designer:	Unknown
Modeller:	Unknown
Height:	2 ½", 6.4 cm
Colour:	Blue overalls, red and white striped shirt and hat; purple coat; yellow knapsack
Issued:	2003 to the present
Series:	High Hills Collection

Doulton Number	Price			
	U.S. $	Can. $	U.K. £	Aust. $
DBH 56	N/I	95.00	25.00	N/I

DBH 57
ON THE LEDGE™

Designer:	Unknown
Modeller:	Unknown
Height:	4 ¾", 12.1 cm
Colour:	Wilfred: Purple coat, blue overalls; red and white striped shirt and hat Mr. Apple: Tan coat, black trousers and waistcoat; blue and white striped shirt; red neckerchief
Issued:	2003 to the present
Series:	High Hills Collection

Doulton Number	Price			
	U.S. $	Can. $	U.K. £	Aust. $
DBH 57	N/I	185.00	40.00	N/I

DBH58
LILY WEAVER SPINNING™

Designer:	Unknown
Modeller:	Unknown
Height:	4 ¼", 10.8 cm
Colour:	Mustard skirt, brown top, pink, yellow and white striped sleeves; white apron, cap and neckerchief; brown spinning wheel
Issed:	2003 to the present
Series:	High Hills Collection

Doulton Number	Price			
	U.S. $	Can. $	U.K. £	Aust. $
DBH 58	N/I	95.00	40.00	N/I

DBH 59
TEA AT HORNBEAM TREE™

Designer:	Unknown
Modeller:	Unknown
Height:	4", 10.1 cm
Colour:	White skirt with yellow and orange design, green blouse with grey dots, white apron, white bonnet with yellow ribbon, tray with blue and white striped crockery
Issued:	2003 to the present
Series:	High Hills Collection

Doulton	Price			
Number	U.S. $	Can. $	U.K. £	Aust. $
DBH 59	N/I	95.00	25.00	N/I

DBH 60
A CHEERFUL BLAZE™

Designer:	Unknown
Modeller:	Unknown
Height:	3 ½", 8.9 cm
Colour:	Browns, green, red, and blue
Issued:	2003 to the present
Series:	High Hills Collection

Doulton	Price			
Number	U.S. $	Can. $	U.K. £	Aust. $
DBH 60	N/I	220.00	50.00	N/I

DBH 61
SHOOTING THE RAPIDS™

Designer:	Unknown
Modeller:	Unknown
Height:	3 ¾", 9.5 cm
Colour:	Browns, purple, blues and white
Issued:	2003 in a limited edition of 2,000
Series:	High Hills Collection

Doulton	Price			
Number	U.S. $	Can. $	U.K. £	Aust. $
DBH 61	N/I	260.00	65.00	N/I

Mr. Toadflax
Front view

Third Version
Tail at the back; with cushion

First Version
Tail at the front

Second Version
Tail at the back

Mr. Toadflax
back view

Third Version
With cushion

First Version
With cushion

Second Version
Without cushion

THE CAT'S CHORUS

CC1
PURRFECT PITCH™

Modeller:	Shane Ridge
Height:	4", 10.1 cm
Colour:	White cat; black dress and hair, red gloves and shoes
Issued:	1998 - 2001

U.S.	**$50.00**
Can.	**$70.00**
U.K.	**£35.00**
Aust.	**$75.00**

CC2
CALYPSO KITTEN™

Modeller:	Shane Ridge
Height:	4", 10.1 cm
Colour:	Black cat, patterned yellow shirt, beige trousers, red and yellow drum
Issued:	1998 - 2001

U.S.	**$50.00**
Can.	**$70.00**
U.K.	**£35.00**
Aust.	**$75.00**

CC3
ONE COOL CAT™

Modeller:	Shane Ridge
Height:	4", 10.1 cm
Colour:	Ginger cat, blue suit with black trim, black shoes, yellow saxophone
Issued:	1998 - 2001

U.S.	**$50.00**
Can.	**$70.00**
U.K.	**£35.00**
Aust.	**$75.00**

CC4
RATCATCHER BILK

Modeller:	Shane Ridge
Height:	4", 10.1 cm
Colour:	White cat, blue shirt and hat, yellow waistcoat, black trousers and clarinet
Issued:	1998 - 2001

U.S.	**$50.00**
Can.	**$70.00**
U.K.	**£35.00**
Aust.	**$75.00**

CC5
TRAD JAZZ TOM™

Modeller:	Shane Ridge
Height:	4", 10.1 cm
Colour:	Grey cat, trousers and waistcoat, lemon shirt, black hat, yellow trumpet
Issued:	1998 - 2001

U.S.	**$50.00**
Can.	**$70.00**
U.K.	**£35.00**
Aust.	**$75.00**

CC6
CATWALKING BASS™

Modeller:	Shane Ridge
Height:	4", 10.1 cm
Colour:	White cat, yellow jacket, green shirt, red trousers, black hat, tan bass
Issued:	1998 - 2001

U.S.	**$50.00**
Can.	**$70.00**
U.K.	**£35.00**
Aust.	**$75.00**

CC7
FELINE FLAMENCO™

Modeller:	Shane Ridge
Height:	4", 10.1 cm
Colour:	Ginger cat, lemon shirt, black trousers and waistcoat, red/white cumberbund, tan guitar
Issued:	1998 - 2001

U.S.	**$50.00**
Can.	**$70.00**
U.K.	**£35.00**
Aust.	**$75.00**

CC8
BRAVURA BRASS™

Modeller:	Shane Ridge
Height:	4", 10.1 cm
Colour:	Ginger cat, black suit and shoes, white shirt, yellow french horn
Issued:	1998 - 2001

U.S.	**$50.00**
Can.	**$70.00**
U.K.	**£35.00**
Aust.	**$75.00**

CC9
FAT CAT™

Modeller:	Shane Ridge
Height:	3 ¾", 9.5 cm
Colour:	Brown, yellow and blue
Issued:	1999 - 2001
U.S.	**$50.00**
Can.	**$70.00**
U.K.	**£35.00**
Aust.	**$75.00**

CC10
GLAM GUITAR™

Modeller:	Shane Ridge
Height:	4 ¼", 10.8 cm
Colour:	Red, yellow and white
Issued:	1999 - 2001
U.S.	**$50.00**
Can.	**$70.00**
U.K.	**£35.00**
Aust.	**$75.00**

COMPTON & WOODHOUSE

TEDDY BEARS

ARCHIE
by *John Beswick*
Compton & Woodhouse
— 1997 —

BENJAMIN
by
John Beswick
Compton & Woodhouse
— 1996 —

BERTIE
by *John Beswick*
Compton & Woodhouse
— 1997 —

HENRY
by *John Beswick*
Compton & Woodhouse
— 1997 —

ARCHIE™

Designer:	Unknown
Height:	4 ½", 11.9 cm
Colour:	Brown bear; light blue waistcoat; red and white spotted handkerchief
Issued:	1997
U.S.	**$ 85.00**
Can.	**$125.00**
U.K.	**£ 50.00**
Aust.	**$135.00**

BENJAMIN™

Designer:	Unknown
Height:	4 ½", 11.9 cm
Colour:	Brown bear wearing a bright yellow scarf
Issued:	1996
U.S.	**$ 85.00**
Can.	**$125.00**
U.K.	**£ 50.00**
Aust.	**$135.00**

BERTIE™

Designer:	Unknown
Height:	4 ½", 11.9 cm
Colour:	Dark brown bear; straw hat with red and purple band; yellow cane
Issued:	1997
U.S.	**$ 85.00**
Can.	**$125.00**
U.K.	**£ 50.00**
Aust.	**$135.00**

HENRY™

Designer:	Unknown
Height:	4 ½", 11.9 cm
Colour:	Dark brown bear; purple tie, brown satchel
Issued:	1998
U.S.	**$ 85.00**
Can.	**$125.00**
U.K.	**£ 50.00**
Aust.	**$135.00**

COUNTRY COUSINS

BESWICK INTERNATIONAL
COUNTRY COUSINS
**SWEET
SUZIE**
"Thank you"
PM 2101
Made in China © 1994

BESWICK INTERNATIONAL
COUNTRY COUSINS
PETER
*"Once upon
a time"*
PM 2102
Made in China © 1994

BESWICK INTERNATIONAL
COUNTRY COUSINS
HARRY
*"A new home
for Fred"*
PM 2103
Made in China © 1994

BESWICK INTERNATIONAL
COUNTRY COUSINS
MICHAEL
*"Happily
ever after"*
PM 2104
Made in China © 1994

PM 2101	PM 2102	PM 2103	PM 2104
SWEET SUZIE™	**PETER™**	**HARRY™**	**MICHAEL™**
Thank You	**Once Upon A Time**	**A New Home for Fred**	**Happily Ever After**

PM 2101
SWEET SUZIE™
Thank You
Designer: Unknown
Height: 2 ¾", 7.0 cm
Colour: Brown rabbit wearing a brown and yellow pinafore
Issued: 1994 - 1994

U.S. **$35.00**
Can. **$50.00**
U.K. **£20.00**
Aust. **$55.00**

PM 2102
PETER™
Once Upon A Time
Designer: Unknown
Height: 2 ½", 5.6 cm
Colour: Brown hedgehog wearing a blue suit and a white bowtie
Issued: 1994 - 1994

U.S. **$35.00**
Can. **$50.00**
U.K. **£20.00**
Aust. **$55.00**

PM 2103
HARRY™
A New Home for Fred
Designer: Unknown
Height: 2", 5.0 cm
Colour: Brown hedgehog wearing a blue and white jumper and brown trousers
Issued: 1994 - 1994

U.S. **$35.00**
Can. **$50.00**
U.K. **£20.00**
Aust. **$55.00**

PM 2104
MICHAEL™
Happily Ever After
Designer: Unknown
Height: 2 ½", 6.4 cm
Colour: Brown rabbit wearing a green jacket
Issued: 1994 - 1994

U.S. **$35.00**
Can. **$50.00**
U.K. **£20.00**
Aust. **$55.00**

BESWICK INTERNATIONAL
COUNTRY COUSINS

BERTRAM
"Ten out of ten"
PM 2105
Made in China © 1994

BESWICK INTERNATIONAL
COUNTRY COUSINS

LEONARDO
"Practice
makes perfect"
PM 2106
Made in China © 1994

BESWICK INTERNATIONAL
COUNTRY COUSINS

LILY
"Flowers picked
just for you"
PM 2107
Made in China © 1994

BESWICK INTERNATIONAL
COUNTRY COUSINS

PATRICK
"This way's best"
PM 2108
Made in China © 1994

PM 2105
BERTRAM™
Ten Out of Ten

Designer:	Unknown
Height:	3", 7.6 cm
Colour:	Brown owl wearing a green and blue striped waistcoat, a red bow tie and blue mortar board with red tassel
Issued:	1994 - 1994

U.S.	**$35.00**
Can.	**$50.00**
U.K.	**£20.00**
Aust.	**$55.00**

PM 2106
LEONARDO
Practice Makes Perfect

Designer:	Unknown
Height:	2 ¾", 7.0 cm
Colour:	Brown owl wearing a brown hat; white palette and blue paintbrush
Issued:	1994 - 1994

U.S.	**$35.00**
Can.	**$50.00**
U.K.	**£20.00**
Aust.	**$55.00**

PM 2107
LILY
Flowers Picked Just for You™

Designer:	Unknown
Height:	3", 7.6 cm
Colour:	Brown hedgehog wearing a pink dress with matching bonnet with white ribbon, yellow pinafore with white collar
Issued:	1994 - 1994

U.S.	**$35.00**
Can.	**$50.00**
U.K.	**£20.00**
Aust.	**$55.00**

PM 2108
PATRICK™
This Way's Best

Designer:	Unknown
Height:	3", 7.6 cm
Colour:	Brown owl wearing a blue and yellow checked waistcoat, white collar and blue bow tie, yellow hat with red band
Issued:	1994 - 1994

U.S.	**$35.00**
Can.	**$50.00**
U.K.	**£20.00**
Aust.	**$55.00**

PM 2109
JAMIE™
Hurrying Home

Designer:	Unknown
Height:	3", 7.6 cm
Colour:	Brown hedgehog wearing a pink sailor top with white stripes, blue trousers
Issued:	1994 - 1994
U.S.	**$35.00**
Can.	**$50.00**
U.K.	**£20.00**
Aust.	**$55.00**

PM 2111
MUM AND LIZZIE™
Let's Get Busy

Designer:	Unknown
Height:	3 ¼", 8.3 cm
Colour:	Large brown rabbit wearing a blue dress and white pinafore Small brown rabbit wearing a white pinafore
Issued:	1994 - 1994
U.S.	**$50.00**
Can.	**$70.00**
U.K.	**£30.00**
Aust.	**$75.00**

PM 2112
MOLLY AND TIMMY™
Picnic Time

Designer:	Unknown
Height:	2 ¾", 7 cm
Colour:	Large brown mouse wearing pink dress, yellow bonnet, and blue pinafore, Small brown mouse wearing yellow dungarees, white top, blue hat
Issued:	1994 - 1994
U.S.	**$50.00**
Can.	**$70.00**
U.K.	**£30.00**
Aust.	**$75.00**

PM 2113
POLLY AND SARAH™
Good News!

Designer:	Unknown
Height:	3 ¼", 8.3 cm
Colour:	Brown rabbit wearing blue dress and pink apron Brown hedgehog wearing blue dress and scarf, green jacket, white pinafore
Issued:	1994 - 1994
U.S.	**$50.00**
Can.	**$70.00**
U.K.	**£30.00**
Aust.	**$75.00**

BILL & TED
"Working together"
PM 2114
Made in China © 1994

JACK & DAISY
"How does your garden grow?"
PM 2115
Made in China © 1994

ALISON & DEBBIE
"Friendship is fun"
PM 2116
Made in China © 1994

ROBERT & ROSIE
"Perfect Partners"
PM 2119
Made in China © 1994

PM 2114
BILL AND TED™
Working Together

Designer:	Unknown
Height:	3 ¼", 8.3 cm
Colour:	Brown mouse in blue dungarees Brown hedgehog in green dungarees
Issued:	1994 - 1994
U.S.	**$50.00**
Can.	**$70.00**
U.K.	**£30.00**
Aust.	**$75.00**

PM 2115
JACK AND DAISY™
How Does Your Garden Grow?

Designer:	Unknown
Height:	2 ¾", 7 cm
Colour:	Male - brown mouse, white shirt, blue dungarees Female - brown mouse, pink and white striped dress, white pinafore
Issued:	1994 - 1994
U.S.	**$50.00**
Can.	**$70.00**
U.K.	**£30.00**
Aust.	**$75.00**

PM 2116
ALISON AND DEBBIE™
Friendship is Fun

Designer:	Unknown
Height:	2 ¾", 7 cm
Colour:	Rabbit - brown, pink dress, white pinafore Squirrel - brown, blue dress, pink apron
Issued:	1994 - 1994
U.S.	**$50.00**
Can.	**$70.00**
U.K.	**£30.00**
Aust.	**$75.00**

PM 2119
ROBERT AND ROSIE™
Perfect Partners

Designer:	Unknown
Height:	3 ¼", 8.3 cm
Colour:	Male - brown squirrel, blue dungarees, blue hat with red band Female - brown squirrel, pink dress with white collar, yellow hat
Issued:	1994 - 1994
U.S.	**$50.00**
Can.	**$70.00**
U.K.	**£30.00**
Aust.	**$75.00**

PM 2120
SAMMY™
Treasure Hunting

Designer:	Unknown
Height:	2 ¼", 5.7 cm
Colour:	Brown squirrel wearing a green shirt, blue sack
Issued:	1994 - 1994

Back Stamp	Beswick Number	Price U.S. $	Can. $	U.K. £	Aust. $
BK-1	PM2120	35.00	50.00	20.00	55.00

BESWICK INTERNATIONAL
COUNTRY COUSINS
SAMMY
"Treasure hunting"
PM 2120
Made in China © 1994

DAVID HAND'S
ANIMALAND

1148
DINKUM PLATYPUS™

Designer:	Arthur Gredington
Height:	4 ¼", 10.8 cm
Colour:	Brown and beige platypus, green base
Issued:	1949 - 1955

Beswick Number	Price			
	U.S. $	Can. $	U.K. £	Aust. $
1148	325.00	450.00	200.00	475.00

1150
ZIMMY LION™

Designer:	Arthur Gredington
Height:	3 ¾", 9.5 cm
Colour:	Brown lion with white face
Issued:	1949 - 1955

Beswick Number	Price			
	U.S. $	Can. $	U.K. £	Aust. $
1150	575.00	800.00	350.00	850.00

1151
FELIA™

Designer:	Arthur Gredington
Height:	4", 10.1 cm
Colour:	Green cat
Issued:	1949 - 1955

Beswick Number	Price			
	U.S. $	Can. $	U.K. £	Aust. $
1151	750.00	1,000.00	450.00	1,100.00

1152
GINGER NUTT™

Designer:	Arthur Gredington
Height:	4", 10.1 cm
Colour:	Brown and beige squirrel, green base
Issued:	1949 - 1955

Beswick Number	Price			
	U.S. $	Can. $	U.K. £	Aust. $
1152	775.00	1,100.00	500.00	1,200.00

1153
HAZEL NUTT™

Designer:	Arthur Gredington
Height:	3 ¾", 9.5 cm
Colour:	Brown and beige squirrel, green base
Issued:	1949 - 1955

Beswick Number	Price			
	U.S. $	Can. $	U.K. £	Aust. $
1153	775.00	1,100.00	500.00	1,200.00

1154
OSCAR OSTRICH™

Designer:	Arthur Gredington
Height:	3 ¾", 9.5 cm
Colour:	Beige and mauve ostrich, brown base
Issued:	1949 - 1955

Beswick Number	Price			
	U.S. $	Can. $	U.K. £	Aust. $
1154	900.00	1,250.00	550.00	1,350.00

1155
DUSTY MOLE™

Designer:	Arthur Gredington
Height:	3 ½", 8.9 cm
Colour:	Blue mole, white face
Issued:	1949 - 1955

Beswick Number	Price			
	U.S. $	Can. $	U.K. £	Aust. $
1155	500.00	700.00	300.00	750.00

1156
LOOPY HARE™

Designer:	Arthur Gredington
Height:	4 ¼", 10.8 cm
Colour:	Brown and beige hare
Issued:	1949 - 1955

Beswick Number	Price			
	U.S. $	Can. $	U.K. £	Aust. $
1156	725.00	1,000.00	450.00	1,100.00

ENGLISH COUNTRY FOLK

ECF 1
HUNTSMAN FOX

ECF 2
FISHERMAN OTTER

ECF 3
GARDENER RABBIT

ECF 4
GENTLEMAN PIG

ECF 1
HUNTSMAN FOX™
Beswick No.: 9150
Designer: A. Hughes-Lubeck
Height: 5 ¾", 14.6 cm
Colour: Dark green jacket
          and cap, blue-grey
          trousers, green
          wellingtons
Issued: 1993 - 1998

U.S.	**$100.00**
Can.	**$135.00**
U.K.	**£ 55.00**
Aust.	**$145.00**

ECF 2
FISHERMAN OTTER™
Beswick No.: 9152
Designer: Warren Platt
Height: 5 ¾", 14.6 cm
Colour: Yellow shirt and hat,
          dark green
          waistcoat, blue-grey
          trousers
Issued: 1993 - 1998

U.S.	**$100.00**
Can.	**$135.00**
U.K.	**£ 55.00**
Aust.	**$145.00**

ECF 3
GARDENER RABBIT™
First Variation
Beswick No.: 9155
Designer: Warren Platt
Height: 6", 15.0 cm
Colour: White shirt, red
          pullover, blue
          trousers, grey hat
Issued: 1993 - 1999
Varieties: ECF 12

U.S.	**$100.00**
Can.	**$135.00**
U.K.	**£ 55.00**
Aust.	**$145.00**

ECF 4
GENTLEMAN PIG™
First Variation
Beswick No.: 9149
Designer: A. Hughes-Lubeck
Height: 5 ¾", 14.6 cm
Colour: Dark brown suit,
          yellow waistcoat
Issued: 1993 - 1999
Varieties: ECF 10

U.S.	**$100.00**
Can.	**$135.00**
U.K.	**£ 55.00**
Aust.	**$145.00**

ECF 5

SHEPHERD SHEEPDOG

ECF 6

HIKER BADGER

ECF 7

MRS RABBIT BAKING

ECF 8

THE LADY PIG

ECF 5
SHEPHERD SHEEPDOG™

Beswick No.:	9156
Designer:	Warren Platt
Height:	6 ¾", 17.2 cm
Colour:	Yellow smock
Issued:	1993 - 1999

U.S.	**$100.00**
Can.	**$135.00**
U.K.	**£ 55.00**
Aust.	**$145.00**

ECF 6
HIKER BADGER™
First Variation

Beswick No.:	9157
Designer:	Warren Platt
Height:	5 ¼", 13.3 cm
Colour:	Yellow shirt, blue waistcoat, red cap and socks
Issued:	1993 - 1999
Varieties:	ECF 9

U.S.	**$100.00**
Can.	**$135.00**
U.K.	**£ 55.00**
Aust.	**$145.00**

ECF 7
MRS. RABBIT BAKING™
First Variation

Beswick No.:	Unknown
Designer:	Martyn Alcock
Height:	5 ½", 14.0 cm
Colour:	Mauve dress, white apron and cap
Issued:	1994 - 1999
Varieties:	ECF 13

U.S.	**$100.00**
Can.	**$135.00**
U.K.	**£ 55.00**
Aust.	**$145.00**

ECF 8
THE LADY PIG™
First Variation

Designer:	Amanda Hughes-Lubeck
Height:	5 ½", 14.0 cm
Colour:	Green jacket, skirt and hat, brown umbrella
Issued:	1995 - 1999
Varieties:	ECF 11

U.S.	**$100.00**
Can.	**$135.00**
U.K.	**£ 55.00**
Aust.	**$145.00**

ECF 9
HIKER BADGER™
Second Variation

Beswick No.: 9157
Designer: Warren Platt
Height: 5 ¼", 13.3 cm
Colour: Green, red, black
Issued: 1997 in a special edition of 1,000
Varieties: ECF 6

U.S.	**$135.00**
Can.	**$200.00**
U.K.	**£ 85.00**
Aust.	**$225.00**

ECF 10
GENTLEMAN PIG™
Second Variation

Beswick No.: 9149
Designer: A. Hughes-Lubeck
Height: 5 ¾", 14.6 cm
Colour: Light brown
Issued: 1998 in a limited edition of 2,000
Varieties: ECF 4

U.S.	**$ 85.00**
Can.	**$125.00**
U.K.	**£ 50.00**
Aust.	**$135.00**

ECF 11
THE LADY PIG™
Second Variation

Beswick No.: Unknown
Designer: A. Hughes-Lubeck
Height: 5 ½", 14.0 cm
Colour: Browns
Issued: 1998 in a limited edition of 2,000
Varieties: ECF 8

U.S.	**$ 85.00**
Can.	**$125.00**
U.K.	**£ 50.00**
Aust.	**$135.00**

ECF 12
GARDENER RABBIT™
Second Variation

Beswick No.: 9155
Designer: Warren Platt
Height: 6", 15.0 cm
Colour: Black and slate
Issued: 1998 in a limited edition of 2,000
Varieties: ECF 3

U.S.	**$ 85.00**
Can.	**$125.00**
U.K.	**£ 50.00**
Aust.	**$135.00**

ECF 13
MRS. RABBIT BAKING™
Second Variation

Beswick No. Unknown
Designer: Martyn Alcock
Height: 5 ½", 14.0 cm
Colour: Grey, yellow, rust
Issued: 1998 in a limited edition of 2,000
Varieties: ECF 7

U.S.	**$110.00**
Can.	**$150.00**
U.K.	**£ 65.00**
Aust.	**$165.00**

ENID BLYTON'S
NODDY™ COLLECTION

3676
BIG EARS™

Designer:	Enid Blyton
Modeller:	Andy Moss
Height:	5", 12.7 cm
Colour:	Red, white, dark blue and yellow
Issued:	1997 in a special edition of 1,500

U.S.	**$110.00**
Can.	**$150.00**
U.K.	**£ 65.00**
Aust.	**$165.00**

3678
NODDY™

Designer:	Enid Blyton
Modeller	Andy Moss
Height:	5", 12.7 cm
Colour:	Red, blue and light brown
Issued:	1997 in a special edition of 1,500

U.S.	**$110.00**
Can.	**$150.00**
U.K.	**£ 65.00**
Aust.	**$165.00**

3679
MR. PLOD™

Designer:	Enid Blyton
Modeller:	Andy Moss
Height:	5", 12.7 cm
Colour:	Navy and yellow
Issued:	1998 in a special edition of 1,500

U.S.	**$125.00**
Can.	**$175.00**
U.K.	**£ 75.00**
Aust.	**$200.00**

3770
TESSIE BEAR™

Designer:	Enid Blyton
Modeller:	Andy Moss
Height:	5", 12.7 cm
Colour:	Yellow, pink, green and white
Issued:	1998 in a special edition of 1,500

U.S.	**$125.00**
Can.	**$175.00**
U.K.	**£ 75.00**
Aust.	**$200.00**

NODDY AND BIG EARS™

Designer:	Enid Blyton
Modeller:	Andy Moss
Height:	3 ½", 8.9 cm
Colour:	Red, yellow, blue, brown and black
Issued:	2002 in a limited edition of 750 (C of A)

Doulton	Price			
Number	U.S. $	Can. $	U.K. £	Aust. $
–	150.00	200.00	85.00	225.00

2694
RUPERT BEAR™
Style One

Designer:	Harry Sales
Height:	4 ¼", 10.8 cm
Colour:	Red sweater, yellow check trousers and scarf
Issued:	1980 - 1986
U.S.	**$425.00**
Can.	**$600.00**
U.K.	**£275.00**
Aust.	**$650.00**

2710
ALGY PUG™

Designer:	Harry Sales
Height:	4", 10.1 cm
Colour:	Grey jacket, yellow waistcoat, brown trousers
Issued:	1981 - 1986
U.S.	**$400.00**
Can.	**$550.00**
U.K.	**£250.00**
Aust.	**$575.00**

2711
PONG PING™

Designer:	Harry Sales
Height:	4 ¼", 10.8 cm
Colour:	Dark green jacket, gold trousers
Issued:	1981 - 1986
U.S.	**$400.00**
Can.	**$550.00**
U.K.	**£250.00**
Aust.	**$575.00**

2720
BILL BADGER™
Style One

Designer:	Harry Sales
Height:	2 ¾", 7.0 cm
Colour:	Dark grey jacket, light grey trousers and red bowtie
Issued:	1981 - 1986
U.S.	**$475.00**
Can.	**$675.00**
U.K.	**£300.00**
Aust.	**$700.00**

2779
RUPERT BEAR
SNOWBALLING™

Designer:	Harry Sales
Height:	4 ¼", 10.8 cm
Colour:	Red coat, yellow with brown check trousers and scarf
Issued:	1982 - 1986
U.S.	**$400.00**
Can.	**$550.00**
U.K.	**£250.00**
Aust.	**$575.00**

RUPERT BEAR™
Style Two

Designer:	Martyn Alcock
Height:	5 ¾", 14.6 cm
Colour:	Red sweater, yellow check trousers and scarf
Issued:	1998 in a limited edition of 1,920
U.S.	**$ 85.00**
Can.	**$125.00**
U.K.	**£ 50.00**
Aust.	**$135.00**

PODGY PIG™

Modeller:	Martyn Alcock
Height:	5 ¾", 14.6 cm
Colour:	Brown suit, red scarf, black socks, white shoes
Issued:	1998 in a limited edition of 1,920
U.S.	**$ 85.00**
Can.	**$125.00**
U.K.	**£ 50.00**
Aust.	**$135.00**

BILL BADGER™
Style Two

Modeller:	Martyn Alcock
Height:	5", 12.7 cm
Colour:	Turquoise, yellow and purple
Issued:	2000 in a limited edition of 1,920
Comm. by:	Doulton-Direct
U.S.	**$ 85.00**
Can.	**$125.00**
U.K.	**£ 50.00**
Aust.	**$135.00**

EDWARD TRUNK™

Modeller:	Martyn Alcock
Height:	5 ¼", 13.3 cm
Colour:	Blue coat, red scarf, yellow check trousers
Issued:	2000 in a limited edition of 1,920
Comm. by:	Doulton-Direct

U.S.	**$ 85.00**
Can.	**$125.00**
U.K.	**£ 50.00**
Aust.	**$135.00**

RUPERT BEAR AND ALGY PUG GO-CARTING™

Modeller:	Martyn Alcock
Size:	4 ½" x 5"
Colour:	Red, yellow, blue burgundy, brown
Issued:	2000 in a limited edition of 2,500
Comm. by:	Doulton-Direct

U.S.	**$225.00**
Can.	**$300.00**
U.K.	**£125.00**
Aust.	**$325.00**

RUPERT WITH SATCHEL™

Modeller:	Martyn Alcock
Height:	5", 12.7 cm
Colour:	Red, yellow, white, brown
Issued:	2000 in a limited edition of 2,000
Comm. by:	Doulton-Direct

U.S.	**$ 85.00**
Can.	**$125.00**
U.K.	**£ 50.00**
Aust.	**$135.00**

FOOTBALLING
FELINES

FF2
MEE-OUCH

Designer:	Andy Moss
Height:	3 ¼", 8.3 cm
Colour:	Blue shirt/socks, white shorts
Issued:	1998 in a special edition of 1,500

U.S.	**$55.00**
Can.	**$75.00**
U.K.	**£35.00**
Aust.	**$80.00**

Note: FF1 not issued.

FF3
KITCAT

Designer:	Andy Moss
Height:	4 ¼", 10.8 cm
Colour:	Red shirt/socks, white shorts
Issued:	1998 in a special edition of 1,500

U.S.	**$55.00**
Can.	**$75.00**
U.K.	**£35.00**
Aust.	**$80.00**

FF4
DRIBBLE

Designer:	Andy Moss
Height:	4 ¼", 10.8 cm
Colour:	White shirt/socks, black shorts
Issued:	1998 in a special edition of 1,500

U.S.	**$150.00**
Can.	**$225.00**
U.K.	**£100.00**
Aust.	**$250.00**

FF5
THROW IN

Designer:	Andy Moss
Height:	6", 15.0 cm
Colour:	Yellow shirt/socks, white shorts
Issued:	1999 in a special edition of 1,500

U.S.	**$55.00**
Can.	**$75.00**
U.K.	**£35.00**
Aust.	**$80.00**

FF6
REFFEREE: RED CARD

Designer:	Andy Moss
Height:	6 ¼", 15.9 cm
Colour:	Black uniform; black and white socks
Issued:	1999 in a special edition of 1,500

U.S.	**$55.00**
Can.	**$75.00**
U.K.	**£35.00**
Aust.	**$80.00**

HANNA-BARBERA

THE FLINTSTONES
TOP CAT

THE FLINTSTONES
1996-1997

3577
PEBBLES FLINTSTONE™

Designer:	Simon Ward
Height:	3 ½", 8.9 cm
Colour:	Green dress, blue pants, red hair, light brown base
Issued:	1997 in a limited edition of 2,000

U.S.	**$ 70.00**
Can.	**$100.00**
U.K.	**£ 45.00**
Aust.	**$125.00**

3579
BAMM-BAMM RUBBLE™

Designer:	Simon Ward
Height:	3", 7.6 cm
Colour:	Light and dark brown pants, white hair, yellow club, light brown base
Issued:	1997 in a limited edition of 2,000

u.s.	**$ 70.00**
Can.	**$100.00**
U.K.	**£ 45.00**
Aust.	**$125.00**

3583
WILMA FLINTSTONE™

Designer:	Simon Ward
Height:	4 ¾", 12.1 cm
Colour:	White dress, red hair, light brown base
Issued:	1996 in a limited edition of 2,000

U.S.	**$ 70.00**
Can.	**$100.00**
U.K.	**£ 45.00**
Aust.	**$125.00**

3584
BETTY RUBBLE™

Designer:	Simon Ward
Height:	4", 10.1 cm
Colour:	Blue dress, black hair, light brown base
Issued:	1996 in a limited edition of 2,000

U.S.	**$ 70.00**
Can.	**$100.00**
U.K.	**£ 45.00**
Aust.	**$125.00**

3587
BARNEY RUBBLE™

Designer:	Simon Ward
Height:	3 ½", 8.9 cm
Colour:	Reddish brown shirt, yellow hair, light brown base
Issued:	1996 in a limited edition of 2,000

U.S.	**$ 70.00**
Can.	**$100.00**
U.K.	**£ 45.00**
Aust.	**$125.00**

3588
FRED FLINTSTONE™

Designer:	Simon Ward
Height:	4 ¾", 12.1 cm
Colour:	Light brown shirt with dark patches, black hair, blue tie, light brown base
Issued:	1996 in a limited edition of 2,000

U.S.	**$ 70.00**
Can.	**$100.00**
U.K.	**£ 45.00**
Aust.	**$125.00**

3590
DINO™

Designer:	Simon Ward
Height:	4 ¾", 12.1 cm
Colour:	Purple, white and black
Issued:	1997 in a limited edition of 2,000

U.S.	**$100.00**
Can.	**$150.00**
U.K.	**£ 65.00**
Aust.	**$165.00**

TOP CAT
1996-1998

John Beswick
TOP CAT™
© 1996 H-B PROD., INC
LICENSED BY CPL
© 1996 ROYAL DOULTON
EXCLUSIVE EDITION OF 2,000
FOR THE DOULTON &
BESWICK FAIRS IN ENGLAND

John Beswick
CHOO-CHOO™
© 1996 H-B PROD., INC.
LICENSED BY CPL
© 1996 ROYAL DOULTON
EXCLUSIVE EDITION OF 2,000
FOR THE DOULTON &
BESWICK FAIRS IN ENGLAND

John Beswick
FANCY FANCY™
© 1997 H-B PROD., INC.
LICENSED BY CPL
© 1997 ROYAL DOULTON
EXCLUSIVE EDITION OF 2,000
FOR THE DOULTON &
BESWICK FAIRS IN ENGLAND

John Beswick
BENNY™
© 1997 H-B PROD., INC.
LICENSED BY CPL
© 1997 ROYAL DOULTON
EXCLUSIVE EDITION OF 2,000
FOR THE DOULTON &
BESWICK FAIRS IN ENGLAND

3581
TOP CAT™

Designer:	Andy Moss
Height:	4 ½", 11.9 cm
Colour:	Yellow cat wearing a mauve waistcoat and hat
Issued:	1996 in a limited edition of 2,000
Series:	Top Cat
U.S.	**$ 85.00**
Can.	**$125.00**
U.K.	**£ 60.00**
Aust.	**$135.00**

3586
CHOO-CHOO™

Designer:	Andy Moss
Height:	4 ½", 11.9 cm
Colour:	Pink cat wearing a white shirt
Issued:	1996 in a limited edition of 2,000
Series:	Top Cat
U.S.	**$ 85.00**
Can.	**$125.00**
U.K.	**£ 60.00**
Aust.	**$135.00**

3624
FANCY FANCY™

Designer:	Andy Moss
Height:	4 ½", 11.9 cm
Colour:	Pink cat with black tip on tail, white scarf
Issued:	1997 in a limited edition of 2,000
Series:	Top Cat
U.S.	**$ 65.00**
Can.	**$ 90.00**
U.K.	**£ 45.00**
Aust.	**$100.00**

3627
BENNY™

Designer:	Andy Moss
Height:	3 ¾", 8.5 cm
Colour:	Lilac cat wearing a white jacket
Issued:	1997 in a limited edition of 2,000
Series:	Top Cat
U.S.	**$ 65.00**
Can.	**$ 90.00**
U.K.	**£ 45.00**
Aust.	**$100.00**

3671
OFFICER DIBBLE™

Designer:	Andy Moss
Height:	6 ¾", 17.5 cm
Colour:	Dark blue police officer's uniform
Issued:	1998 in a limited edition of 2,000

U.S.	**$165.00**
Can.	**$225.00**
U.K.	**£100.00**
Aust.	**$250.00**

3673
SPOOK™

Designer:	Andy Moss
Height:	4 ½", 11.9 cm
Colour:	Beige cat wearing black tie
Issued:	1998 in a limited edition of 2,000

U.S.	**$ 85.00**
Can.	**$125.00**
U.K.	**£ 60.00**
Aust.	**$135.00**

3674
BRAIN™

Designer:	Andy Moss
Height:	4", 10.1 cm
Colour:	Yellow cat wearing a purple shirt
Issued:	1998 in a limited edition of 2,000

U.S.	**$ 85.00**
Can.	**$125.00**
U.K.	**£ 60.00**
Aust.	**$135.00**

HARRY POTTER™

HP 1
THE REMEMBRALL™
RECOVERY

Designer:	Unknown
Height:	4", 10.1 cm
Colour:	Black, blue and brown
Issued:	2001 - 2003
U.S.	**$60.00**
Can.	**$85.00**
U.K.	**£35.00**
Aust.	**$95.00**

HP 2
HARRY CASTS A MAGICAL
SPELL™

Designer:	Unknown
Height:	4 ½", 11.9 cm
Colour:	Black, blue, red beige and brown
Issued:	2001 - 2003
U.S.	**$50.00**
Can.	**$70.00**
U.K.	**£30.00**
Aust.	**$75.00**

HP 3
HERMIONE STUDIES FOR
POTIONS CLASS™

Designer:	Unknown
Height:	5", 12.7 cm
Colour:	Black, blue, pink, green, brown and gold
Issued:	2001 - 2003
U.S.	**$50.00**
Can.	**$70.00**
U.K.	**£30.00**
Aust.	**$75.00**

HP 4
RON FOLLOWS THE WEASLEY
FAMILY TRADITION™

Designer:	Unknown
Height:	5 ¼", 13.3 cm
Colour:	Black, blue and purple
Issued:	2001 - 2002
U.S.	**$50.00**
Can.	**$70.00**
U.K.	**£30.00**
Aust.	**$75.00**

HP 5
PROFESSOR SEVERUS SNAPE™

Designer:	Unknown
Height:	6 ¼" 15.9 cm
Colour:	Black
Issued:	2001 - 2002
U.S.	**$60.00**
Can.	**$85.00**
U.K.	**£35.00**
Aust.	**$95.00**

HP 6
HEADMASTER ALBUS
DUMBLEDORE™

Designer:	Unknown
Height:	6 ½", 16.5 cm
Colour:	Purple, green, white and brown
Issued:	2001 - 2003
U.S.	**$60.00**
Can.	**$85.00**
U.K.	**£35.00**
Aust.	**$95.00**

HP 7
WIZARD-IN-TRAINING™

Designer:	Unknown
Height:	5 ¼", 13.3 cm
Colour:	Black, blue, red, white, brown and gold
Issued:	2001 - 2003
U.S.	**$60.00**
Can.	**$85.00**
U.K.	**£35.00**
Aust.	**$95.00**

HP 8
THE FRIENDSHIP BEGINS™

Designer:	Unknown
Height:	5 ¼", 13.3 cm
Colour:	Blue, red, white, purple, green and brown
Issued:	2001 in a limited edition of 5,000
U.S.	**$125.00**
Can.	**$175.00**
U.K.	**£ 75.00**
Aust.	**$200.00**

HP 9
HARRY'S 11TH BIRTHDAY™

Designer: Unknown
Height: 6 ¼", 15.9 cm
Colour: Brown, white, red,
blue, olive green
and pink
Issued: 2001 in a limited
edition of 5,000

U.S. **$200.00**
Can. **$275.00**
U.K. **£120.00**
Aust. **$300.00**

HP 10
STRUGGLING THROUGH
POTIONS CLASS™

Designer: Unknown
Height: 3 ¾", 9.5 cm
Colour: Black, green, red
and tan
Issued: 2002 -2003

U.S. **$ 90.00**
Can. **$125.00**
U.K. **£ 55.00**
Aust. **$135.00**

HP 11
SLYTHERIN OR GRYFFINDOR™

Designer: Unknown
Height: 4 ¾", 12.1 cm
Colour: Black, blue, red
and beige
Issued: 2002 - 2003

U.S. **$50.00**
Can. **$70.00**
U.K. **£30.00**
Aust. **$75.00**

HP 12
RON AND SCRABBERS™

Designer: Unknown
Height: 4 ½", 11.9 cm
Colour: Purple, blue
and green
Issued: 2002 - 2003

U.S. **$60.00**
Can. **$85.00**
U.K. **£35.00**
Aust. **$95.00**

HP 13
HERMIONE LEARNS TO
LEVITATE™

Designer: Unknown
Height: 4 ½", 11/9 cm
Colour: Black, pink,
blue and brown
Issued: 2002 - 2003

U.S. **$50.00**
Can. **$70.00**
U.K. **£30.00**
Aust. **$75.00**

HP 14
PROFESSOR McGONAGALL™

Designer: Unknown
Height: 5 ¼", 13.3 cm
Colour: Dark green
Issued: 2002 - 2003

U.S. **$60.00**
Can. **$85.00**
U.K. **£35.00**
Aust. **$95.00**

HP 15
PROFESSOR QUIRRELL™

Designer: Unknown
Height: 5", 12.7 cm
Colour: Dark blue
and purple
Issued: 2002 - 2003

U.S. **$60.00**
Can. **$85.00**
U.K. **£35.00**
Ausr. **$95.00**

HP 16
HEDWIG™

Designer: Unknown
Height: 3 ½", 8.9 cm
Colour: White, yellow
and beige
Issued: 2002 - 2003

U.S. **$50.00**
Can. **$70.00**
U.K. **£30.00**
Aust. **$75.00**

HP 17
THE BIRTH OF NORBERT™

Designer:	Unknown
Height:	4 ¼", 10.8 cm
Colour:	Green, grey, purple and brown
Issued:	2002 - 2003
U.S.	**$60.00**
Can.	**$85.00**
U.K.	**£35.00**
Aust.	**$95.00**

HP 18
THE MIRROR HOLDS THE ANSWER™

Designer:	Unknown
Height:	10", 25.4 cm
Colour:	Gold, black, blue, yellow and grey
Issued:	2002 in a limited edition of 5,000
U.S.	**$135.00**
Can.	**$200.00**
U.K.	**£ 85.00**
Aust.	**$225.00**

HP 19
THE JOURNEY TO HOGWARTS™

Designer:	Unknown
Height:	3 ½", 8.9 cm
Colour:	Black, brown and blue
Issued:	2002 in a limited edition of 5,000
U.S.	**$150.00**
Can.	**$225.00**
U.K.	**£ 95.00**
Aust.	**$250.00**

HP 20
MADAME HOOCH™

Designer:	Unknown
Height:	5 ¼", 13.3 cm
Colour:	Black and white
Issued:	2002 - 2003
Comm. by:	Doulton-Direct
U.S.	**$60.00**
Can.	**$85.00**
U.K.	**£35.00**
Aust.	**$95.00**

HP 21
PROFESSOR SPROUT™

Designer:	Unknown
Height:	5", 12.7 cm
Colour:	Olive green and orange
Issued:	2002 - 2003
Comm. by:	Doulton-Direct
U.S.	**$60.00**
Can.	**$85.00**
U.K.	**£35.00**
Aust.	**$95.00**

HP 22
HARRY POTTER™ PLAYING QUIDDITCH

Designer:	Unknown
Height:	4 ¾", 12.1 cm
Colour:	Red, teal blue, black and brown
Issued:	2002 - 2003
Comm. by:	Doulton-Direct
U.S.	**$60.00**
Can.	**$85.00**
U.K.	**£35.00**
Aust.	**$95.00**

HP 23
DOBBY™

Designer:	Unknown
Height:	2 ¼", 5.7 cm
Colour:	Blue and lilac
Issued:	2002 - 2003
Comm. by:	Doulton-Direct
U.S.	**$60.00**
Can.	**$85.00**
U.K.	**£35.00**
Aust.	**$95.00**

HP 24
DURSLEY FAMILY™

Designer:	Unknown
Height:	6", 15.0 cm
Colour:	Black, blue, red, green, white, yellow and brown
Issued:	2002 in a limited edition of 1,000
Comm. by:	Doulton-Direct
U.S.	**$150.00**
Can.	**$225.00**
U.K.	**£ 95.00**
Aust.	**$250.00**

HP 25
WHOMPING WILLOW™

Designer:	Unknown
Height:	9 ½", 24.0 cm
Colour:	Brown, green and turquoise
Issued:	2002 in a limited edition of 1,000
Comm. by:	Doulton-Direct

U.S.	**$475.00**
Can.	**$650.00**
U.K.	**£295.00**
Aust.	**$675.00**

HP 26
RESCUE IN THE FORBIDDEN FOREST™

Designer:	Unknown
Height:	7 ¼", 18.4 cm
Colour:	Cream, brown, black and blue
Issued:	2002 in a limited edition of 5,000
Comm. by:	Doulton-Direct

U.S.	**$150.00**
Can.	**$225.00**
U.K.	**£ 95.00**
Aust.	**$250.00**

THE HERBS
(Parsley and the Herbs)

H 1
PARSLEY THE LION™

Beswick No.: 4058
Designer: Ivor Wood
Modeller: Shane Ridge
Height: 3 ¾", 9.5 cm
Colour: Greens, yellow and white
Issued: 2001 in a limited edition of 2,500
Comm. by: Doulton-Direct

U.S.	**$100.00**
Can.	**$145.00**
U.K.	**£ 70.00**
Aust.	**$160.00**

H 2
BAYLEAF THE GARDENER™

Beswick No.: 4059
Designer: Ivor Wood
Modeller: Shane Ridge
Height: 5 ¾", 14.6 cm
Colour: Red, white, brown, cream, grey, black
Issued: 2001 in a limited edition of 2,500
Comm. by: Doulton-Direct

U.S.	**$100.00**
Can.	**$145.00**
U.K.	**£ 70.00**
Aust.	**$160.00**

H 3
DILL THE DOG™

Beswick No.: 4057
Designer: Ivor Wood
Modeller: Shane Ridge
Height: 3 ½", 8.9 cm
Colour: Brown, grey, yellow and cream
Issued: 2001 in a limited edition of 2,500
Comm. by: Doulton-Direct

U.S.	**$175.00**
Can.	**$235.00**
U.K.	**£110.00**
Aust.	**$265.00**

H 4
SAGE THE OWL™

Beswick No.: 4056
Designer: Ivor Wood
Modeller: Shane Ridge
Height: 3", 7.5 cm
Colour: Green, brown, yellow and white
Issued: 2001 in a limited edition of 2,500
Comm. by: Doulton-Direct

U.S.	**$100.00**
Can.	**$145.00**
U.K.	**£ 70.00**
Aust.	**$160.00**

HIPPOS ON HOLIDAY

HH1
GRANDMA™

Modeller:	A. Hughes-Lubeck
Height:	5", 12.7 cm
Colour:	Orange, grey, black and brown
Issued:	1999 in a limited edition of 3,500

U.S.	**$55.00**
Can.	**$75.00**
U.K.	**£35.00**
Aust.	**$80.00**

HH2
GRANDPA™

Modeller:	Warren Platt
Height:	5", 12.7 cm
Colour:	White jacket and cap, blue trousers
Issued:	1999 in a limited edition of 3,500

U.S.	**$55.00**
Can.	**$75.00**
U.K.	**£35.00**
Aust.	**$80.00**

HH3
MA™

Modeller:	A. Hughes-Lubeck
Height:	5", 12.7 cm
Colour:	Purple, grey, pink and yellow
Issued:	1999 in a limited edition of 3,500

U.S.	**$55.00**
Can.	**$75.00**
U.K.	**£35.00**
Aust.	**$80.00**

HH4
PA™

Modeller:	Martyn Alcock
Height:	5", 12.7 cm
Colour:	Yellow, green and grey
Issued:	1999 in a limited edition of 3,500

U.S.	**$55.00**
Can.	**$75.00**
U.K.	**£35.00**
Aust.	**$80.00**

HH5
HARRIET™

Modeller:	Martyn Alcock
Height:	5", 12.7 cm
Colour:	Pink and grey
Issued:	1999 in a limited edition of 3,500

U.S.	**$55.00**
Can.	**$75.00**
U.K.	**£35.00**
Aust.	**$80.00**

HH6
HUGO™

Modeller:	Warren Platt
Height:	4", 10.1 cm
Colour:	Grey, white, blue and yellow
Issued:	1999 in a limited edition of 3,500

U.S.	**$55.00**
Can.	**$75.00**
U.K.	**£35.00**
Aust.	**$80.00**

JANE HISSEY'S
OLD BEAR™
AND FRIENDS

OB4601
OLD BEAR™

Designer:	Jane Hissey
Modeller:	Paul Gurney
Height:	4", 10.1 cm
Colour:	Light brown bear
Issued:	1997 - 2001
U.S.	**$40.00**
Can.	**$55.00**
U.K.	**£25.00**
Aust.	**$60.00**

OB4602
TIME FOR BED™

Designer:	Jane Hissey
Modeller:	Paul Gurney
Height:	4", 10.1 cm
Colour:	Golden brown giraffe, light brown bear wearing blue and white striped pyjamas, yellow toothbrush
Issued:	1997 - 1999
U.S.	**$45.00**
Can.	**$65.00**
U.K.	**£30.00**
Aust.	**$75.00**

OB4603
BRAMWELL BROWN HAS A GOOD IDEA™

Designer:	Jane Hissey
Modeller:	Paul Gurney
Height:	4", 10.1 cm
Colour:	Brown bear, beige teddy bear wearing red trousers, green and white base
Issued:	1997 - 1998
U.S.	**$45.00**
Can.	**$65.00**
U.K.	**£30.00**
Aust.	**$75.00**

OB4604
DON'T WORRY, RABBIT™

Designer:	Jane Hissey
Modeller:	Paul Gurney
Height:	4", 10.1 cm
Colour:	Light brown bear, beige rabbit, yellow and red blocks, green base
Issued:	1997 - 2000
U.S.	**$60.00**
Can.	**$85.00**
U.K.	**£40.00**
Aust.	**$95.00**

Royal Doulton

JANE HISSEY'S
OLD BEAR
AND FRIENDS
THE LONG RED SCARF
OB5
© Jane Hissey 1997
Made in Thailand

JANE HISSEY'S
OLD BEAR
AND FRIENDS
WAITING FOR SNOW
OB6

JANE HISSEY'S
OLD BEAR
AND FRIENDS
OB7

Royal Doulton

JANE HISSEY'S
OLD BEAR
AND FRIENDS
WELCOME HOME
OLD BEAR
OB8
© Jane Hissey 1997
Made in Thailand

OB4605
THE LONG RED SCARF™

Designer:	Jane Hissey
Modeller:	Paul Gurney
Height:	4", 10.1 cm
Colour:	Golden brown giraffe wearing long red scarf, dark brown bear
Issued:	1997 - 1999
U.S.	**$60.00**
Can.	**$85.00**
U.K.	**£40.00**
Aust.	**$95.00**

OB4606
WAITING FOR SNOW™

Designer:	Jane Hissey
Modeller:	Paul Gurney
Height:	4", 10.1 cm
Colour:	Golden brown giraffe, light brown bear, white duck with brown beak
Issued:	1997 - 1999
U.S.	**$60.00**
Can.	**$85.00**
U.K.	**£40.00**
Aust.	**$95.00**

OB4607
THE SNOWFLAKE BISCUITS™

Designer:	Jane Hissey
Modeller:	Paul Gurney
Height:	4", 10.1 cm
Colour:	Golden brown giraffe wearing red scarf, light brown bear wearing red dungarees, white donkey with black stripes, brown biscuits
Issued:	1997 - 2001
U.S.	**$ 65.00**
Can.	**$ 95.00**
U.K.	**£ 40.00**
Auat.	**$100.00**

OB4608
WELCOME HOME OLD BEAR™

Designer:	Jane Hissey
Modeller:	Paul Gurney
Height:	4", 10.1 cm
Colour:	Brown bear with two light brown bears and a white duck
Issued:	1997 - 2001
U.S.	**$60.00**
Can.	**$85.00**
U.K.	**£40.00**
Aust.	**$95.00**

Royal Doulton

JANE HISSEY'S
OLD BEAR
AND FRIENDS
RUFF'S PRIZE
OB9
© Jane Hissey 1997
Made in Thailand

JANE HISSEY'S
OLD BEAR
AND FRIENDS
OB10

Royal Doulton

JANE HISSEY'S
OLD BEAR
AND FRIENDS
DON'T FORGET
OLD BEAR
OB11
© Jane Hissey 1998
Made in Thailand

JANE HISSEY'S
OLD BEAR
AND FRIENDS
HOLD ON TIGHT
OB12

OB4609
RUFF'S PRIZE™

Designer:	Jane Hissey
Modeller:	Paul Gurney
Height:	2 ½", 6.5 cm
Colour:	Light brown dog wearing a dark brown coat, light brown bear wearing red dungarees
Issued:	1997 - 1999

U.S.	**$60.00**
Can.	**$85.00**
U.K.	**£40.00**
Aust.	**$95.00**

OB4610
TIME FOR A CUDDLE, HUG ME TIGHT™

Designer:	Jane Hissey
Modeller:	Paul Gurney
Height:	3 ½", 8.9 cm
Colour:	Golden brown bear, light brown bear wearing blue and white striped pyjamas
Issued:	1997 - 2000

U.S.	**$45.00**
Can.	**$65.00**
U.K.	**£30.00**
Aust.	**$75.00**

OB4611
DON'T FORGET OLD BEAR™

Designer:	Jane Hissey
Modeller:	Paul Gurney
Height:	3", 7.6 cm
Colour:	Brown bear in brown box, red book covers
Issued:	1998 - 2001

U.S.	**$60.00**
Can.	**$85.00**
U.K.	**£40.00**
Aust.	**$95.00**

OB4612
HOLD ON TIGHT™

Designer:	Jane Hissey
Modeller:	Paul Gurney
Height:	3", 7.6 cm
Colour:	White owl wearing blue apron, light brown bear wearing blue and white striped pyjamas
Issued:	1998 - 2001

U.S.	**$45.00**
Can.	**$65.00**
U.K.	**£30.00**
Auat.	**$75.00**

OB4613
RESTING WITH CAT™

Designer:	Jane Hissey
Modeller:	Paul Gurney
Height:	2 ½", 6.4 cm
Colour:	Black cat with red inner ears and necktie, light brown bear wearing red trousers
Issued:	1998 - 2001
U.S.	**$45.00**
Can.	**$65.00**
U.K.	**£30.00**
Aust.	**$75.00**

OB4614
LOOKING FOR A SAILOR™

Designer:	Jane Hissey
Modeller:	Paul Gurney
Height:	5", 12.7 cm
Colour:	Red and blue horse, light brown bear
Issued:	1998 - 2001
U.S.	**$60.00**
Can.	**$85.00**
U.K.	**£40.00**
Aust.	**$95.00**

OB4615
TOO MUCH FOOD™

Designer:	Jane Hissey
Modeller:	Paul Gurney
Height:	4", 10.1 cm
Colour:	Golden brown bear on a brown basket, light brown bear wearing red trousers
Issued:	1998 - 2001
U.S.	**$60.00**
Can.	**$85.00**
U.K.	**£40.00**
Aust.	**$95.00**

OB4616
NEST OF SOCKS™

Designer:	Jane Hissey
Modeller:	Paul Gurney
Height:	2 ¾", 7.0 cm
Colour:	Pale brown, blue, green, white yellow and red
Issued:	2000 - 2001
U.S.	**$60.00**
Can.	**$85.00**
U.K.	**£40.00**
Aust.	**$95.00**

OB4617
SNOW DECORATIONS™
Designer:	Jane Hissey
Modeller:	Paul Gurney
Height:	3 ½", 8.9 cm
Colour:	Brown bear
Issued:	2000 - 2001
U.S.	**$45.00**
Can.	**$65.00**
U.K.	**£30.00**
Aust.	**$75.00**

OB4618
STORYTIME™
Designer:	Jane Hissey
Modeller:	Paul Gurney
Height:	2 ½", 6.4 cm
Colour:	Black, beige, red, light blue, and white
Issued:	2000 - 2001
U.S.	**$45.00**
Can.	**$65.00**
U.K.	**£30.00**
Aust.	**$75.00**

OB4619
DUCK™
Designer:	Jane Hissey
Modeller:	Paul Gurney
Height:	3", 7.6 cm
Colour:	White, brown and yellow duck, multicoloured quilt
Issued:	2000 - 2001
U.S.	**$45.00**
Can.	**$65.00**
U.K.	**£30.00**
Aust.	**$75.00**

OB4620
UP, UP AND AWAY™
Designer:	Jane Hissey
Modeller:	Paul Gurney
Height:	3 ½", 8.9 cm
Colour:	White, red, brown, blue and silver
Issued:	2000 - 2001
U.S.	**$60.00**
Can.	**$85.00**
U.K.	**£40.00**
Aust.	**$95.00**

JOAN WALSH ANGLUND

2272
ANGLUND BOY™

Designer:	Albert Hallam
Height:	4 ½", 11.9 cm
Colour:	Green dungarees, brown hat
Issued:	1970 - 1971

U.S.	**$150.00**
Can.	**$200.00**
U.K.	**£ 95.00**
U.S.	**$225.00**

2293
ANGLUND GIRL WITH DOLL™

Designer:	Albert Hallam
Height:	4 ½", 11.9 cm
Colour:	Green dress and bow, white apron
Issued:	1970 - 1971

U.S.	**$150.00**
Can.	**$200.00**
U.K.	**£ 95.00**
Aust.	**$225.00**

2317
ANGLUND GIRL WITH FLOWERS™

Designer:	Albert Hallam
Height:	4 ¾", 12.1 cm
Colour:	White dress, blue leggings, straw hat with blue ribbon
Issued:	1971 - 1971

U.S.	**$150.00**
Can.	**$200.00**
U.K.	**£ 95.00**
Aust.	**$225.00**

KITTY MACBRIDE

2526
A FAMILY MOUSE™

Designer:	Graham Tongue
Height:	3 ½", 8.9 cm
Colour:	Brown, mauve, turquoise, light and dark green
Issued:	1975 - 1983
U.S.	**$145.00**
Can.	**$200.00**
U.K.	**£ 90.00**
Aust.	**$225.00**

2527
A DOUBLE ACT™

Designer:	Graham Tongue
Height:	3 ½", 8.9 cm
Colour:	Yellow, orange, brown, green and blue
Issued:	1975 - 1983
U.S.	**$145.00**
Can.	**$200.00**
U.K.	**£ 90.00**
Aust.	**$225.00**

2528
THE RACEGOER™

Designer:	David Lyttleton
Height:	3 ½", 8.9 cm
Colour:	Brown, yellow, and green
Issued:	1975 - 1983
U.S.	**$145.00**
Can.	**$200.00**
U.K.	**£ 90.00**
Aust.	**$225.00**

2529
A GOOD READ™

Designer:	David Lyttleton
Height:	2 ½", 6.4 cm
Colour:	Yellow, blue, brown and white
Issued:	1975 - 1983
U.S.	**$325.00**
Can.	**$450.00**
U.K.	**£200.00**
Aust.	**$475.00**

2530
LAZYBONES™

Designer:	David Lyttleton
Height:	1 ½", 3.8 cm
Colour:	Blue, black, brown, green and white
Issued:	1975 - 1983

U.S.	**$145.00**
Can.	**$200.00**
U.K.	**£ 90.00**
Aust.	**$225.00**

2531
A SNACK™

Designer:	David Lyttleton
Height:	3 ¼", 8.3 cm
Colour:	Brown, blue, yellow and green
Issued:	1975 - 1983

U.S.	**$145.00**
Can.	**$200.00**
U.K.	**£ 90.00**
Aust.	**$225.00**

2532
STRAINED RELATIONS™

Designer:	David Lyttleton
Height:	3", 7.6 cm
Colour:	Brown, blue and green
Issued:	1975 - 1983

U.S.	**$145.00**
Can.	**$200.00**
U.K.	**£ 90.00**
Aust.	**$225.00**

2533
JUST GOOD FRIENDS™

Designer:	David Lyttleton
Height:	3", 7.6 cm
Colour:	Brown, yellow, blue, red and green
Issued:	1975 - 1983

U.S.	**$200.00**
Can.	**$275.00**
U.K.	**£125.00**
Aust.	**$300.00**

Backstamp not
available
at press time

Backstamp not
available
at press time

2565
THE RING™

Designer:	David Lyttleton
Height:	3 ¼", 8.3 cm
Colour:	Brown, white, purple and yellow
Issued:	1976 - 1983

U.S.	**$250.00**
Can.	**$350.00**
U.K.	**£150.00**
Aust.	**$375.00**

2566
GUILTY SWEETHEARTS™

Designer:	David Lyttleton
Height:	2 ¼", 5.7 cm
Colour:	Brown, yellow, green and white
Issued:	1976 - 1983

U.S.	**$225.00**
Can.	**$300.00**
U.K.	**£140.00**
Aust.	**$325.00**

2589
ALL I DO IS THINK OF YOU™

Designer:	David Lyttleton
Height:	2 ½", 6.4 cm
Colour:	Brown, yellow and white
Issued:	1976 - 1983

U.S.	**$500.00**
Can.	**$700.00**
U.K.	**£325.00**
Aust.	**$750.00**

LITTLE LIKEABLES

LL1
FAMILY GATHERING™
(Hen and Two Chicks)

Designer:	Diane Griffiths
Height:	4 ½", 11.9 cm
Colour:	White hen and chicks with yellow beaks; gold comb on hen
Issued:	1985 - 1987

Beswick Number	Price U.S. $	Can. $	U.K. £	Aust. $
LL1	75.00	115.00	45.00	125.00

LL2
WATCHING THE WORLD GO BY™
(Frog)

Designer:	Robert Tabbenor
Height:	3 ¾", 9.5 cm
Colour:	White frog, black and green eyes
Issued:	1985 - 1987

Beswick Number	Price U.S. $	Can. $	U.K. £	Aust. $
LL2	75.00	115.00	45.00	125.00

LL3
HIDE AND SLEEP™
(Pig and Two Piglets)

Designer:	Robert Tabbenor
Height:	3 ¼", 8.3 cm
Colour:	White pigs with pink noses, ears and tails
Issued:	1985 - 1987

Beswick Number	Price U.S. $	Can. $	U.K. £	Aust. $
LL3	75.00	115.00	45.00	125.00

LL4
MY PONY™
(Pony)

Designer:	Diane Griffiths
Height:	7 ¼", 18.4 cm
Colour:	White pony with blue highlights in mane and tail
Issued:	1985 - 1987

| Beswick Number | Price | | | |
	U.S. $	Can. $	U.K. £	Aust. $
LL4	75.00	115.00	45.00	125.00

LL5
ON TOP OF THE WORLD™
(Elephant)

Designer:	Diane Griffiths
Height:	3 ¾", 9.5 cm
Colour:	White elephant with black eyes and gold nails
Issued:	1985 - 1987

| Beswick Number | Price | | | |
	U.S. $	Can. $	U.K. £	Aust. $
LL5	75.00	115.00	45.00	125.00

LL6
TREAT ME GENTLY™
(Fawn)

Designer:	Diane Griffiths
Height:	4 ½", 11.9 cm
Colour:	White fawn with black and brown eyes, black nose and gold hoof
Issued:	1985 - 1987

| Beswick Number | Price | | | |
	U.S. $	Can. $	U.K. £	Aust. $
LL6	75.00	115.00	45.00	125.00

LL7
OUT AT LAST™
(Duckling)

Designer:	Robert Tabbenor
Height:	3 ¼", 8.3 cm
Colour:	White duck with black and brown eyes and gold beak
Issued:	1985 - 1987

Beswick	Price			
Number	U.S. $	Can. $	U.K. £	Aust. $
LL7	75.00	115.00	45.00	125.00

LL8
CATS CHORUS™
(Cats)

Designer:	Robert Tabbenor
Height:	4 ¾", 12.1 cm
Colour:	Two white cats with black and green eyes, black nose, pink ears and mouth
Issued:	1985 - 1987

Beswick	Price			
Number	U.S. $	Can. $	U.K. £	Aust. $
LL8	75.00	115.00	45.00	125.00

LITTLE LOVABLES

HAPPY BIRTHDAY

I LOVE YOU

GOD LOVES ME

JUST FOR YOU

BESWICK
B
ENGLAND
LL 1

BESWICK
B
ENGLAND
LL 2

BESWICK
B
ENGLAND
LL 3

BESWICK
B
ENGLAND
LL 4

LL1
HAPPY BIRTHDAY™

Beswick No.: 3328
Designer: A. Hughes-Lubeck
Height: 4 ½", 11.9 cm
Colour: White, pink and
           orange (gloss)
Issued: 1992 - 1994
Varieties: LL8; LL15; also
           unnamed LL22

U.S.	**$ 65.00**
Can.	**$ 90.00**
U.K.	**£ 40.00**
Aust.	**$100.00**

LL2
I LOVE YOU™

Beswick No.: 3320
Designer: A. Hughes-Lubeck
Height: 4 ½", 11.9 cm
Colour: White, green and
           pink (gloss)
Issued: 1992 - 1994
Varieties: LL9, LL16; also
           unnamed LL23

U.S.	**$ 65.00**
Can.	**$ 90.00**
U.K.	**£ 40.00**
Aust.	**$100.00**

LL3
GOD LOVES ME™

Beswick No.: 3336
Designer: A. Hughes-Lubeck
Height: 3 ¾", 9.5 cm
Colour: White, green and
           turquoise (gloss)
Issued: 1992 - 1993
Varieties: LL10, LL17; also
           called Please, LL33,
           LL34; also unnamed
           LL24

U.S.	**$165.00**
Can.	**$225.00**
U.K.	**£100.00**
Aust.	**$250.00**

LL4
JUST FOR YOU™

Beswick No.: 3361
Designer: Warren Platt
Height: 4 ½", 11.9 cm
Colour: White, pink and
           blue (gloss)
Issued: 1992 - 1994
Varieties: LL11, LL18; also
           unnamed LL25

U.S.	**$55.00**
Can.	**$80.00**
U.K.	**£35.00**
Aust.	**$90.00**

LL 5

LL 6

LL 7

LL 8

LL5
TO MOTHER™

Beswick No.:	3331
Designer:	A. Hughes-Lubeck
Height:	4 ½", 11.9 cm
Colour:	White, blue and purple (gloss)
Issued:	1992 - 1994
Varieties:	LL12, LL19; also called To Daddy, also unnamed LL26

U.S.	$55.00
Can.	$80.00
U.K.	£35.00
Aust.	$90.00

LL6
CONGRATULATIONS™

Beswick No.:	3340
Designer:	Warren Platt
Height:	4 ½", 11.9 cm
Colour:	White, green and pink (gloss)
Issued:	1992 - 1994
Varieties:	LL13, LL20; also unnamed LL27

U.S.	$55.00
Can.	$80.00
U.K.	£35.00
Aust.	$90.00

LL7
PASSED™

Beswick No.:	3334
Designer:	A. Hughes-Lubeck
Height:	3", 7.6 cm
Colour:	White, lilac and pink (gloss)
Issued:	1992 - 1994
Varieties:	LL14, LL21; also unnamed LL28

U.S.	$ 80.00
Can	$125.00
U.K.	£ 50.00
Aust.	$135.00

LL8
HAPPY BIRTHDAY™

Beswick No.:	3328
Designer:	A. Hughes-Lubeck
Height:	4 ½", 11.9 cm
Colour:	White, yellow and green (gloss)
Issued:	1992 - 1994
Varieties:	LL1, LL15; also unnamed LL22

U.S.	$55.00
Can.	$80.00
U.K.	£35.00
Aust.	$90.00

LL9
I LOVE YOU™

Beswick No.: 3320
Designer: A. Hughes-Lubeck
Height: 4 ½", 11.9 cm
Colour: White, blue and orange (gloss)
Issued: 1992 - 1994
Varieties: LL2, LL16; also unnamed LL23

U.S.	**$55.00**
Can.	**$80.00**
U.K.	**£35.00**
Aust.	**$90.00**

LL10
GOD LOVES ME™

Beswick No.: 3336
Designer: A. Hughes-Lubeck
Height: 3 ¾", 9.5 cm
Colour: White, gold and blue (gloss)
Issued: 1992 - 1993
Varieties: LL3, LL17; also called Please, LL33, LL34; also unnamed LL24

U.S.	**$ 95.00**
Can.	**$135.00**
U.K.	**£ 60.00**
Aust.	**$150.00**

LL11
JUST FOR YOU™

Beswick No.: 3361
Designer: Warren Platt
Height: 4 ½", 11.9 cm
Colour: White, yellow and pale green (gloss)
Issued: 1992 - 1994
Varieties: LL4, LL18; also unnamed LL25

U.S.	**$55.00**
Can.	**$80.00**
U.K.	**£35.00**
Aust.	**$90.00**

LL12
TO MOTHER™

Beswick No.: 3331
Designer: A. Hughes-Lubeck
Height: 4 ½", 11.9 cm
Colour: White, yellow and pink (gloss)
Issued: 1992 - 1994
Varieties: LL5, LL19; also called To Daddy, LL29; also unnamed LL26

U.S.	**$55.00**
Can.	**$80.00**
U.K.	**£35.00**
Aust.	**$90.00**

LL 13

LL 14

LL 15

LL 16

LL13
CONGRATULATIONS™

Beswick No.:	3340
Designer:	Warren Platt
Height:	4 ½", 11.9 cm
Colour:	White, pale blue and yellow (gloss)
Issued:	1992 - 1994
Varieties:	LL6, LL20; also unnamed LL27

U.S.	**$55.00**
Can.	**$80.00**
U.K.	**£35.00**
Aust.	**$90.00**

LL14
PASSED™

Beswick No.:	3334
Designer:	A. Hughes-Lubeck
Height:	3", 7.6 cm
Colour:	White, light blue and orange (gloss)
Issued:	1992 - 1994
Varieties:	LL7, LL21; also unnamed LL28

U.S.	**$ 80.00**
Can.	**$125.00**
U.K.	**£ 50.00**
Aust.	**$135.00**

LL15
HAPPY BIRTHDAY™

Beswick No.:	3407
Designer:	A. Hughes-Lubeck
Height:	4 ½", 11.9 cm
Colour:	White, salmon and green (matt)
Issued:	1992 - 1993
Varieties:	LL8, LL15; also unnamed LL22

U.S.	**$125.00**
Can.	**$175.00**
U.K.	**£ 75.00**
Aust.	**$175.00**

LL16
I LOVE YOU™

Beswick No.:	3406
Designer:	A. Hughes-Lubeck
Height:	4 ½", 11.9 cm
Colour:	White, green and yellow (matt)
Issued:	1992 - 1993
Varieties:	LL2, LL9; also unnamed LL23

U.S.	**$125.00**
Can.	**$175.00**
U.K.	**£ 75.00**
Aust.	**$175.00**

LL17
GOD LOVES ME™

Beswick No.:	3410
Designer:	A. Hughes-Lubeck
Height:	3 ¾", 9.5 cm
Colour:	White, purple and yellow (matt)
Issued:	1992 - 1993
Varieties:	LL3, LL10; also called Please, LL33, LL34; also unnamed LL24

U.S.	**$125.00**
Can.	**$175.00**
U.K.	**£ 75.00**
Aust.	**$175.00**

LL18
JUST FOR YOU™

Beswick No.:	3412
Designer:	Warren Platt
Height:	4 ½", 11.9 cm
Colour:	White, yellow and dark blue (matt)
Issued:	1992 - 1993
Varieties:	LL4, LL11; also unnamed LL25

U.S.	**$125.00**
Can.	**$175.00**
U.K.	**£ 75.00**
Aust.	**$175.00**

LL19
TO MOTHER™

Beswick No.:	3408
Designer:	A. Hughes-Lubeck
Height:	4 ½", 11.9 cm
Colour:	White, green and orange (matt)
Issued:	1992 - 1993
Varieties:	LL5, LL12; also called To Daddy, LL29; also unnamed LL26

U.S.	**$125.00**
Can.	**$175.00**
U.K.	**£ 75.00**
Aust.	**$175.00**

LL20
CONGRATULATIONS™

Beswick No.:	3411
Designer:	Warren Platt
Height:	4 ½", 11.9 cm
Colour:	White, blue and red (matt)
Issued:	1992 - 1993
Varieties:	LL6, LL13; also unnamed LL27

U.S.	**$125.00**
Can.	**$175.00**
U.K.	**£ 75.00**
Aust.	**$175.00**

LL21
PASSED™

Beswick No.:	3409
Designer:	A. Hughes-Lubeck
Height:	3", 7.6 cm
Colour:	White, blue and orange (matt)
Issued:	1992 - 1993
Varieties:	LL7, LL14; also unnamed LL28

U.S.	**$125.00**
Can.	**$175.00**
U.K.	**£ 75.00**
Aust.	**$175.00**

LL22
(No Name)

Beswick No.:	3329
Designer:	A. Hughes-Lubeck
Height:	4 ½", 11.9 cm
Colour:	White, pink and orange (gloss)
Issued:	1993 - 1993
Varieties:	Also called Happy Birthday, LL1, LL8, LL15

U.S.	**$ 85.00**
Can.	**$135.00**
U.K.	**£ 60.00**
Aust.	**$145.00**

LL23
(No Name)

Beswick No.:	3320
Designer:	A. Hughes-Lubeck
Height:	4 ½", 11.9 cm
Colour:	White, green and pink (gloss)
Issued:	1993 - 1993
Varieties:	Also called I Love You, LL2, LL9, LL16

U.S.	**$ 85.00**
Can.	**$135.00**
U.K.	**£ 60.00**
Aust.	**$145.00**

LL24
(No Name)

Beswick No.:	3336
Designer:	A. Hughes-Lubeck
Height:	3 ¾", 9.5 cm
Colour:	White, green and turquoise (gloss)
Issued:	1993 - 1993
Varieties:	Also called God Loves Me, LL3. LL10, LL17; Please, LL33, LL34

U.S.	**$ 85.00**
Can.	**$135.00**
U.K.	**£ 60.00**
Aust.	**$145.00**

LL25
(No Name)

Beswick No.: 3361
Designer: Warren Platt
Height: 4 ½", 11.9 cm
Colour: White, pink and blue (gloss)
Issued: 1993 - 1993
Varieties: Also called Just For You, LL4, LL11, LL18

U.S.	$ 85.00
Can.	$135.00
U.K.	£ 60.00
Aust.	$145.00

LL26
(No Name)

Beswick No.: 3331
Designer: A. Hughes-Lubeck
Height: 4 ¼", 10.8 cm
Colour: White, blue and purple (gloss)
Issued: 1993 - 1993
Varieties: Also called To Mother, LL5, LL12, LL19;To Daddy, LL29

U.S.	$ 85.00
Can.	$135.00
U.K.	£ 60.00
Aust.	$145.00

LL27
(No Name)

Beswick No.: 3340
Designer: Warren Platt
Height: 4 ½", 11.9 cm
Colour: White, green and pink (gloss)
Issued: 1993 - 1993
Varieties: Also called Congratulations, LL6, LL13, LL20

U.S.	$ 85.00
Can.	$135.00
U.K.	£ 60.00
Aust	$145.00

LL28
(No Name)

Beswick No.: 3334
Designer: A. Hughes-Lubeck
Height: 3", 7.6 cm
Colour: White, lilac and pink (gloss)
Issued: 1993 - 1993
Varieties: Also called Passed, LL7, LL14, LL21

U.S.	$ 85.00
Can.	$135.00
U.K.	£ 60.00
Aust.	$145.00

LL 29

LL 30

LL 31

LL 32

LL29
TO DADDY™

Beswick No.:	3331
Designer:	A. Hughes-Lubeck
Height:	4 ½", 11.9 cm
Colour:	White, light blue and green (gloss)
Issued:	1994 - 1994
Varieties:	Also called To Mother, LL5, LL12, LL19; also unnamed LL26

U.S.	**$ 65.00**
Can.	**$ 90.00**
U.K.	**£ 40.00**
Aust.	**$100.00**

LL30
MERRY CHRISTMAS™

Beswick No.:	3389
Designer:	A. Hughes-Lubeck
Height:	4", 10.1 cm
Colour:	White, red and green (gloss)
Issued:	1993 - 1994

U.S.	**$ 75.00**
Can.	**$110.00**
U.K.	**£ 45.00**
Aust.	**$110.00**

LL31
GOOD LUCK™

Beswick No.:	3388
Designer:	A. Hughes-Lubeck
Height:	4 ¼", 10.8 cm
Colour:	White, pink and green (gloss)
Issued:	1993 - 1994

U.S.	**$60.00**
Can.	**$85.00**
U.K.	**£40.00**
Aust.	**$95.00**

LL32
GET WELL SOON™

Beswick No.:	3390
Designer:	A. Hughes-Lubeck
Height:	4 ¼", 10.8 cm
Colour:	White, green and purple (gloss)
Issued:	1994 - 1994

U.S.	**$ 80.00**
Can.	**$125.00**
U.K.	**£ 50.00**
Aust.	**$135.00**

LL 33

LL 34

LL 36
B.C.C. 10th ANNIVERSARY

LL33
PLEASE™

Beswick No.: 3336
Designer: A. Hughes-Lubeck
Height: 3 ¾", 9.5 cm
Colour: White, green and
blue (gloss)
Issued: 1993 - 1994
Varieties: LL34; also called
God Loves Me, LL3,
LL10, LL17; also
unnamed LL24

U.S.	**$ 80.00**
Can.	**$125.00**
U.K.	**£ 50.00**
Aust.	**$135.00**

LL34
PLEASE™

Beswick No.: 3336
Designer: A. Hughes-Lubeck
Height: 3 ¾", 9.5 cm
Colour: White, gold and
light blue (gloss)
Issued: 1993 - 1994
Varieties: LL33; also called
God Loves Me,
LL3, LL10, LL17;
also unnamed LL24

U.S.	**$ 80.00**
Can.	**$125.00**
U.K.	**£ 50.00**
Aust.	**$135.00**

LL35 is the prototype for "I Love
Beswick." Colourway not issued.

LL36
I LOVE BESWICK™

Beswick No.: 3320
Designer: A. Hughes-Lubeck
Height: 4 ½", 11.9 cm
Colour: White, green and
pink (gloss)
Issued: 1995 - 1995
Varieties: Also called I Love
You, LL2, LL9, LL16;
also unnamed LL23

U.S.	**$145.00**
Can.	**$200.00**
U.K.	**£ 90.00**
Aust.	**$225.00**

Note: This piece was specially
commissioned for the 10th
Anniversary of the Beswick
Collectors Circle.

NORMAN THELWELL

EARTHENWARE SERIES 1981-1989
RESIN STUDIO SCULPTURES 1985
EARTHENWARE SERIES 2001

NORMAN THELWELL
EARTHENWARE SERIES 1981-1989

2704A
AN ANGEL ON HORSEBACK™
First Variation

Designer:	Harry Sales
Modeller:	David Lyttleton
Height:	4 ½", 11.4 cm
Colour:	Grey horse, rider wears brown jacket, yellow jodhpurs
Issued:	1981 - 1989
Varieties:	2704B

U.S.	**$275.00**
Can.	**$375.00**
U.K.	**£175.00**
Aust.	**$400.00**

2704B
AN ANGEL ON HORSEBACK™
Second Variation

Designer:	Harry Sales
Modeller:	David Lyttleton
Height:	4 ½", 11.4 cm
Colour:	Bay horse, rider wears red jacket, yellow jodhpurs
Issued:	1981 - 1989
Varieties:	2704A

U.S.	**$250.00**
Can.	**$350.00**
U.K.	**£150.00**
Aust.	**$400.00**

2769A
KICK-START™
First Variation

Designer:	Harry Sales
Modeller:	David Lyttleton
Height:	3 ½", 8.9 cm
Colour:	Grey horse, rider wears red jacket and yellow jodhpurs
Issued:	1982 - 1989
Varieties:	2769B

U.S.	**$275.00**
Can.	**$375.00**
U.K.	**£175.00**
Aust.	**$400.00**

2769B
KICK-START™
Second Variation

Designer:	Harry Sales
Modeller:	David Lyttleton
Height:	3 ½", 8.9 cm
Colour:	Bay horse, rider wears red jacket and yellow jodhpurs
Issued:	1982 - 1989
Varieties:	2769B

U.S.	**$250.00**
Can.	**$350.00**
U.K.	**£150.00**
Aust.	**$400.00**

2789A
PONY EXPRESS™
First Variation

Designer:	Harry Sales
Modeller:	David Lyttleton
Height:	4 ½", 11.4 cm
Colour:	Grey horse, rider wears green jacket and yellow jodhpurs
Issued:	1982 - 1989
Varieties:	2789B

U.S.	**$500.00**
Can.	**$700.00**
U.K.	**£300.00**
Aust.	**$800.00**

2789B
PONY EXPRESS™
Second Variation

Designer:	Harry Sales
Modeller:	David Lyttleton
Height:	4 ½", 11.4 cm
Colour:	Bay horse, rider wears red jacket and yellow jodhpurs
Issued:	1982 - 1989
Varieties:	2789A

U.S.	**$325.00**
Can.	**$500.00**
U.K.	**£200.00**
Aust.	**$550.00**

NORMAN THEWELL
RESIN STUDIO SCULPTURES 1985-1985

SS7A
I FORGIVE YOU™
First Variation

Designer:	Harry Sales
Modeller:	David Lyttleton
Height:	4", 10.1 cm
Colour:	Grey horse, rider wears red jacket and yellow jodhpurs
Issued:	1985 - 1985
Series:	Studio Sculptures
Varieties:	SS7B

U.S.	**$250.00**
Can.	**$350.00**
U.K.	**£150.00**
Aust.	**$375.00**

SS7B
I FORGIVE YOU™
Second Variation

Designer:	Harry Sales
Modeller:	David Lyttleton
Height:	4", 10.1 cm
Colour:	Bay horse, rider wears red jacket and yellow jodhpurs
Issued:	1985 - 1985
Series:	Studio Sculptures
Varieties:	SS7A

U.S.	**$250.00**
Can.	**$350.00**
U.K.	**£150.00**
Aust.	**$375.00**

SS12A
EARLY BATH™
First Variation

Designer:	Harry Sales
Modeller:	David Lyttleton
Height:	4 ¾", 12.1 cm
Colour:	Grey horse, rider wears red jacket and yellow jodhpurs
Issued:	1985 - 1985
Series:	Studio Sculptures
Varieties:	SS12B

U.S.	**$250.00**
Can.	**$350.00**
U.K.	**£150.00**
Aust.	**$375.00**

SS12B
EARLY BATH™
Second Variation

Designer:	Harry Sales
Modeller:	David Lyttleton
Height:	4 ¾", 12.1 cm
Colour:	Bay horse, rider wears red jacket and yellow jodhpurs
Issued:	1985 - 1985
Series:	Studio Sculptures
Varieties:	SS12A

U.S.	**$250.00**
Can.	**$350.00**
U.K.	**£150.00**
Aust.	**$375.00**

NORMAN THELWELL
EARTHENWARE SERIES 2001 to date

NT 1
LOSING HURTS™

Designer:	A. Hughes-Lubeck
Height:	5", 12.7 cm
Colour:	Palomino horse, rider wears navy jacket and hat, yellow jodhpurs
Issued:	2001 in a limited edition of 1,000

U.S.	**$175.00**
Can.	**$325.00**
U.K.	**£100.00**
Aust.	**$350.00**

NT 2
POWERFUL HINDQUARTERS ARE A DISTINCT ADVANTAGE™

Designer:	A. Hughes-Lubeck
Height:	5 ¼", 13.3 cm
Colour:	Grey horse; rider has blonde hair and wears a black cap
Issued:	2001 in a limited edition of 1,000

U.S.	**$175.00**
Can.	**$325.00**
U.K.	**£100.00**
Aust.	**$350.00**

NT 3
EXHAUSTED™

Designer:	A. Hughes-Lubeck
Height:	4 ¼", 10.8 cm
Colour:	Brown horse; rider wears red jacket, yellow jodhpurs, black hat and shoes
Issued:	2001 in a limited edition of 1,000

U.S.	**$175.00**
Can.	**$325.00**
U.K.	**£100.00**
Aust.	**$350.00**

NT 4
CHOOSING GOOD FEET™

Designer:	A. Hughes-Lubeck
Height:	4 ¼", 10.8 cm
Colour:	Chestnut horse; rider wears a burgundy jacket, white jodhpurs, black hat and shoes
Issued:	2001 in a limited edition of 1,000

U.S.	**$175.00**
Can.	**$325.00**
U.K.	**£100.00**
Aust.	**$350.00**

Backstamp not
available
at press time

Backstamp not
available
at press time

NT 5
EXCESSIVE PRAISE™

Designer:	A. Hughes-Lubeck
Height:	5 ¼", 13.3 cm
Colour:	Brown horse; rider wears blue jersey and pale yellow jodhpurs
Issued:	2001 in a limited edition of 1,000
U.S.	**$175.00**
Can.	**$325.00**
U.K.	**£100.00**
Aust.	**$350.00**

NT 6
SUPPLING EXERCISES™

Designer:	A. Hughes-Lubeck
Height:	4 ¾", 12.1 cm
Colour:	Black horse; rider wears red jersey, yellow jodhpurs; blonde hair
Issued:	2001 in a limited edition of 1,000
U.S.	**$175.00**
Can.	**$325.00**
U.K.	**£100.00**
Aust.	**$350.00**

NT 7
BODY BRUSH™

Designer:	Shane Ridge
Height:	5 ¼", 13.3 cm
Colour:	Grey horse; rider wears black jacket and yellow jodhpurs
Issued:	2003 to the present
U.S.	**N/I**
Can.	**N/I**
U.K.	**£40.00**
Aust.	**N/I**

NT 8
DETECTING AILMENTS™

Designer:	Warren Platt
Height:	5 ¼", 13.3 cm
Colour:	Chestnut horse; doctor wears white medical coat, blue tie, grey trousers
Issued:	2003 to the present
U.S.	**N/I**
Can.	**N/I**
U.K.	**£40.00**
Aust.	**N/I**

thelwell

by ROYAL DOULTON

Ice Cream Treat

NT 9

.t.

HAND MADE & HAND DECORATED — © 2003 NORMAN THELWELL, LICENSED BY MOMENTUM LICENSING

Backstamp not
available
at press time

thelwell

by ROYAL DOULTON

So Treat Him
Like A Friend

NT 11

.t.

HAND MADE & HAND DECORATED — © 2003 NORMAN THELWELL, LICENSED BY MOMENTUM LICENSING

Backstamp not
available
at press time

NT 9
ICE CREAM TREAT™

Designer:	Martyn Alcock
Height:	5", 12.7 cm
Colour:	Dun horse; rider wears black jacket and cap, white jodhpurs
Issued:	2003 to the present
U.S.	**N/I**
Can.	**N/I**
U.K.	**£40.00**
Aust.	**N/I**

NT 10
IDEAL PONY FOR A NERVOUS CHILD™

Designer:	Martyn Alcock
Height:	5 ¼", 13.3 cm
Colour:	Brown horse; rider wears black hat and yellow jodhpurs
Issued:	2003 to the present
U.S.	**N/I**
Can.	**N/I**
U.K.	**£40.00**
Aust.	**N/I**

NT 11
SO TREAT HIM LIKE A FRIEND™

Designer:	Shane Ridge
Height:	5", 12.7 cm
Colour:	Black and white horse
Issued:	2003 to the present
U.S.	**N/I**
Can.	**N/I**
U.K.	**£40.00**
Aust.	**N/I**

NT 12
HE'LL FIND YOU™

Designer:	Shane Ridge
Height:	4 ¼", 10.8 cm
Colour:	Grey horse; rider wears black jacket and hat, yellow jodhpurs
Issued:	2003 to the present
U.S.	**N/I**
Can.	**N/I**
U.K.	**£40.00**
Aust.	**N/I**

NURSERY RHYMES
COLLECTION

DNR 1
HUMPTY DUMPTY™

Designer:	Andy Moss
Height:	5 ½", 14.0 cm
Colour:	Red, pink, orange and black
Issued:	1998 in a special edition of 1,500

U.S.	**$150.00**
Can.	**$225.00**
U.K.	**£ 95.00**
Aust.	**$250.00**

DNR 2
LITTLE MISS MUFFET™

Designer:	Andy Moss
Height:	6", 15.0 cm
Colour:	Pink, white, red and black
Issued:	1998 in a special edition of 1,500

U.S.	**$150.00**
Can.	**$225.00**
U.K.	**£ 95.00**
Aust.	**$250.00**

DNR 3
OLD MOTHER HUBBARD™

Designer:	Andy Moss
Height:	7 ½", 19.1 cm
Colour:	Red, green, blue, white and black
Issued:	1999 in a special edition of 1,500

U.S.	**$150.00**
Can.	**$225.00**
U.K.	**£ 95.00**
Aust.	**$250.00**

DNR 4
THE CAT AND THE FIDDLE™

Designer:	Andy Moss
Height:	6", 15.0 cm
Colour:	Black, white red and grey
Issued:	1999 in a special edition of 1,500

U.S.	**$150.00**
Can.	**$225.00**
U.K.	**£ 95.00**
Aust.	**$250.00**

DNR 5
OLD KING COLE™

Designer:	Andy Moss
Height:	7", 17.8 cm
Colour:	Red, white, yellow and brown
Issued:	2000 in a special edition of 1,500

Doulton	Price			
Number	U.S. $	Can. $	U.K. £	Aust. $
DNR5	150.00	225.00	95.00	250.00

PADDINGTON BEAR CO. LTD.

RESIN SERIES 1996-1998
CERAMIC SERIES 1999

RESIN SERIES
1996 - 1998

Royal Doulton
Paddington ™
"At the Station"
PB1
© Paddington & Co. Ltd. 1996
Licensed by ©OPYRIGHTS

PB1
PADDINGTON™ "AT THE STATION"
Style One

Designer:	Zoe Annand
Modeller:	Zoe Annand
Height:	4 ¼", 10.8 cm
Colour:	Brown bear, blue coat, yellow hat, brown cobbled base
Issued:	1996 - 1998

Doulton Number	Price			
	U.S. $	Can. $	U.K. £	Aust. $
PB1	40.00	55.00	25.00	60.00

Royal Doulton
Paddington ™
"Bakes a Cake"
PB2
© Paddington & Co. Ltd. 1996
Licensed by ©OPYRIGHTS

PB2
PADDINGTON™ "BAKES A CAKE"

Designer:	Zoe Annand
Modeller:	Zoe Annand
Height:	4 ¼", 10.8 cm
Colour:	Red jacket, black hat, multicoloured cake, blue and white striped bowl
Issued:	1996 - 1998

Doulton Number	Price			
	U.S. $	Can. $	U.K. £	Aust. $
PB2	40.00	55.00	25.00	60.00

Royal Doulton
Paddington ™
"Decorating"
PB3
© Paddington & Co. Ltd. 1996
Licensed by ©OPYRIGHTS

PB3
PADDINGTON™ "DECORATING"

Designer:	Zoe Annand
Modeller:	Zoe Annand
Height:	4 ¾", 12.0 cm
Colour:	Blue coat, red hat, silver bucket, cream paint
Issued:	1996 - 1998

Doulton Number	Price			
	U.S. $	Can. $	U.K. £	Aust. $
PB3	40.00	55.00	25.00	60.00

PB4
PADDINGTON™ "SURFING"

Designer:	Zoe Annand
Modeller:	Zoe Annand
Height:	4", 10.1 cm
Colour:	Multicoloured shorts, blue hat, yellow surfboard, red rubber ring, brown suitcase
Issued:	1996 - 1998

Doulton Number	Price			
	U.S. $	Can. $	U.K. £	Aust. $
PB4	40.00	55.00	25.00	60.00

PB5
PADDINGTON™ "GARDENING"

Designer:	Zoe Annand
Modeller:	Zoe Annand
Height:	4", 10.1 cm
Colour:	Blue jacket, red hat, green watering can, yellow and red bucket and spade
Issued:	1996 - 1998

Doulton Number	Price			
	U.S. $	Can. $	U.K. £	Aust. $
PB5	40.00	55.00	25.00	60.00

PB6
PADDINGTON™ "BATHTIME"

Designer:	Zoe Annand
Modeller:	Zoe Annand
Height:	3 ¼", 8.5 cm
Colour:	Blue coat, yellow hat, brown scrubbing brush, yellow duck, pink soap
Issued:	1996 - 1998

Doulton Number	Price			
	U.S. $	Can. $	U.K. £	Aust. $
PB6	40.00	55.00	25.00	60.00

PB7
PADDINGTON™ "THE GOLFER"

Designer:	Zoe Annand
Modeller:	Zoe Annand
Height:	3 ¾", 9.5 cm
Colour:	White top, red and yellow sweater, red hat, green trousers, white shoes
Issued:	1996 - 1998

Doulton Number	Price			
	U.S. $	Can. $	U.K. £	Aust. $
PB7	40.00	55.00	25.00	60.00

PB8
PADDINGTON™ "THE MUSICIAN"

Designer:	Zoe Annand
Modeller:	Zoe Annand
Height:	3 ¾", 9.5 cm
Colour:	Black jacket, red waistcoat, brown trousers, brown violin, brass trumpet
Issued:	1996 - 1998

Doulton Number	Price			
	U.S. $	Can. $	U.K. £	Aust. $
PB8	40.00	55.00	25.00	60.00

PB9
PADDINGTON™ "AT CHRISTMAS TIME"

Designer:	Zoe Annand
Modeller:	Zoe Annand
Height:	3 ½", 8.9 cm
Colour:	Red coat, blue boots, yellow sleigh
Issued:	1996 - 1998

Doulton Number	Price			
	U.S. $	Can. $	U.K. £	Aust. $
PB9	40.00	55.00	25.00	60.00

PB10
PADDINGTON™ "MARMALADE SANDWICH"

Designer:	Zoe Annand
Modeller:	Zoe Annand
Height:	3 ½", 8.9 cm
Colour:	Dark blue coat, yellow hat, green book, orange and white sandwiches
Issued:	1997 - 1998

Doulton Number	Price			
	U.S. $	Can. $	U.K. £	Aust. $
PB10	40.00	55.00	25.00	60.00

PB11
PADDINGTON™ "GOING TO BED"

Designer:	Zoe Annand
Modeller:	Zoe Annand
Height:	3 ¾", 9.5 cm
Colour:	Turquoise, red and yellow pyjamas, red hat
Issued:	1997 - 1998

Doulton Number	Price			
	U.S. $	Can. $	U.K. £	Aust. $
PB11	40.00	55.00	25.00	60.00

PB12
PADDINGTON™ "THE FISHERMAN"

Designer:	Zoe Annand
Modeller:	Zoe Annand
Height:	3 ½", 8.9 cm
Colour:	Red jacket with yellow buttons; dark blue hat and wellingtons
Issued:	1997 - 1998

Doulton Number	Price			
	U.S. $	Can. $	U.K. £	Aust. $
PB12	40.00	55.00	25.00	60.00

CERAMIC SERIES
1999

PADDINGTON™ "AT THE STATION"
Style Two

Modeller:	Warren Platt
Height:	3 ¼", 8.5 cm
Colour:	Brown bear, blue coat, red hat, grey sack, gold suitcase corners
Issued:	1999 in a special edition of 2,000
Series:	Gold edition

Doulton Number	Price			
	U.S. $	Can. $	U.K. £	Aust. $
—	80.00	115.00	50.00	125.00

Note: Commissioned by Paddington and Friends.

THE PIG PROMENADE

Beswick Ware
JOHN
PP 1

Beswick Ware
MATTHEW
PP 2

Beswick Ware
DAVID
PP 3

Beswick Ware
ANDREW
PP 4

PP 1
JOHN THE CONDUCTOR™
(Vietnamese Pot Bellied Pig)

Designer:	Martyn Alcock
Height:	4 ¾", 12.1 cm
Colour:	Black jacket and bowtie
Issued:	1993 - 1996
U.S.	**$ 70.00**
Can.	**$100.00**
U.K.	**£ 45.00**
Aust.	**$110.00**

PP 2
MATTHEW THE TRUMPET PLAYER™
(Large White Pig)

Designer:	A. Hughes-Lubeck
Height:	5", 12.7 cm
Colour:	Light red waistcoat, black bowtie
Issued:	1993 - 1996
U.S.	**$ 70.00**
Can.	**$100.00**
U.K.	**£ 45.00**
Aust.	**$110.00**

PP 3
DAVID THE FLUTE PLAYER™
(Tamworth Pig)

Designer:	A. Hughes-Lubeck
Height:	5 ¼", 13.3 cm
Colour:	Dark green waistcoat, black bowtie
Issued:	1993 - 1996
U.S.	**$ 70.00**
Can.	**$100.00**
U.K.	**£ 45.00**
Aust.	**$110.00**

PP 4
ANDREW THE CYMBAL PLAYER™
(Gloucester Old Spotted Pig)

Designer:	Martyn Alcock
Height:	4 ¾", 12.1 cm
Colour:	Blue waistcoat, yellow cymbals, black bowtie
Issued:	1993 - 1996
Varieties:	Also called George, PP10
U.S.	**$ 70.00**
Can.	**$100.00**
U.K.	**£ 45.00**
Aust.	**$110.00**

DANIEL
PP 5

MICHAEL
PP 6

PP 7
JAMES

PP 8
RICHARD

PP 5
DANIEL THE VIOLINIST™
(Saddleback Pig)

Designer:	A. Hughes-Lubeck
Height:	5 ¼", 13.3 cm
Colour:	Pale blue waistcoat, brown violin
Issued:	1993 - 1996

U.S.	**$ 70.00**
Can.	**$100.00**
U.K.	**£ 45.00**
Aust.	**$110.00**

PP 6
MICHAEL THE BASS DRUM PLAYER™ (Large Black Pig)

Designer:	Martyn Alcock
Height:	4 ¾", 12.1 cm
Colour:	Yellow waistcoat, red and white drum
Issued:	1993 - 1996

U.S.	**$ 70.00**
Can.	**$100.00**
U.K.	**£ 45.00**
Aust.	**$110.00**

PP 7
JAMES THE TRIANGLE PLAYER™
(Tamworth Piglet)

Designer:	Warren Platt
Height:	4", 10.1 cm
Colour:	Purple waistcoat, black bowtie
Issued:	1995 - 1996

U.S.	**$ 70.00**
Can.	**$100.00**
U.K.	**£ 45.00**
Aust.	**$110.00**

PP 8
RICHARD THE FRENCH HORN PLAYER™

Designer:	Shane Ridge
Height:	5", 12.7 cm
Colour:	Pale pink with dark grey spots, tan and beige waistcoat
Issued:	1996 - 1996
Varieties:	Also called Benjamin, PP12

U.S.	**$ 70.00**
Can.	**$100.00**
U.K.	**£ 45.00**
Aust.	**$110.00**

PP 9
CHRISTOPHER THE GUITAR PLAYER™

Designer:	Warren Platt
Height:	5 ½", 13.3 cm
Colour:	Dark grey, yellow and cream waistcoat, black bowtie
Issued:	1996 - 1996
Varieties:	Also called Thomas, PP11

U.S.	**$ 70.00**
Can.	**$100.00**
U.K.	**£ 45.00**
Aust.	**$110.00**

PP 10
GEORGE™

Designer:	Martyn Alcock
Height:	4 ¾", 12.1 cm
Colour:	Dark green waistcoat, yellow cymbals, black bowtie
Issued:	1996 in a limited edition of 2,000
Varieties:	Also called Andrew, PP4

U.S.	**$ 70.00**
Can.	**$100.00**
U.K.	**£ 45.00**
Aust.	**$110.00**

PP 11
THOMAS™

Designer:	Warren Platt
Height:	5", 12.7 cm
Colour:	Black pig with green waistcoat, yellow bowtie, white guitar
Issued:	1997 in a special edition of 2,000
Varieties:	Also called Christopher the Guitar Player, PP9

U.S.	**$ 70.00**
Can.	**$100.00**
U.K.	**£ 45.00**
Aust.	**$110.00**

PP 12
BENJAMIN™

Designer:	Shane Ridge
Height:	5", 12.7 cm
Colour:	White and black pig, orange bowtie, gold french horn
Issued:	1997 in a special edition of 2,000
Varieties:	Also called Richard the French Horn Player, PP8

U.S.	**$ 70.00**
Can.	**$100.00**
U.K.	**£ 45.00**
Aust.	**$110.00**

PUNCH AND JUDY

JUDY™

Designer:	Unknown
Modeller:	Shane Ridge
Height:	5 ¼", 13.3 cm
Colour:	Blue and white striped dress, white apron and mob cap, brown hair and rolling pin
Issued:	2001 in a limited edition of 2,500
Comm. by:	Doulton-Direct

Beswick Number	Price			
	U.S. $	Can. $	U.K. £	Aust. $
—	100.00	145.00	65.00	165.00

PUNCH™

Designer:	Unknown
Modeller:	Shane Ridge
Height:	5 ½", 14.0 cm
Colour:	Red and yellow tunic and hat, red and white striped stockings, brown shoes, green crocodile
Issued:	2001 in a limited edition of 2,500
Comm. by:	Doulton-Direct

Beswick Number	Price			
	U.S. $	Can. $	U.K. £	Aust. $
—	100.00	145.00	65.00	165.00

ST. TIGGYWINKLES

Royal Doulton
St. Tiggywinkles®
Henry Hedgehog
TW1/ 1999
© St.Tiggywinkles 1996
Made in Thailand

Royal Doulton
St. Tiggywinkles®
Harry Hedgehog
TW2/ 1269
© St.Tiggywinkles 1996
Made in Thailand

Royal Doulton
St. Tiggywinkles®
Fred Fox
TW3/ 1094
© St.Tiggywinkles 1996
Made in Thailand

Royal Doulton
St. Tiggywinkles®
Bob Badger
TW4/ 1698
© St.Tiggywinkles 1996
Made in Thailand

TW1
HENRY HEDGEHOG™
(Standing)

Designer:	Unknown
Modeller:	A. Hughes-Lubeck
Height:	3 ½", 8.5 cm
Colour:	Light and dark brown hedgehog wearing a purple sweater
Issued:	1997 - 1999
Series:	Wildlife Hospital Trust

U.S.	**$30.00**
Can.	**$45.00**
U.K.	**£20.00**
Aust.	**$50.00**

TW2
HARRY HEDGEHOG™
(Sitting)

Designer:	Unknown
Modeller:	A. Hughes-Lubeck
Height:	3 ½", 8.9 cm
Colour:	Light and dark brown hedgehog wearing a purple sweater, red cap
Issued:	1997 - 1999
Series:	Wildlife Hospital Trust

U.S.	**$30.00**
Can.	**$45.00**
U.K.	**£20.00**
Aust.	**$50.00**

TW3
FRED FOX™

Designer:	Unknown
Modeller:	Warren Platt
Height:	4", 10.1 cm
Colour:	Light brown fox wearing light blue overalls, pink shirt, white bandage around his head and tail
Issued:	1997 - 1998
Series:	Wildlife Hospital Trust

U.S.	**$30.00**
Can.	**$45.00**
U.K.	**£20.00**
Aust.	**$50.00**

TW4
BOB BADGER™

Designer:	Unknown
Modeller:	A. Hughes-Lubeck
Height:	3 ¾", 9.5 cm
Colour:	Brown, black and white badger wearing a yellow jumper and brown scarf; beige crutch
Issued:	1997 - 1999
Series:	Wildlife Hospital Trust

U.S.	**$30.00**
Can.	**$45.00**
U.K.	**£20.00**
Aust.	**$50.00**

Royal Doulton
St. Tiggywinkles
Rosie Rabbit
TW5/ 1456
© St.Tiggywinkles 1996
Made in Thailand

Royal Doulton
St. Tiggywinkles
Sarah Squirrel
TW6/ 0183
© St.Tiggywinkles 1996
Made in Thailand

Royal Doulton
St. Tiggywinkles
Daniel Duck
TW7/ 1925
© St.Tiggywinkles 1996
Made in Thailand

Royal Doulton
St. Tiggywinkles
Oliver Owl
TW8/ 1703
© St.Tiggywinkles 1996
Made in Thailand

	TW5 ROSIE RABBIT™	TW6 SARAH SQUIRREL™	TW7 DANIEL DUCK™	TW8 OLIVER OWL™
Designer:	Unknown	Unknown	Unknown	Unknown
Modeller:	A. Hughes-Lubeck	A. Hughes-Lubeck	Shane Ridge	Warren Platt
Height:	3 ½", 8.9 cm	3 ¼", 8.3 cm	3 ½", 8.5 cm	4", 10.1 cm
Colour:	Grey rabbit wearing a light blue dress and rose pinafore	Brown squirrel wearing a pink and white dress	Yellow duck, white and red bandage, brown satchel	Dark and light brown owl, white arm sling, red book
Issued:	1997 - 1999	1997 - 1998	1997 - 1999	1997 - 1999
Series:	Wildlife Hospital Trust	Wildlife Hospital Trust	Wildlife Hospital Trust	Wildlife Hospital Trust
U.S.	$30.00	$30.00	$30.00	$30.00
Can.	$45.00	$45.00	$45.00	$45.00
U.K.	£20.00	£20.00	£20.00	£20.00
Aust.	$50.00	$50.00	$50.00	$50.00

Royal Doulton
St. Tiggywinkles
Friends
TW9/ 1430
© St.Tiggywinkles 1996
Made in Thailand

Royal Doulton
St. Tiggywinkles
A Helping Hand
TW10/ 0303
© St.Tiggywinkles 1996
Made in Thailand

Royal Doulton
St. Tiggywinkles
Deborah Dormouse
TW11/ 458
© St.Tiggywinkles 1998
Made in Thailand

Royal Doulton
St. Tiggywinkles
Monty Mole
TW12/ 549
© St.Tiggywinkles 1998
Made in Thailand

TW9
FRIENDS™

Designer:	Unknown
Modeller:	A. Hughes-Lubeck
Height:	4", 10.1 cm
Colour:	Light /dark brown hedgehog, green and yellow jacket, maroon hat; yellow ducklings, white bandages
Issued:	1997 - 1999
Series:	Wildlife Hospital Trust
U.S.	**$50.00**
Can.	**$70.00**
U.K.	**£30.00**
Aust.	**$75.00**

TW10
A HELPING HAND™

Designer:	Unknown
Modeller:	A. Hughes-Lubeck
Height:	4", 10.1 cm
Colour:	Light and dark brown hedgehog, white and grey rabbits, blue, pink and yellow clothing
Issued:	1997 - 1999
Series:	Wildlife Hospital Trust
U.S.	**$ 65.00**
Can.	**$100.00**
U.K.	**£ 40.00**
Aust.	**$115.00**

TW11
DEBORAH DORMOUSE™

Designer:	Unknown
Modeller:	Rob Simpson
Height:	3 ¼", 8.3 cm
Colour:	Brown dormouse, pink dress, white apron, brown basket
Issued:	1998 - 1999
Series:	Wildlife Hospital Trust
U.S.	**$30.00**
Can.	**$45.00**
U.K.	**£20.00**
Aust.	**$50.00**

TW12
MONTY MOLE™

Designer:	Unknown
Modeller:	Rob Simpson
Height:	3 ½", 8.5 cm
Colour:	Dark brown mole wearing a blue jacket, yellow hat, white arm sling
Issued:	1998 - 1999
Series:	Wildlife Hospital Trust
U.S.	**$30.00**
Can.	**$45.00**
U.K.	**£20.00**
Aust.	**$50.00**

TW13
FRANCHESCA FAWN™

Designer:	Unknown
Modeller:	Rob Simpson
Height:	3", 7.6 cm
Colour:	Pale brown fawn; white bandages
Issued:	1998 - 1999
Series:	Wildlife Hospital Trust

Royal Doulton
St. Tiggywinkles
Franchesca Fawn
TW13/ 48
© St.Tiggywinkles 1998
Made in Thailand

Doulton Number	Price			
	U.S. $	Can. $	U.K. £	Aust. $
TW13	30.00	45.00	20.00	50.00

THE SNOWMAN
GIFT COLLECTION

DS 1
JAMES™
Style One

Designer:	Harry Sales
Modeller:	David Lyttleton
Height:	3 ¾", 9.5 cm
Colour:	Brown dressing-gown, blue and white striped pyjamas,
Issued:	1985 - 1993
U.S.	**$165.00**
Can.	**$225.00**
U.K.	**£100.00**
Aust.	**$250.00**

DS 2
THE SNOWMAN™
Style One

Designer:	Harry Sales
Modeller:	David Lyttleton
Height:	5", 12.7 cm
Colour:	White snowman wearing a green hat and scarf
Issued:	1985 - 1994
U.S.	**$165.00**
Can.	**$225.00**
U.K.	**£100.00**
Aust.	**$250.00**

DS 3
STYLISH SNOWMAN™

Designer:	Harry Sales
Modeller:	David Lyttleton
Height:	5", 12.7 cm
Colour:	White snowman wearing blue trousers, lilac braces, grey hat, yellow tie with red stripes
Issued:	1985 - 1993
U.S.	**$200.00**
Can.	**$300.00**
U.K.	**£125.00**
Aust.	**$325.00**

DS 4
THANK YOU SNOWMAN™

Designer:	Harry Sales
Modeller:	David Lyttleton
Height:	5", 12.7 cm
Colour:	Snowman - green hat and scarf James - brown dressing-gown
Issued:	1985 - 1994
U.S.	**$135.00**
Can.	**$185.00**
U.K.	**£ 85.00**
Aust.	**$200.00**

HARRY POTTER

THE REMEMBRALL RECOVERY

HARRY CASTS A MAGICAL SPELL

HERMIONE STUDIES FOR
POTIONS CLASS

RON FOLLOWS THE WEASLEY
FAMILY TRADITION

PROFESSOR SEVERUS SNAPE

HEADMASTER ALBUS DUMBLEDORE

WIZARD-IN-TRAINING

THE FRIENDSHIP BEGINS

HARRY'S 11TH BIRTHDAY

HARRY POTTER

STRUGGLING THROUGH
POTIONS CLASS

SLYTHERIN OR GRYFFINDOR

RON AND SCABBERS

HERMIONE LEARNS TO LEVITATE

PROFESSOR McGONAGALL

PROFESSOR QUIRRELL

HEDWIG

THE BIRTH OF NORBERT

THE MIRROR HOLDS THE ANSWER

HARRY POTTER

THE JOURNEY TO HOGWARTS

MADAME HOOCH

PROFESSOR SPROUT

HARRY POTTER PLAYING QUIDDITCH

DOBBY

DURSLEY FAMILY

WHOMPING WILLOW

RESCUE IN THE FORBIDDEN FOREST

NORMAN THELWELL

LOSING HURTS

POWERFUL HINDQUARTERS ARE
A DISTINCT ADVANTAGE

EXHAUSTED

CHOOSING GOOD FEET

EXCESSIVE PRAISE

SUPPLING EXERCISES

NORMAN THELWELL

BODY BRUSH

DETECTING AILMENTS

SO TREAT HIM LIKE A FRIEND

ICE CREAM TREAT

IDEAL PONY FOR A NERVOUS CHILD

HE'LL FIND YOU

JOHN BESWICK – TEDDY BEARS

HENRY

EDWARD

GEORGE

WILLIAM

THE HERBS

PARSLEY THE LION

BAYLEAF THE GARDENER

DILL THE DOG

SAGE THE OWL

TRUMPTONSHIRE

MICKEY MURPHY

MRS. DINGLE

JONATHAN BELL

MRS. HONEYMAN

PC McGARRY

CAPTAIN FLACK

DR. MOPP

MRS. COBBIT

WINDY MILLER

THE MAYOR

Backstamp not
available
at press time

Royal Doulton®
THE SNOWMAN™
GIFT COLLECTION
COWBOY SNOWMAN
DS 6
© 1986 ROYAL DOULTON (UK)
© S ENT 1985

Royal Doulton©
THE SNOWMAN™
GIFT COLLECTION
HIGHLAND SNOWMAN
DS 7
© 1985 ROYAL DOULTON (UK)
© S ENT 1985

Royal Doulton€
THE SNOWMAN™
GIFT COLLECTION
LADY SNOWMAN
DS 8
© 1986 ROYAL DOULTON (UK)
© S ENT 1985

DS 5
SNOWMAN MAGIC MUSIC BOX™

Designer:	Harry Sales
Modeller:	David Lyttleton
Height:	8", 20.3 cm
Colour:	White snowman wearing a green hat and scarf, cream music box with blue, green and pink balloon design
Issued:	1985 - 1994
Tune:	Walking in the Air

U.S.	**$165.00**
Can.	**$225.00**
U.K.	**£100.00**
Aust.	**$250.00**

DS 6
COWBOY SNOWMAN™

Designer:	Harry Sales
Modeller:	David Lyttleton
Height:	5", 12.7 cm
Colour:	White snowman wearing a brown hat and holster belt
Issued:	1986 - 1992

U.S.	**$275.00**
Can.	**$400.00**
U.K.	**£175.00**
Aust.	**$425.00**

DS 7
HIGHLAND SNOWMAN™

Designer:	Harry Sales
Modeller:	David Lyttleton
Height:	5 ¼", 13.3 cm
Colour:	White snowman wearing a red, blue and white kilt
Issued:	1987 - 1993

U.S.	**$250.00**
Can.	**$350.00**
U.K.	**£150.00**
Aust.	**$375.00**

DS 8
LADY SNOWMAN™

Designer:	Harry Sales
Modeller:	David Lyttleton
Height:	5", 12.7 cm
Colour:	White snowman wearing a pink apron and blue hat
Issued:	1987 - 1992

U.S.	**$325.00**
Can.	**$450.00**
U.K.	**£200.00**
Aust.	**$475.00**

Royal Doulton®
**THE SNOWMAN™
GIFT COLLECTION
BASS DRUMMER SNOWMAN**
D S 9
© 1987 ROYAL DOULTON
© S ENT 1987

Royal Doulton®
**THE SNOWMAN™
GIFT COLLECTION
FLAUTIST SNOWMAN**
D S 10
© 1987 ROYAL DOULTON
© S ENT 1987

Royal Doulton®
**THE SNOWMAN™
GIFT COLLECTION
VIOLINIST SNOWMAN**
D S 11
© 1987 ROYAL DOULTON
© S ENT 1987

Royal Doulton®
**THE SNOWMAN™
GIFT COLLECTION
PIANIST SNOWMAN**
D S 12
© 1987 ROYAL DOULTON
© S ENT 1987

DS 9
BASS DRUMMER SNOWMAN™

Designer:	Graham Tongue
Modeller:	Warren Platt
Height:	5 ¼", 13.3 cm
Colour:	White snowman wearing a pale blue hat; pink and yellow drum, pale brown straps
Issued:	1987 - 1993
U.S.	**$250.00**
Can.	**$350.00**
U.K.	**£150.00**
Aust.	**$375.00**

DS 10
FLAUTIST SNOWMAN™

Designer:	Graham Tongue
Modeller:	Warren Platt
Height:	5 ½", 14.0 cm
Colour:	White snowman wearing a yellow and red hat and a brown tie
Issued:	1987 - 1993
U.S.	**$250.00**
Can.	**$350.00**
U.K.	**£150.00**
Aust.	**$375.00**

DS 11
VIOLINIST SNOWMAN™

Designer:	Graham Tongue
Modeller:	Warren Platt
Height:	5 ¼", 13.3 cm
Colour:	White snowman wearing a green waistcoat with yellow collar, blue bowtie, brown hat, playing a violin
Issued:	1987 - 1994
U.S.	**$165.00**
Can.	**$225.00**
U.K.	**£100.00**
Aust.	**$250.00**

DS 12
PIANIST SNOWMAN™

Designer:	Graham Tongue
Modeller:	Warren Platt
Height:	5", 12.7 cm
Colour:	White snowman wearing a blue crown / orange tie
Issued:	1987 - 1994
U.S.	**$165.00**
Can.	**$225.00**
U.K.	**£100.00**
Aust.	**$250.00**

Royal Doulton®
THE SNOWMAN™
GIFT COLLECTION
SNOWMAN'S PIANO
DS 13
© 1987 ROYAL DOULTON
© S. ENT 1987

Royal Doulton®
THE SNOWMAN™
GIFT COLLECTION
CYMBAL PLAYER SNOWMAN
DS 14
© 1988 ROYAL DOULTON
© S ENT 1988

Royal Doulton®
THE SNOWMAN™
GIFT COLLECTION
DRUMMER SNOWMAN
DS 15
© 1988 ROYAL DOULTON
© S ENT 1988

Royal Doulton®
THE SNOWMAN™
GIFT COLLECTION
TRUMPETER SNOWMAN
DS 16
© 1988 ROYAL DOULTON
© S ENT 1988

DS 13
SNOWMAN'S PIANO™

Designer:	Graham Tongue
Modeller:	Warren Platt
Height:	5 ¼", 13.3 cm
Colour:	White piano
Issued:	1987 - 1994
U.S.	**$ 85.00**
Can.	**$125.00**
U.K.	**£ 50.00**
Aust.	**$150.00**

DS 14
CYMBAL PLAYER SNOWMAN™

Designer:	Graham Tongue
Modeller:	Warren Platt
Height:	5 ¼", 13.3 cm
Colour:	White snowman wearing a brown waistcoat, green hat and bowtie, playing yellow cymbals
Issued:	1988 - 1993
U.S.	**$250.00**
Can.	**$350.00**
U.K.	**£150.00**
Aust.	**$375.00**

DS 15
DRUMMER SNOWMAN™

Designer:	Graham Tongue
Modeller:	Warren Platt
Height:	5 ¾", 14.6 cm
Colour:	White snowman wearing a red and black hat, purple bowtie, playing pink and yellow drum
Issued:	1988 - 1994
U.S.	**$200.00**
Can.	**$275.00**
U.K.	**£125.00**
Aust.	**$300.00**

DS 16
TRUMPETER SNOWMAN™

Designer:	Graham Tongue
Modeller:	Warren Platt
Height:	5", 12.7 cm
Colour:	White snowman wearing a pink hat playing a yellow trumpet
Issued:	1988 - 1993
U.S.	**$250.00**
Can.	**$350.00**
U.K.	**£150.00**
Aust.	**$375.00**

Royal Doulton®
THE SNOWMAN ™
GIFT COLLECTION
CELLIST SNOWMAN
DS 17
© 1988 ROYAL DOULTON
© S ENT 1988

Backstamp not
available
at press time

Royal Doulton®
THE SNOWMAN ™
GIFT COLLECTION
THE SNOWMAN
MONEY BOX
DS 19
© 1990 ROYAL DOULTON
© S ENT 1990

Royal Doulton®
THE SNOWMAN ™
GIFT COLLECTION
THE SNOWMAN
TOBOGGANING
DS 20
© 1990 ROYAL DOULTON
© S ENT 1990

DS 17
CELLIST SNOWMAN™

Designer: Graham Tongue
Modeller: Warren Platt
Height: 5 ¼", 13.3 cm
Colour: White snowman
wearing a green
waistcoat with
yellow collar, blue
bowtie, playing a
brown cello
Issued: 1988 - 1993

U.S.	$200.00
Can.	$275.00
U.K.	£125.00
Aust.	$300.00

DS 18
SNOWMAN MUSICAL BOX™

Designer: Unknown
Height: 8", 22.5 cm
Colour: White snowman
wearing a red, blue
and white kilt,
green, pink and
blue balloons on
box
Issued: 1988 - 1990
Tune: Blue Bells of
Scotland

U.S.	$325.00
Can.	$450.00
U.K.	£200.00
Aust.	$475.00

DS 19
SNOWMAN MONEY BOX™

Designer: Graham Tongue
Modeller: Warren Platt
Height: 8 ½", 21.6 cm
Colour: White snowman
wearing a green
hat with grey band
and green scarf
Issued: 1990 - 1994

U.S.	$250.00
Can.	$350.00
U.K.	£150.00
Auat.	$375.00

DS 20
THE SNOWMAN TOBOGGANING™

Designer: Graham Tongue
Modeller: Warren Platt
Height: 5", 12.7 cm
Colour: White snowman
wearing a green
hat and scarf,
rose-pink toboggan
Issued: 1990 - 1994

U.S.	$250.00
Can.	$350.00
U.K.	£150.00
Aust.	$375.00

Royal Doulton®
THE SNOWMAN™
GIFT COLLECTION
THE SNOWMAN
SKIING
DS 21
© 1990 ROYAL DOULTON
© S. ENT 1990

Royal Doulton®
THE SNOWMAN™
GIFT COLLECTION
THE SNOWMAN
SNOWBALLING
DS 22
© 1990 ROYAL DOULTON
© S. ENT 1990

Royal Doulton®
THE SNOWMAN™
GIFT COLLECTION
BUILDING THE
SNOWMAN
DS 23
© 1990 ROYAL DOULTON
© S. ENT 1990

Backstamp not
available
at press time

DS 21
THE SNOWMAN SKIING™

Designer:	Graham Tongue
Modeller:	Warren Platt
Height:	5", 12.7 cm
Colour:	White snowman wearing a green hat and scarf, yellow and black goggles
Issued:	1990 - 1992
U.S.	**$600.00**
Can.	**$850.00**
U.K.	**£375.00**
Aust.	**$900.00**

DS 22
THE SNOWMAN SNOWBALLING™

Designer:	Graham Tongue
Modeller:	Warren Platt
Height:	5", 12.7 cm
Colour:	White snowman wearing a green hat and scarf, brown tree stump
Issued:	1990 - 1994
U.S.	**$165.00**
Can.	**$225.00**
U.K.	**£100.00**
Aust.	**$250.00**

DS 23
BUILDING THE SNOWMAN™

Designer:	Graham Tongue
Modeller:	Warren Platt
Height:	4", 10.1 cm
Colour:	White snowman wearing a green hat and scarf
Issued:	1990 - 1994
U.S.	**$165.00**
Can.	**$225.00**
U.K.	**£100.00**
Aust.	**$250.00**

DANCING IN THE SNOW™

Des./Mod.:	Shane Ridge
Height:	5 ¾", 14.6 cm
Colour:	White, green, brown and blue
Issued:	1999 ltd. ed. 2,500
Series:	Tableau
Comm. by:	Doulton-Direct
U.S.	**$165.00**
Can.	**$225.00**
U.K.	**£100.00**
Aust.	**$250.00**

Note: Issued to commemorate the 21st Anniversary of Raymond Briggs' Tale.

JAMES™
Style Two

Designer:	Shane Ridge
Modeller:	Shane Ridge
Height:	4 ¼", 10.8 cm
Colour:	Brown, white and blue
Issued:	1999 in a limited edition of 2,500

U.S.	**$ 75.00**
Can.	**$100.00**
U.K.	**£ 50.00**
Aust.	**$125.00**

Note: Issued as a pair with The Snowman (Style Two).

THE SNOWMAN™
Style Two

Designer:	Shane Ridge
Modeller:	Shane Ridge
Height:	5 ¾", 14.6 cm
Colour:	White and green
Issued:	1999 in a limited edition of 2,500

U.S.	**$ 75.00**
Can.	**$100.00**
U.K.	**£ 50.00**
Aust.	**$125.00**

Note: Issued as a pair with James (Style Two).

JAMES™
Style Three
(James Builds a Snowman)

Des./Mod.:	Shane Ridge
Height:	4", 10.1 cm
Colour	Maroon/blue/black
Issued:	2000 ltd. ed. 2,500
Comm. by:	Doulton-Direct

U.S.	**$ 75.00**
Can.	**$100.00**
U.K.	**£ 50.00**
Aust.	**$125.00**

Note: Issued, numbered and sold as a pair with The Snowman (Style Three).

THE SNOWMAN™
Style Three
(James Builds a Snowman)

Designer:	Shane Ridge
Modeller:	Shane Ridge
Height:	6", 15.0 cm
Colour:	White and green
Issued:	2000 ltd. ed. 2,500
Comm. by:	Doulton-DIrect

U.S.	**$ 75.00**
Can.	**$100.00**
U.K.	**£ 50.00**
Aust.	**$125.00**

Note: Issued, numbered and sold as a pair with James (Style Three).

SNOWMAN AND JAMES
THE ADVENTURE BEGINS™

Des./Mod.:	Shane Ridge
Height:	6", 15.0 cm
Colour:	White, green, brown and blue
Issued:	2000 in a limited edition of 2,500
Series:	Tableau
Comm. by:	Doulton-Direct

U.S.	**$165.00**
Can.	**$225.00**
U.K.	**£100.00**
Aust.	**$250.00**

WALKING IN THE AIR™
Wall Plaque

Designer:	Shane Ridge
Modeller:	Shane Ridge
Height:	8" x 13 ½"
Colour:	Blue, white, tan, brown, green
Issued:	2001 ltd. ed. 2,500
Comm. by:	Doulton-Direct

U.S.	**$165.00**
Can.	**$225.00**
U.K.	**£100.00**
Aust.	**$250.00**

DRESSING THE SNOWMAN™

Designer:	Shane Ridge
Modeller:	Shane Ridge
Height:	6". 15.0 cm
Colour:	White, green, red, blue, black
Issued:	2002 in a limited edition of 2,500
Comm. by:	Doulton-Direct

U.S.	**$185.00**
Can.	**$275.00**
U.K.	**£115.00**
Aust.	**$300.00**

THE JOURNEY ENDS™

Designer:	Shane Ridge
Modeller:	Shane Ridge
Height:	4", 10.0 cm
Colour:	Blue, white, tan, brown, green
Issued:	2002 in a limited edition of 2,500
Comm. by:	Doulton-Direct

U.S.	**$185.00**
Can.	**$275.00**
U.K.	**£ 85.00**
Aust.	**$300.00**

SPORTING CHARACTERS

SC1
FLY FISHING

Designer: Andy Moss
Height: 3 ¼", 8.3 cm
Colour: Green, slate blue, and black
Issued: 1998 in a special edition of 1,500

U.S.	$ 75.00
Can.	$100.00
U.K.	£ 50.00
Aust.	$115.00

SC2
LAST LION OF DEFENCE

Designer: Andy Moss
Height: 4 ¼", 10.8 cm
Colour: Red and white
Issued: 1998 in a special edition of 1,500

U.S.	$ 75.00
Can.	$100.00
U.K.	£ 50.00
Aust.	$115.00

SC3
IT'S A KNOCKOUT

Designer: Andy Moss
Height: 4 ¼", 10.8 cm
Colour: Red, white and black
Issued: 1998 in a special edition of 1,500

U.S.	$ 75.00
Can.	$100.00
U.K.	£ 50.00
Aust.	$115.00

SC4
SLOPING OFF

Designer: Andy Moss
Height: 5 ¼", 13.3 cm
Colour: White, black and yellow
Issued: 1999 in a special edition of 1,500

U.S.	$ 75.00
Can.	$100.00
U.K.	£ 50.00
Aust.	$115.00

SC5
A ROUND WITH FOXY

Designer: Andy Moss
Height: 6", 15.0 cm
Colour: Green, yellow and brown
Issued: 2000 in a special edition of 1,500

U.S.	$ 75.00
Can.	$100.00
U.K.	£ 50.00
Aust.	$115.00

SC6
OUT FOR A DUCK

Designer: Andy Moss
Height: 5 ½", 14.0 cm
Colour: Cream
Issued: 2000 in a special edition of 1,500

U.S.	$ 75.00
Can.	$100.00
U.K.	£ 50.00
Aust.	$115.00

TEDDY BEARS

4130
HENRY

Designer:	Robert Tabbenor
Height:	5 ½", 14.0 cm
Colour:	Light brown
Issued:	2001 in a limited edition of 2,500
Comm. by:	Doulton-Direct

U.S.	**$100.00**
Can.	**$150.00**
U.K.	**£ 60.00**
Aust.	**$165.00**

4131
EDWARD

Designer:	Robert Tabbenor
Height:	6", 15.0 cm
Colour:	Dark brown
Issued:	2001 in a limited edition of 2,500
Comm. by:	Doulton-Direct

U.S.	**$100.00**
Can.	**$150.00**
U.K.	**£ 60.00**
Aust.	**$165.00**

4132
GEORGE

Designer:	Robert Tabbenor
Height:	6", 15.0 cm
Colour:	Golden Brown
Issued:	2001 in a limited edition of 2,500
Comm. by:	Doulton-Direct

U.S.	**$100.00**
Can.	**$150.00**
U.K.	**£ 60.00**
Aust.	**$165.00**

4133
WILLIAM

Designer:	Robert Tabbenor
Height:	6", 15.0 cm
Colour:	Light brown
Issued:	2001 in a limited edition of 2,500
Comm. by:	Doulton-Direct

U.S.	**$100.00**
Can.	**$150.00**
U.K.	**£ 60.00**
Aust.	**$165.00**

THUNDERBIRDS

3337
LADY PENELOPE™

Designer:	William K. Harper
Height:	4", 10.1 cm
Colour:	Pink hat and coat, blonde hair
Issued:	1992 in a limited edition of 2,500

| Beswick Number | Price | | | |
	U.S. $	Can. $	U.K. £	Aust. $
3337	200.00	275.00	125.00	300.00

3339
BRAINS™

Designer:	William K. Harper
Height:	4", 10.1 cm
Colour:	Black and blue uniform, blue glasses, black hair
Issued:	1992 in a limited edition of 2,500

| Beswick Number | Price | | | |
	U.S. $	Can. $	U.K. £	Aust. $
3339	185.00	250.00	115.00	275.00

3344
SCOTT TRACY™

Designer:	William K. Harper
Height:	4", 10.1 cm
Colour:	Blue uniform, light blue band
Issued:	1992 in a limited edition of 2,500

| Beswick Number | Price | | | |
	U.S. $	Can. $	U.K. £	Aust. $
3344	200.00	275.00	125.00	300.00

3345
VIRGIL TRACY™

Designer:	William K. Harper
Height:	4", 10.1 cm
Colour:	Blue uniform, yellow band
Issued:	1992 in a limited edition of 2,500

Beswick Number	Price			
	U.S. $	Can. $	U.K. £	Aust. $
3345	185.00	250.00	115.00	275.00

3346
PARKER™

Designer:	William K. Harper
Height:	4", 10.1 cm
Colour:	Blue-grey uniform
Issued:	1992 in a limited edition of 2,500

Beswick Number	Price			
	U.S. $	Can. $	U.K. £	Aust. $
3346	165.00	225.00	100.00	250.00

3348
THE HOOD™

Designer:	William K. Harper
Height:	4", 10.1 cm
Colour:	Browns
Issued:	1992 in a limited edition of 2,500

Beswick Number	Price			
	U.S. $	Can. $	U.K. £	Aust. $
3348	165.00	225.00	100.00	250.00

TRUMPTONSHIRE

4054
PC MCGARRY™

Designer:	Gordon Murray
Modeller:	Robert Simpson
Height:	5 ¾", 14.6 cm
Colour:	Navy and white
Issued:	2001 in a limited edition of 2,500
Comm. by:	Doulton-Direct

U.S.	**$65.00**
Can.	**$95.00**
U.K.	**£40.00**
Aust.	**$95.00**

4055
WINDY MILLER™

Designer:	Gordon Murray
Modeller:	Robert Simpson
Height:	5 ½", 14.0 cm
Colour:	Blue, red and black
Issued:	2001 in a limited edition of 2,500
Comm. by:	Doutlon-Direct

U.S.	**$65.00**
Can.	**$95.00**
U.K.	**£40.00**
Aust.	**$95.00**

4063
CAPTAIN FLACK™

Designer:	Gordon Murray
Modeller:	Robert Simpson
Height:	6", 15.0 cm
Colour:	Navy, gold, yellow and black
Issued:	2001 in a limited edition of 2,500
Comm. by:	Doulton-Direct

U.S.	**$65.00**
Can.	**$95.00**
U.K.	**£40.00**
Aust.	**$95.00**

4065
DR. MOPP™

Designer:	Gordon Murray
Modeller:	Robert Simpson
Height:	5 ¾", 14.6 cm
Colour:	Purple, blue, white, yellow and black
Issued:	2001 in a limited edition of 2,500
Comm. by:	Doulton-Direct

U.S.	**$65.00**
Can.	**$95.00**
U.K.	**£40.00**
Aust.	**$95.00**

4066
THE MAYOR™

Designer:	Gordon Murray
Modeller:	Robert Simpson
Height:	5 ½", 14.0 cm
Colour:	Black, red, blue and gold
Issued:	2001 in a limited edition of 2,500
Comm. by:	Doulton-Direct

U.S.	**$65.00**
Can.	**$95.00**
U.K.	**£40.00**
Aust.	**$95.00**

4067
MRS. HONEYMAN™

Designer:	Gordon Murray
Modeller:	Robert Simpson
Height:	5 ½", 14.0 cm
Colour:	Pink, black, white, yellow and purple
Issued:	2001 in a limited edition of 2,500
Comm. by:	Doulton-Direct

U.S.	**$65.00**
Can.	**$95.00**
U.K.	**£40.00**
Aust.	**$95.00**

4184
MRS. DINGLE™

Designer:	Gordon Murray
Modeller:	Robert Simpson
Height:	5 ¼", 13.3 cm
Colour:	Blue, red and white
Issued:	2001 in a limited edition of 2,500
Comm. by:	Doulton-Direct

U.S.	**$65.00**
Can.	**$95.00**
U.K.	**£40.00**
Aust.	**$95.00**

4185
JONATHAN BELL™

Designer:	Gordon Murray
Modeller:	Robert Simpson
Height:	5 ¼", 13.3 cm
Colour:	Brown, yellow, green and black
Issued:	2001 in a limited edition of 2,500
Comm. by:	Doulton-Direct

U.S.	**$65.00**
Can.	**$95.00**
U.K.	**£40.00**
Aust.	**$95.00**

4186
MICKEY MURPHY™

Designer:	Gordon Murray
Modeller:	Robert Simpson
Height:	5 ½", 14.0 cm
Colour:	White, blue and yellow
Issued:	2001 in a limited edition of 2,500
Comm. by:	Doulton-Direct

U.S.	**$65.00**
Can.	**$95.00**
U.K.	**£40.00**
Aust.	**$95.00**

4187
MRS COBBIT™

Designer:	Gordon Murray
Modeller:	Robert Simpson
Height:	5 ¼", 13.3 cm
Colour:	Yellow, navy and light blue
Issued:	2001 in a limited edition of 2,500
Comm. by:	Doulton-Direct

U.S.	**$65.00**
Can.	**$95.00**
U.K.	**£40.00**
Aust.	**$95.00**

TURNER ENTERTAINMENT

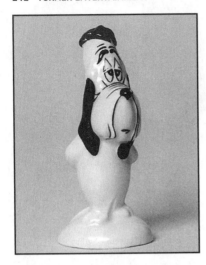

3547
DROOPY™

Designer:	Simon Ward
Height:	4 ½", 11.4 cm
Colour:	White dog with black ears, red cap
Issued:	1995 in a special edition of 2,000

Beswick Number	Price			
	U.S. $	Can. $	U.K. £	Aust. $
3547	60.00	85.00	40.00	90.00

3549
JERRY™

Designer:	Simon Ward
Height:	3", 7.6 cm
Colour	Red-brown and cream mouse, white base
Issued:	1995 in special edition of 2,000
Series:	Tom and Jerry

Beswick Number	Price			
	U.S. $	Can. $	U.K. £	Aust. $
3549	60.00	85.00	40.00	90.00

3552
TOM™

Designer:	Simon Ward
Height:	4 ½", 11.4 cm
Colour:	Grey-blue and pink cat, white base
Issued:	1995 in a special edition of 2,000
Series:	Tom and Jerry

Beswick Number	Price			
	U.S. $	Can. $	U.K. £	Aust. $
3552	60.00	85.00	40.00	90.00

THE WIZARD OF OZ™

3709
SCARECROW™

Designer:	Andy Moss
Height:	6 ½", 16.5 cm
Colour:	Black hat and shirt, brown pants and shoes
Issued:	1998 in a special edition of 1,500
Series:	The Wizard of Oz

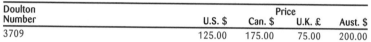

Doulton Number	Price			
	U.S. $	Can. $	U.K. £	Aust. $
3709	125.00	175.00	75.00	200.00

3731
LION™

Designer:	Andy Moss
Height:	6", 15.0 cm
Colour:	Light and dark brown
Issued:	1998 in a special edition of 1,500
Series:	The Wizard of Oz

Doulton Number	Price			
	U.S. $	Can. $	U.K. £	Aust. $
3731	125.00	175.00	75.00	200.00

3732
DOROTHY™

Designer:	Andy Moss
Height:	5", 12.7 cm
Colour:	Blue and white dress, red shoes, black dog
Issued:	1998 in a special edition of 1,500
Series:	The Wizard of Oz

Doulton Number	Price			
	U.S. $	Can. $	U.K. £	Aust. $
3732	125.00	175.00	75.00	200.00

3738
TINMAN™

Designer:	Andy Moss
Height:	7", 17.8 cm
Colour:	Grey
Issued:	1998 in a special edition of 1,500
Series:	The Wizard of Oz

Doulton Number	Price			
	U.S. $	Can. $	U.K. £	Aust. $
3738	125.00	175.00	75.00	200.00

20TH CENTURY ADVERTISING CLASSICS

AC 1
FATHER WILLIAM™

Modeller:	William K. Harper
Height:	6 ¼", 15.9 cm
Colour:	Black, yellow, red and grey
Issued:	1999 in a limited edition of 2,000
Slogan:	Get YOUNGER every day
U.S.	**$250.00**
Can.	**$350.00**
U.K.	**£150.00**
Aust.	**$375.00**

AC 2
GOLLY™

Modeller:	William K. Harper
Height:	5 ½", 14.0 cm
Colour:	Blue, red, orange and white
Issued:	1999 in a limited edition of 2,000
Slogan:	Golly it's Good!
U.S.	**$325.00**
Can.	**$450.00**
U.K.	**£200.00**
Aust.	**$350.00**

AC 3
SIR KREEMY KNUT™
(Sharps Toffee-Trebor Bassett Ltd)

Modeller:	William K. Harper
Height:	6 ¼", 15.9 cm
Colour:	Blue, white, red black and brown
Issued:	1999 in a limited edition of 2,000
Slogan:	Sharps the word for Toffee!
U.S.	**$250.00**
Can.	**$350.00**
U.K.	**£150.00**
Aust.	**$375.00**

AC 4
FOX'S POLAR BEAR™
(Fox's Glacier Mints - Nestlé)

Modeller:	William K. Harper
Height:	4 ¼", 10.8 cm
Colour:	White
Issued:	1999 in a limited edition of 2,000
Slogan:	FOX
U.S.	**$250.00**
Can.	**$350.00**
U.K.	**£150.00**
Aust.	**$375.00**

AC 5
PLAYER'S 'HERO' SAILOR™
(John Player & Sons Ltd - Imperial Tobacco Ltd)

Modeller:	William K. Harper
Height:	6", 15.0 cm
Colour:	Navy and white
Issued:	1999 in a limited edition of 2,000
Slogan:	Player's / Please
U.S.	**$250.00**
Can.	**$350.00**
U.K.	**£150.00**
Aust.	**$375.00**

AC 6
JOHN GINGER™
(Huntley & Palmers - Jacobs Bakery Ltd)

Modeller:	William K. Harper
Height:	6", 15.0 cm
Colour:	Dark green, white
Issued:	2000 ltd. ed. 2,000
Slogan:	There are no ifs, nor ands, not buts, they are the finest Ginger Nuts!
U.S.	**$250.00**
Can.	**$350.00**
U.K.	**£150.00**
Aust.	**$375.00**

AC 7
THE MILKY BAR KID™
(Nestlé)

Modeller:	William K. Harper David Biggs
Height:	5", 12.7 cm
Colour:	Blue, red, brown
Issued:	2000 ltd. ed. 2,000
Slogan:	The Milkybars are on me!
U.S.	**$250.00**
Can.	**$350.00**
U.K.	**£150.00**
Aust.	**$375.00**

AC 8
GUINNESS TOUCAN™
(©Guinness Ltd)

Modeller:	William K. Harper
Height:	6", 15.0 cm
Colour:	Black, white, blue and orange
Issued:	2000 in a limited edition of 2,000
Slogan:	Lovely day for a / GUINNESS
U.S.	**$350.00**
Can.	**$500.00**
U.K.	**£200.00**
Aust.	**$525.00**

MCL 1
PENFOLD GOLFER™

Modeller:	Shane Ridge
Height:	6", 15.0 cm
Colour:	Grey, white, tan, black and green
Issued:	2001 ltd. ed. 2,000
Slogan:	He Played A Penfold
Comm. by:	Millennium Collectables Ltd.

U.S.	**$160.00**
Can.	**$225.00**
U.K.	**£100.00**
Aust.	**$250.00**

MCL 2
DUNLOP CADDIE™

Modeller:	Shane Ridge
Height:	5 ½", 14.0 cm
Colour:	Blue, red, white, black and green
Issued:	2001 ltd. ed. 2,000
Slogan:	We Plan Dunlop 65
Comm. by:	Millennium Collectables Ltd.

U.S.	**$160.00**
Can.	**$225.00**
U.K.	**£100.00**
Aust.	**$250.00**

MCL 3
BIG CHIEF TOUCAN™

Modeller:	Shane Ridge
Height:	6 ¼", 15.9 cm
Colour:	Black, white, yellow, red and blue
Issued:	2002 ltd. ed. 2,000
Slogan:	Guinness – Him Strong
Comm. by:	Millennium Collectables Ltd.

U.S.	**$350.00**
Can.	**$500.00**
U.K.	**£200.00**
Aust.	**$525.00**

MCL 5
P..P..P..PICK UP A..PENGUIN™

Modeller:	Martyn Alcock
Height:	4 ¼", 10.8 cm
Colour:	Black, white, yellow
Issued:	2002 in a limited edition of 1,500
Slogan:	P... P... P... PICK UP A ...PENGUIN
Comm. by:	Millennium Collectables Ltd.

U.S.	**$165.00**
Can.	**$225.00**
U.K.	**£100.00**
Aust.	**$250.00**

MCL 6
CHRISTMAS TOUCAN™

Modeller:	Warren Platt
Height:	5 ½", 14.0 cm
Colour:	Black, white, red, orange, green, blue
Issued:	2001 ltd. ed. 2,000
Slogan:	GUINNESS / is good for yule
Comm. by:	Millennium Collectables Ltd.

U.S.	**$350.00**
Can.	**$500.00**
U.K.	**£200.00**
Aust.	**$525.00**

MCL 7
SEASIDE TOUCAN™

Modeller:	Shane Ridge
Height:	6 ¼", 15.9 cm
Colour:	Black, white, yellow, red and beige
Issued:	2003 ltd. ed. 2,000
Slogan:	GUINNESS / Goodness-on-sea
Comm. by:	Millennium Collectables Ltd.

U.S.	**$350.00**
Can.	**$500.00**
U.K.	**£200.00**
Aust.	**$525.00**

BISTO KIDS™

Modeller:	Rob Donaldson
Height:	4 ¾", 12.1 cm
Colour:	Black, red, green, blue, brown, yellow
Issued:	2002 in a limited edition of 1,000
Comm. by:	Millennium Collectables Ltd.

U.S.	**$250.00**
Can.	**$350.00**
U.K.	**£150.00**
Aust.	**$375.00**

TONY THE TIGER™

Modeller:	Martyn Alcock
Height:	5 ¾", 14.5 cm
Colour:	Orange and black
Issued:	2003 ltd. ed. 2,000
Slogan:	"THEY'RE GR-R-REAT!"
Comm. by:	Millennium Collectables Ltd.

U.S.	**$160.00**
Can.	**$225.00**
U.K.	**£100.00**
Aust.	**$250.00**

HIS MASTER'S VOICE 'NIPPER'™

Modeller:	David Biggs
Size:	6 ¼" x 12", 15.9 X 30.5 CM
Colour:	White dog with brown ears; brown and copper phonograph
Issued:	2001 in a limited edition of 2,000
Comm. by:	Millennium Collectables Ltd.

Back Stamp	Price			
	U.S. $	Can. $	U.K. £	Aust. $
Doulton	200.00	275.00	125.00	300.00

Note: Issued to commemorate the 100th anniversary of the use of the dog "Nipper" in the advertising of EMI's products (EMI REcords Ltd.)

DISNEY FIGURINES

101 DALMATIANS
DISNEY CHARACTERS
DISNEY PRINCESS COLLECTION
DISNEY SHOWCASE COLLECTION
DISNEY VILLAINS COLLECTION
FANTASIA 2000
FILM CLASSICS COLLECTION
MICKEY MOUSE COLLECTION
PETER PAN
SNOW WHITE AND THE SEVEN DWARFS
WINNIE THE POOH

101 DALMATIANS
1997 to the present

DM 1
CRUELLA DE VIL™
Style One

Designer:	Martyn Alcock
Modeller:	Martyn Alcock
Height:	6 ¼", 15.9 cm
Colour:	Black dress, pale yellow coat with red lining, red gloves
Issued:	1997 - 2001
Series:	101 Dalmatians Collection

Doulton Number	Price			
	U.S. $	Can. $	U.K. £	Aust. $
DM 1	150.00	225.00	100.00	250.00

DM 2
PENNY™

Designer:	Shane Ridge
Modeller:	Shane Ridge
Height:	2 ¾", 7.0 cm
Colour:	White and black dalmatian, red collar
Issued:	1997 - 2001
Series:	101 Dalmatians Collection

Doulton Number	Price			
	U.S. $	Can. $	U.K. £	Aust. $
DM 2	45.00	60.00	30.00	65.00

DM 3
PENNY™ AND FRECKLES™

Designer:	Martyn Alcock
Modeller:	Martyn Alcock
Height:	2 ¼", 5.5 cm
Colour:	Two white and black dalmatians with red collars
Issued:	1997 - 2001
Series:	101 Dalmatians Collection

Doulton Number	Price			
	U.S. $	Can. $	U.K. £	Aust. $
DM 3	55.00	80.00	35.00	85.00

DM 4
ROLLY™

Designer:	Shane Ridge
Modeller:	Shane Ridge
Height:	2 ¾", 7.0 cm
Colour:	White and black dalmatian, red collar, black base
Issued:	1997 - 1999
Series:	101 Dalmatians Collection

Doulton Number	Price			
	U.S. $	Can. $	U.K. £	Aust. $
DM 4	45.00	60.00	30.00	65.00

DM 5
PATCH™**, ROLLY**™ **AND FRECKLES**™

Designer:	Shane Ridge
Modeller:	Shane Ridge
Height:	3 ¾", 9.5 cm
Length:	7 ½", 19.0 cm
Colour:	Three white and black dalmatians wearing red collars
Issued:	1997 in a limited edition of 3,500
Series:	1. 101 Dalmatians Collection
	2. Tableau

Doulton Number	Price			
	U.S. $	Can. $	U.K. £	Aust. $
DM 5	250.00	350.00	150.00	375.00

DM 6
PONGO™

Designer:	Martyn Alcock
Modeller:	Martyn Alcock
Height:	4 ½", 11.9 cm
Colour:	White and black dalmatian, red collar
Issued:	1997 - 1998
Series:	101 Dalmatians Collection

Doulton Number	Price			
	U.S. $	Can. $	U.K. £	Aust. $
DM 6	55.00	80.00	35.00	85.00

DM 7
PERDITA™

Designer:	Martyn Alcock
Modeller:	Martyn Alcock
Height:	2 ½", 6.4 cm
Colour:	White and black dalmatian, dark turquoise collar and blanket
Issued:	1997 - 2001
Series:	101 Dalmatians Collection

Doulton Number	Price			
	U.S. $	Can. $	U.K. £	Aust. $
DM 7	55.00	80.00	35.00	85.00

DM 8
LUCKY™

Designer:	Martyn Alcock
Modeller:	Martyn Alcock
Height:	2 ¾", 7.0 cm
Colour:	White and black dalmatian, red collar
Issued:	1997 - 2001
Series:	101 Dalmatians Collection

Doulton Number	Price			
	U.S. $	Can. $	U.K. £	Aust. $
DM 8	45.00	60.00	30.00	65.00

DM 9
PATCH™ IN BASKET

Designer:	Graham Tongue
Modeller:	Graham Tongue
Height:	2 ¼", 5.7 cm
Colour:	White and black dalmatian, beige basket
Issued:	1998 - 2001
Series:	101 Dalmatians Collection

Doulton Number	Price			
	U.S. $	Can. $	U.K. £	Aust. $
DM 9	45.00	60.00	30.00	65.00

DM 10
LUCKY™ AND FRECKLES™ ON ICE

Designer:	Warren Platt
Modeller:	Warren Platt
Height:	2 ½", 6.4 cm
Colour:	White and black dalmatians
Issued:	1998 - 1999
Series:	101 Dalmatians Collection

Doulton Number	Price			
	U.S. $	Can. $	U.K. £	Aust. $
DM 10	100.00	150.00	65.00	165.00

DM 11
PUPS IN THE CHAIR™

Designer:	Martyn Alcock
Modeller:	Martyn Alcock
Height:	4", 10.1 cm
Colour:	White and black dalmatians, yellow chair
Issued:	February 1st to May 12th, 1999 (101 days)
Series:	101 Dalmatians Collection

Doulton Number	Price			
	U.S. $	Can. $	U.K. £	Aust. $
DM 11	150.00	200.00	90.00	225.00

DISNEY CHARACTERS

1952-1965

1278
MICKEY MOUSE™
Style One

Designer:	Jan Granoska
Height:	4", 10.1 cm
Colour:	Black, white and red
Issued:	1952 - 1965

Back Stamp	Beswick Number	Price U.S. $	Can. $	U.K. £	Aust. $
Beswick Gold	1278	800.00	1,150.00	500.00	1,200.00

1279
JIMINY CRICKET™
Style One

Designer:	Jan Granoska
Height:	4", 10.1 cm
Colour:	Black, white, beige and blue
Issued:	1952 - 1965

Back Stamp	Beswick Number	Price U.S. $	Can. $	U.K. £	Aust. $
Beswick Gold	1279	650.00	900.00	400.00	950.00

1280
PLUTO™
Style One

Designer:	Jan Granoska
Height:	3 ½", 8.9 cm
Colour:	Brown dog with red collar
Issued:	1953 - 1965

Back Stamp	Beswick Number	Price U.S. $	Can. $	U.K. £	Aust. $
Beswick Gold	1280	650.00	900.00	400.00	950.00

1281
GOOFY™
Style One

Designer:	Jan Granoska
Height:	4 ¼", 10.8 cm
Colour:	Red jersey, blue trousers, black suspenders, white gloves, brown and black hat, brown boots
Issued:	1953 - 1965

Back Stamp	Beswick Number	Price			
		U.S. $	Can. $	U.K. £	Aust. $
Beswick Gold	1281	650.00	900.00	400.00	950.00

1282
PINOCCHIO™
Style One

Designer:	Jan Granoska
Height:	4", 10.1 cm
Colour:	White and yellow jacket, red trousers, blue bowtie and shoes, brown cap
Issued:	1953 - 1965

Back Stamp	Beswick Number	Price			
		U.S. $	Can. $	U.K. £	Aust. $
Beswick Gold	1282	850.00	1,200.00	525.00	1,300.00

1283
DONALD DUCK™
Style One

Designer:	Jan Granoska
Height:	4", 10.1 cm
Colour:	White duck, blue sailors jacket, red bow, blue and black hat
Issued:	1953 - 1965

Back Stamp	Beswick Number	Price			
		U.S. $	Can. $	U.K. £	Aust. $
Beswick Gold	1283	725.00	1,000.00	450.00	1,100.00

1289
MINNIE MOUSE™
Style One

Designer:	Jan Granoska
Height:	4", 10.1 cm
Colour:	Black and white mouse wearing a yellow top and red skirt with white spots, white gloves and hair bow, brown shoes
Issued:	1953 - 1965

Back Stamp	Beswick Number	Price			
		U.S. $	Can. $	U.K. £	Aust. $
Beswick Gold	1289	725.00	1,000.00	450.00	1,100.00

1291
THUMPER™
Style One

Designer:	Jan Granoska
Height:	3 ¾", 9.5 cm
Colour:	Grey and white rabbit, yellow, red and pink flowers on brown base
Issued:	1953 - 1965

Back Stamp	Beswick Number	Price			
		U.S. $	Can. $	U.K. £	Aust. $
Beswick Gold	1291	450.00	600.00	275.00	650.00

THE DISNEY PRINCESS COLLECTION
1995-1996

HN 3677
CINDERELLA™

Designer:	Pauline Parsons
Height:	8", 20.3 cm
Colour:	Blue and white dress, yellow hair
Issued:	1995 in a limited edition of 2,000
Series:	The Disney Princess Collection

Back Stamp	Doulton Number	Price			
		U.S. $	Can. $	U.K. £	Aust. $
Doulton	HN 3677	400.00	600.00	275.00	600.00

HN 3678
SNOW WHITE™
Style Two

Designer:	Pauline Parsons
Height:	8 ¼", 21.0 cm
Colour:	Yellow, blue and white dress, royal blue and red cape, black hair
Issued:	1995 in a limited edition of 2,000
Series:	The Disney Princess Collection

Back Stamp	Doulton Number	Price			
		U.S. $	Can. $	U.K. £	Aust. $
Doulton	HN 3678	500.00	700.00	325.00	750.00

HN 3830
BELLE™

Designer:	Pauline Parsons
Height:	8", 20.3 cm
Colour:	Yellow dress and gloves, brown hair
Issued:	1996 in a limited edition of 2,000
Series:	The Disney Princess Collection

Back Stamp	Doulton Number	Price			
		U.S. $	Can. $	U.K. £	Aust. $
Doulton	HN 3830	400.00	600.00	250.00	650.00

HN 3831
ARIEL™
Style One

Designer:	Pauline Parsons
Height:	8 ¼", 21.0 cm
Colour:	White dress and veil, red hair
Issued:	1996 in a limited edition of 2,000
Series:	The Disney Princess Collection

Back Stamp	Doulton Number	Price			
		U.S. $	Can. $	U.K. £	Aust. $
Doulton	HN 3831	400.00	600.00	250.00	650.00

HN 3832
JASMINE™

Designer:	Pauline Parsons
Height:	7 ½", 19.1 cm
Colour:	Lilac dress
Issued:	1996 in a limited edition of 2,000
Series:	The Disney Princess Collection

Back Stamp	Doulton Number	Price			
		U.S. $	Can. $	U.K. £	Aust. $
Doulton	HN 3832	400.00	600.00	250.00	650.00

HN 3833
AURORA™

Designer:	Pauline Parsons
Height:	7 ½", 19.1 cm
Colour:	Light and dark blue dress with white trim
Issued:	1996 in a limited edition of 2,000
Series:	The Disney Princess Collection

Back Stamp	Doulton Number	Price			
		U.S. $	Can. $	U.K. £	Aust. $
Doulton	HN 3833	250.00	375.00	150.00	400.00

DISNEY SHOWCASE COLLECTION
ALICE IN WONDERLAND

AW1
ALICE™
Style Four

Designer:	Shane Ridge
Modeller:	Shane Ridge
Height:	4 ¾", 12.1 cm
Colour:	Blue dress, white apron; red with white polka-dot mushroom
Issued:	2001 in a limited edition of 2,000
Series:	Alice In Wonderland

Doulton Number	Price			
	U.S. $	Can. $	U.K. £	Aust. $
AW1	125.00	175.00	70.00	190.00

AW2
MAD HATTER™
Style Three

Designer:	Martyn Alcock
Modeller:	Martyn Alcock
Height:	4 ¾", 12.1 cm
Colour:	Yellow coat, black shirt and shoes, green trousers and bowtie, black and green top hat with black band
Issued:	2001 in a limited edition of 2,000
Series:	Alice In Wonderland

Doulton Number	Price			
	U.S. $	Can. $	U.K. £	Aust. $
AW2	125.00	175.00	85.00	190.00

AW3
MARCH HARE™

Designer:	Martyn C. R. Alcock
Modeller:	Martyn C. R. Alcock
Height:	2 ½", 6.4 cm
Colour:	Yellow rabbit; red coat, black leggings, white and red tea pot and cup
Issued:	2001 in a limited edition of 2,000
Series:	Alice In Wonderland

Doulton Number	Price			
	U.S. $	Can. $	U.K. £	Aust. $
AW3	125.00	175.00	70.00	190.00

AW4
WHITE RABBIT™
Style Three

Designer:	Shane Ridge
Modeller:	Shane Ridge
Height:	2 ¾", 7.0 cm
Colour:	Red coat, yellow shirt, black bowtie, grey trousers; yellow and white clock
Issued:	2001 in a limited edition of 2,000
Series:	Alice In Wonderland

Doulton Number	Price			
	U.S. $	Can. $	U.K. £	Aust. $
AW4	85.00	125.00	50.00	135.00

AW5
CHESHIRE CAT™
Style Four

Designer:	Shane Ridge
Modeller:	Shane Ridge
Height:	2 ¾", 7.0 cm
Colour:	Pink and white striped cat
Issued:	2001 in a limited edition of 2,000
Series:	Alice In Wonderland

Doulton Number	Price			
	U.S. $	Can. $	U.K. £	Aust. $
AW5	80.00	120.00	45.00	125.00

DISNEY SHOWCASE COLLECTION
THE JUNGLE BOOK

JB 1
MOWGLI™

Designer:	Shane Ridge
Modeller:	Shane Ridge
Height:	2 ½", 6.4 cm
Colour:	Fleshtones, black and red
Issued:	2000 - 2001
Series:	Jungle Book

Doulton Number	Price			
	U.S. $	Can. $	U.K. £	Aust. $
JB 1	125.00	175.00	75.00	190.00

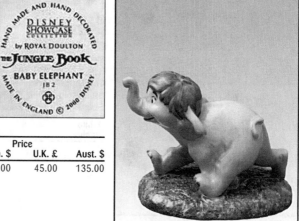

JB 2
BABY ELEPHANT™

Designer:	Martyn Alcock
Modeller:	Martyn Alcock
Height:	3 ¼", 8.3 cm
Colour:	Tan
Issued:	2000 - 2001
Series:	Jungle Book

Doulton Number	Price			
	U.S. $	Can. $	U.K. £	Aust. $
JB 2	75.00	125.00	45.00	135.00

JB 3
BALOO™

Designer:	Shane Ridge
Modeller:	Shane Ridge
Height:	5 ¼", 13.3 cm
Colour:	Grey and white
Issued:	2000 - 2001
Series:	Jungle Book

Doulton Number	Price			
	U.S. $	Can. $	U.K. £	Aust. $
JB 3	125.00	175.00	75.00	190.00

JB 4
BAGHEERA™

Designer:	Shane Ridge
Modeller:	Shane Ridge
Height:	4 ¾", 12.1 cm
Colour:	Black
Issued:	2000 - 2001
Series:	Jungle Book

Doulton Number	Price U.S. $	Can. $	U.K. £	Aust. $
JB 4	125.00	175.00	75.00	190.00

JB 5
SHERE KHAN™

Designer:	Martyn Alcock
Modeller:	Martyn Alcock
Height:	3 ¼", 8.3 cm
Colour:	Yellow with dark brown stripes
Issued:	2000 - 2001
Series:	Jungle Book

Doulton Number	Price U.S. $	Can. $	U.K. £	Aust. $
JB 5	135.00	200.00	85.00	225.00

JB 6
FLOATING ALONG™

Designer:	Martyn Alcock
Modeller:	Martyn Alcock
Height:	2 ¾", 7.0 cm
Colour:	White and grey bear; fleshtones, black and red
Issued:	2001 in a limited edition of 3,500
Series:	1. Jungle Book
	2. Tableau

Doulton Number	Price U.S. $	Can. $	U.K. £	Aust. $
JB 6	165.00	225.00	100.00	250.00

JB 7
KING LOUIE™

Designer:	Warren Platt
Modeller:	Warren Platt
Height:	4", 10.1 cm
Colour:	Orange
Issued:	2001 - 2003
Series:	Jungle Book

Doulton Number	Price			
	U.S. $	Can. $	U.K. £	Aust. $
JB 7	165.00	225.00	100.00	250.00

DISNEY SHOWCASE COLLECTION
THE LITTLE MERMAID

LM 1
ARIEL™
Style Two

Designer:	Unknown
Modeller:	Unknown
Height:	4 ½", 11.9 cm
Colour:	Green, purple, red and yellow
Issued:	2002 - 2003
Series:	The Little Mermaid

Doulton Number	Price			
	U.S. $	Can. $	U.K. £	Aust. $
LM 1	N/I	N/I	35.00	N/I

LM 2
FLOUNDER™

Designer:	Unknown
Modeller:	Unknown
Height:	2 ½", 6.4 cm
Colour:	Yellow fish with blue striped fins
Issued:	2002 - 2003
Series:	The Little Mermaid

Doulton Number	Price			
	U.S. $	Can. $	U.K. £	Aust. $
LM 2	N/I	N/I	25.00	N/I

LM 3
SEBASTIAN™

Designer:	Unknown
Modeller:	Unknown
Height:	2 ¼", 5.5 cm
Colour:	Yellow, red, coral
Issued:	2002 - 2003
Series:	The Little Mermaid

Doulton Number	Price			
	U.S. $	Can. $	U.K. £	Aust. $
LM 3	N/I	N/I	25.00	N/I

LM 4
URSULA™

Designer:	Unknown
Modeller:	Unknown
Height:	4 ¼", 10.8 cm
Colour:	Purple, black and green
Issued:	2002 - 2003
Series:	The Little Mermaid

Doulton Number			Price	
	U.S. $	Can. $	U.K. £	Aust. $
LM 4	N/I	N/I	45.00	N/I

LM 5
SCUTTLE™

Designer:	Unknown
Modeller:	Unknown
Height:	3", 7.6 cm
Colour:	White, purple, black and orange
Issued:	2002 - 2003
Series:	The Little Mermaid

Doulton Number			Price	
	U.S. $	Can. $	U.K. £	Aust. $
LM 5	N/I	N/I	25.00	N/I

DISNEY SHOWCASE COLLECTION
PETER PAN SERIES 2002 to date

PAN 1
PETER PAN™
Style Two

Designer:	Unknown
Modeller:	Unknown
Height:	5 ½", 14.0 cm
Colour:	Light green tunic, darker green tights and cap, brown shoes
Issued:	2002 to the present
Series:	Peter Pan (Series Two)

Doulton Number			Price	
	U.S. $	Can. $	U.K. £	Aust. $
PAN 1	N/I	N/I	40.00	N/I

PAN 2
TINKER BELL™
Style Two

Designer:	Unknown
Modeller:	Unknown
Height:	6", 15.0 cm
Colour:	Green dress and slippers, lilac and white wings
Issued:	2002 to the present
Series:	Peter Pan (Series Two)

Doulton Number			Price	
	U.S. $	Can. $	U.K. £	Aust. $
PAN 2	N/I	N/I	40.00	N/I

PAN 3
THE DUEL™

Designer:	Unknown
Modeller:	Unknown
Height:	6 ¼", 15.9 cm
Colour:	Peter Pan: Green tunic and cap, darker green tights; brown belt Captain: Red and gold coat, pink and lilac hat, white neckerchief and stockings, black shoes
Issued:	2002 in a limited edition of 3,000
Series:	Peter Pan (Series Two)

Doulton Number	Price			
	U.S. $	Can. $	U.K. £	Aust. $
PAN 3	N/I	N/I	80.00	N/I

PAN 4
CAPTAIN HOOK™

Designer:	Unknown
Modeller:	Unknown
Height:	7", 17.8 cm
Colour:	Red and gold coat, pink and lilac hat, white neckerchief and stockings, black shoes
Issued:	2002 to the present
Series:	Peter Pan (Series Two)

Doulton Number	Price			
	U.S. $	Can. $	U.K. £	Aust. $
PAN 4	N/I	N/I	40.00	N/I

PAN 5
WENDY™

Designer:	Unknown
Modeller:	Unknown
Height:	5", 12.7 cm
Colour:	Blue dress, blonde hair, yellow block
Issued:	2002 to the present
Series:	Peter Pan (Series Two)

Doulton Number	Price			
	U.S. $	Can. $	U.K. £	Aust. $
PAN 5	N/I	N/I	30.00	N/I

PAN 6
TIC TOC CROCODILE™

Designer:	Unknown
Modeller:	Unknown
Height:	5 ½", 14.0 cm
Colour:	Green, grey, red, blue and white
Issued:	2002 to the present
Series:	Peter Pan (Series Two)

Doulton Number	Price			
	U.S. $	Can. $	U.K. £	Aust. $
PAN 6	N/I	N/I	35.00	N/I

HAND MADE AND HAND DECORATED
DISNEY SHOWCASE
COLLECTION
by ROYAL DOULTON
PETER PAN
TIC TOC CROCODILE
PAN 6
MADE IN THAILAND © 2002 DISNEY

PAN 7
HEADING FOR SKULL ROCK

Designer:	Unknown
Modeller:	Unknown
Height:	6", 15.0 cm
Colour:	Captain Hook: Red and gold coat; pink and lilac hat
	Princess Tiger Lily: Brown, red and orange dress
	Smee: Blue and white striped shirt, blue shorts, red cap
Issued:	2002 in a limited edition of 3,000
Series:	Peter Pan (Series Two)

Doulton Number	Price			
	U.S. $	Can. $	U.K. £	Aust. $
PAN 7	N/I	N/I	80.00	N/I

HAND MADE AND HAND DECORATED
DISNEY SHOWCASE
COLLECTION
by ROYAL DOULTON
PETER PAN
HEADING FOR SKULL ROCK
PAN 7
LIMITED EDITION
OF 3,000
THIS IS Nº
0767
MADE IN THAILAND © 2002 DISNEY

DISNEY VILLAINS COLLECTION
1997-1998

HN 3839
CRUELLA DE VIL™
Style Two

Designer:	Pauline Parsons
Height:	8", 20.3 cm
Colour:	Black dress, white fur coat, red gloves
Issued:	1997 in a limited edition of 2,000
Series:	The Disney Villains Collection

Back Stamp	Doulton Number	Price			
		U.S. $	Can. $	U.K. £	Aust. $
Doulton	HN 3839	400.00	600.00	250.00	625.00

HN 3840
MALEFICENT™

Designer:	Pauline Parsons
Height:	8", 20.3 cm
Colour:	Black and purple
Issued:	1997 in a limited edition of 2,000
Series:	The Disney Villains Collection

Back Stamp	Doulton Number	Price			
		U.S. $	Can. $	U.K. £	Aust. $
Doulton	HN 3840	400.00	600.00	250.00	625.00

HN 3847
THE QUEEN™

Designer:	Pauline Parson
Height:	8 ¾", 22.2 cm
Colour:	Black, white, purple, red and yellow
Issued:	1998 in a limited edition of 2,000
Series:	The Disney Villains Collection

Back Stamp	Doulton Number	Price			
		U.S. $	Can. $	U.K. £	Aust. $
Doulton	HN 3847	325.00	475.00	200.00	500.00

HN 3848
THE WITCH™

Designer:	Pauline Parsons
Height:	7", 17.8 cm
Colour:	Black robes, red apple
Issued:	1998 in a limited edition of 2,000
Series:	The Disney Villains Collection

Back Stamp	Doulton Number	Price			
		U.S. $	Can. $	U.K. £	Aust. $
Doulton	HN 3848	325.00	475.00	200.00	500.00

FANTASIA 2000

FAN1
BUCKETS OF MISCHIEF™

Designer:	Shane Ridge
Modeller:	Shane Ridge
Height:	4 ½", 11.9 cm
Colour:	Brown broom and buckets, blue water
Issued:	2000 in a limited edition of 2,000
Series:	Fantasia 2000

Back Stamp	Doulton Number	Price			
		U.S. $	Can. $	U.K. £	Aust. $
FAN1	8226	110.00	175.00	65.00	200.00

FAN2
FOLLOW ME™

Designer:	Shane Ridge
Modeller:	Shane Ridge
Height:	5 ¼", 13.3 cm
Colour:	Red, purple, black and white
Issued:	2000 in a limited edition of 2,000
Series:	Fantasia 2000

Back Stamp	Doulton Number	Price			
		U.S. $	Can. $	U.K. £	Aust. $
FAN2	8227	150.00	225.00	90.00	250.00

FAN3
NOAH'S™ HELPER

Designer:	Shane Ridge
Modeller:	Shane Ridge
Height:	4", 10.1 cm
Colour:	Brown, white and yellow
Issued:	2000 in a limited edition of 2,000
Series:	Fantasia 2000

Back Stamp	Doulton Number	Price			
		U.S. $	Can. $	U.K. £	Aust. $
FAN3	8228	125.00	200.00	75.00	225.00

FAN4
HEART ON A STRING™
(Pomp and Circumstance)

Designer:	Shane Ridge
Modeller:	Shane Ridge
Height:	4 ¼", 10.8 cm
Colour:	Blue, yellow and white
Issued:	2000 in a limited edition of 2,000
Series:	Fantasia 2000

Back Stamp	Doulton Number	Price			
		U.S. $	Can. $	U.K. £	Aust. $
FAN4	8325	150.00	225.00	90.00	250.00

FAN5
A FLOWER AND HIS HEART™
(Shostakovich's Piano Concerto No. 2)

Designer:	Shane Ridge
Modeller:	Shane Ridge
Height:	6 ½", 16.5 cm
Colour:	Red, white and pink
Issued:	2000 in a limited edition of 2,000
Series:	1. Fantasia 2000
	2. Tableau

Back Stamp	Doulton Number	Price			
		U.S. $	Can. $	U.K. £	Aust. $
FAN5	8225	325.00	450.00	200.00	475.00

FILM CLASSICS COLLECTION

CN 1
CINDERELLA™ THE DRESS OF DREAMS

Designer:	Shane Ridge
Modeller:	Shane Ridge
Height:	6 ¾", 17.2 cm
Colour:	Pink and white dress
Issued:	2000 in a limited edition of 2,000
Series:	Film Classics Collection

Back Stamp	Doulton Number	Price			
		U.S. $	Can. $	U.K. £	Aust. $
CN 1	–	195.00	295.00	120.00	300.00

FC 1
BAMBI™

Designer:	Martyn Alcock
Modeller:	Martyn Alcock
Height:	4", 10.1 cm
Colour:	Brown deer, yellow spots, black nose and tip on top of ears
Issued:	1999 in a limited edition of 1,500
Series:	Film Classics Collection

Back Stamp	Doulton Number	Price			
		U.S. $	Can. $	U.K. £	Aust. $
FC 1	4440	150.00	225.00	90.00	250.00

FC 2
THUMPER™
Style Two

Designer:	Martyn Alcock
Modeller:	Martyn Alcock
Height:	3 ¼", 8.3 cm
Colour:	Grey, white and cream rabbit, pink nose
Issued:	1999 in a limited edition on 1,500
Series:	Film Classics Collection

Back Stamp	Doulton Number	Price			
		U.S. $	Can. $	U.K. £	Aust. $
FC 2	4432	150.00	225.00	90.00	250.00

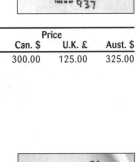

FC 3
DUMBO™

Modeller:	Shane Ridge
Height:	4 ½", 11.9 cm
Colour:	Grey elephant, pink inner ears
Issued:	1999 in a limited edition of 1,500
Series:	Film Classics Collection

Back Stamp	Doulton Number	Price			
		U.S. $	Can. $	U.K. £	Aust. $
FC 3	4427	200.00	300.00	125.00	325.00

FC 4
PINOCCHIO™
Style Two

Designer:	Shane Ridge
Modeller:	Shane Ridge
Height:	5 ½", 14.0 cm
Colour:	Yellow shirt and hat, red trousers and shoes, blue bowtie and book
Issued:	1999 in a limited edition of 1,500
Series:	Film Classics Collection

Back Stamp	Doulton Number	Price			
		U.S. $	Can. $	U.K. £	Aust. $
FC 4	4431	200.00	300.00	125.00	325.00

FC5
JIMINY CRICKET™
Style Two

Designer:	Warren Platt
Modeller:	Warren Platt
Height:	4 ¼", 10.8 cm
Colour:	Dark blue jacket and shoes, tan trousers, orange waistcoat, blue hat with orange band, red umbrella
Issued:	2000 in a limited edition of 1,500
Series:	Film Classics Collection

Back Stamp	Doulton Number	Price			
		U.S. $	Can. $	U.K. £	Aust. $
FC 5	3149	150.00	225.00	90.00	250.00

FC 6
TIMOTHY MOUSE™

Designer:	Amanda Hughes-Lubeck
Modeller:	Amanda Hughes-Lubeck
Height:	3 ¼", 8.3 cm
Colour:	Red and yellow suit and hat
Issued:	2000 in a limited edition of 1,500
Series:	Film Classics Collection

Back Stamp	Doulton Number	Price U.S. $	Can. $	U.K. £	Aust. $
FC 6	–	100.00	150.00	65.00	175.00

FC 7
LADY™

Designer:	Shane Ridge
Modeller:	Shane Ridge
Height:	3 ¼", 8.3 cm
Colour:	Tan and brown dog, blue collar
Issued:	2001 in a limited edition of 1,500
Series:	Film Classics Collection

Back Stamp	Doulton Number	Price U.S. $	Can. $	U.K. £	Aust. $
FC 7	–	100.00	150.00	65.00	175.00

FC 8
TRAMP™

Designer:	Shane Ridge
Modeller:	Shane Ridge
Height:	4", 10.1 cm
Colour:	Grey and white dog, red collar, gold dog tag
Issued:	2001 in a limited edition of 1,500
Series:	Film Classics Collection

Back Stamp	Doulton Number	Price U.S. $	Can. $	U.K. £	Aust. $
FC 8	–	125.00	175.00	75.00	200.00

MICKEY MOUSE COLLECTION
1998-2000

MM 1/MM 7
MICKEY MOUSE™
Style Two

Designer:	Warren Platt
Modeller:	Warren Platt
Height:	4 ¾", 12.1 cm
Colour:	Black, red and light brown
Issued:	1. 1998 - 1998
	2. 1999 - 2000
Series:	Mickey Mouse Collection

Back Stamp	Doulton Number	Price U.S. $	Can. $	U.K. £	Aust. $
BK-1 / 70th Anniv.	MM 1	100.00	150.00	60.00	150.00
BK-2	MM 7	100.00	150.00	60.00	150.00

MM 2/MM 8
MINNIE MOUSE™
Style Two

Designer:	Warren Platt
Modeller:	Warren Platt
Height:	5 ½", 14.0 cm
Colour:	Black, blue and red
Issued:	1. 1998 - 1998
	2. 1999 - 2000
Series:	Mickey Mouse Collection

Back Stamp	Doulton Number	Price U.S. $	Can. $	U.K. £	Aust. $
BK-1 / 70th Anniv.	MM 2	100.00	150.00	60.00	150.00
BK-2	MM 8	100.00	150.00	60.00	150.00

MM 3/MM 9
DONALD DUCK™
Style Two

Designer:	Warren Platt
Modeller:	Shane Ridge
Height:	4 ¾", 12.1 cm
Colour:	Blue, white and red
Issued:	1. 1998 - 1998
	2. 1999 - 2000
Series:	Mickey Mouse Collection

Back Stamp	Doulton Number	Price U.S. $	Can. $	U.K. £	Aust. $
BK-1 / 70th Anniv.	MM 3	100.00	150.00	60.00	150.00
BK-2	MM 9	100.00	150.00	60.00	150.00

MM 4/MM 10
DAISY DUCK™

Designer:	Shane Ridge
Modeller:	Shane Ridge
Height:	5 ½", 14.0 cm
Colour:	Blue, white and pink
Issued:	1. 1998 - 1998
	2. 1999 - 2000
Series:	Mickey Mouse Collection

Back Stamp	Doulton Number	Price			
		U.S. $	Can. $	U.K. £	Aust. $
BK-1 / 70th Anniv.	MM 4	100.00	150.00	60.00	150.00
BK-2	MM 10	100.00	150.00	60.00	150.00

MM 5/MM 11
GOOFY™
Style Two

Designer:	Shane Ridge
Modeller:	Graham Tongue
Height:	5", 12.7 cm
Colour:	Red, blue and black
Issued:	1. 1998 - 1998
	2. 1999 - 2000
Series:	Mickey Mouse Collection

Back Stamp	Doulton Number	Price			
		U.S. $	Can. $	U.K. £	Aust. $
BK-1 / 70th Anniv.	MM 5	100.00	150.00	60.00	150.00
BK-2	MM 11	100.00	150.00	60.00	150.00

MM 6/MM 12
PLUTO™
Style Two

Designer:	Graham Tongue
Modeller:	Graham Tongue
Height:	4 ½", 12.1 cm
Colour:	Light brown
Issued:	1. 1998 - 1998
	2. 1999 - 2000
Series:	Mickey Mouse Collection

Back Stamp	Doulton Number	Price			
		U.S. $	Can. $	U.K. £	Aust. $
BK-1 / 70th Anniv.	MM 6	100.00	150.00	60.00	150.00
BK-2	MM 12	100.00	150.00	60.00	150.00

PETER PAN
1953-1965

1301
NANA™

Designer:	Jan Granoska
Height:	3 ¼", 8.3 cm
Colour:	Brown dog, white frilled cap with blue ribbon
Issued:	1953 - 1965
Series:	Peter Pan (Series One)

Back Stamp	Beswick Number	Price			
		U.S. $	Can. $	U.K. £	Aust. $
Beswick Gold	1301	725.00	1,000.00	450.00	1,100.00

1302
SMEE™

Designer:	Jan Granoska
Height:	4 ¼", 10.8 cm
Colour:	Blue and white shirt, blue pants, red cap, green bottle
Issued:	1953 - 1965
Series:	Peter Pan (Series One)

Back Stamp	Beswick Number	Price			
		U.S. $	Can. $	U.K. £	Aust. $
Beswick Gold	1302	650.00	900.00	400.00	950.00

1307
PETER PAN™
Style One

Designer:	Jan Granoska
Height:	5", 12.7 cm
Colour:	Light green tunic, dark green pants, brown shoes, red and green cap
Issued:	1953 - 1965
Series:	Peter Pan (Series One)

Back Stamp	Beswick Number	Price			
		U.S. $	Can. $	U.K. £	Aust. $
Beswick Gold	1307	950.00	1,300.00	600.00	1,350.00

1312
TINKER BELL™
Style One

Designer:	Jan Granoska
Height:	5", 12.7 cm
Colour:	Light green dress, dark green wings and shoes
Issued:	1953 - 1965
Series:	Peter Pan (Series One)

Back Stamp	Beswick Number	Price			
		U.S. $	Can. $	U.K. £	Aust. $
Beswick Gold	1312	1,200.00	1,800.00	750.00	2,000.00

SNOW WHITE AND THE SEVEN DWARFS

BESWICK SERIES 1954-1967

1325
DOPEY™
Style One

Designer:	Arthur Gredington
Height:	3 ½", 8.9 cm
Colour:	Green coat, maroon cap, grey shoes
Issued:	1954 - 1967
Series:	Snow White and the Seven Dwarfs (Series One)

Back Stamp	Beswick Number	Price			
		U.S. $	Can. $	U.K. £	Aust. $
Beswick Gold	1325	250.00	350.00	150.00	375.00

1326
HAPPY™
Style One

Designer:	Arthur Gredington
Height:	3 ½", 8.9 cm
Colour:	Purple tunic, light blue trousers, light brown cap, brown shoes
Issued:	1954 - 1967
Series:	Snow White and the Seven Dwarfs (Series One)

Back Stamp	Beswick Number	Price			
		U.S. $	Can. $	U.K. £	Aust. $
Beswick Gold	1326	250.00	350.00	150.00	375.00

1327
BASHFUL™
Style One

Designer:	Arthur Gredington
Height:	3 ½", 8.9 cm
Colour:	Brown tunic, purple trousers, grey cap, brown shoes
Issued:	1954 - 1967
Series:	Snow White and the Seven Dwarfs (Series One)

Back Stamp	Beswick Number	Price			
		U.S. $	Can. $	U.K. £	Aust. $
Beswick Gold	1327	250.00	350.00	150.00	375.00

1328
SNEEZY™
Style One

Designer:	Arthur Gredington
Height:	3 ½", 8.9 cm
Colour:	Green tunic, purple trousers, brown cap and shoes
Issued:	1954 - 1967
Series:	Snow White and the Seven Dwarfs (Series One)

Back Stamp	Beswick Number	Price			
		U.S. $	Can. $	U.K. £	Aust. $
Beswick Gold	1328	250.00	350.00	150.00	375.00

1329
DOC™
Style One

Designer:	Arthur Gredington
Height:	3 ½", 8.9 cm
Colour:	Brown tunic, blue trousers, yellow cap, brown shoes
Issued:	1954 - 1967
Series:	Snow White and the Seven Dwarfs (Series One)

Back Stamp	Beswick Number	Price			
		U.S. $	Can. $	U.K. £	Aust. $
Beswick Gold	1329	250.00	350.00	150.00	375.00

1330
GRUMPY™
Style One

Designer:	Arthur Gredington
Height:	3 ¾", 9.5 cm
Colour:	Purple tunic, red trousers, blue cap, brown shoes
Issued:	1954 - 1967
Series:	Snow White and the Seven Dwarfs (Series One)

Back Stamp	Beswick Number	Price			
		U.S. $	Can. $	U.K. £	Aust. $
Beswick Gold	1330	250.00	350.00	150.00	375.00

1331
SLEEPY™
Style One

Designer:	Arthur Gredington
Height:	3 ½", 8.9 cm
Colour:	Tan tunic, red trousers, green hat, grey shoes
Issued:	1954 - 1967
Series:	Snow White and the Seven Dwarfs (Series One)

Back Stamp	Beswick Number	Price			
		U.S. $	Can. $	U.K. £	Aust. $
Beswick Gold	1331	250.00	350.00	150.00	375.00

1332A
SNOW WHITE™
Style One
First Version (Hair in Flounces)

Designer:	Arthur Gredington
Height:	5 ½", 14.0 cm
Colour:	Yellow and purple dress, red cape, white collar
Issued:	1954 - 1955

Back Stamp	Beswick Number	Price			
		U.S. $	Can. $	U.K. £	Aust. $
Beswick Gold	1332A			Extremely rare	

Note: Snow White (Style One) was remodelled February 1955.

1332B
SNOW WHITE™
Style One
Second Version (Hair Flat to Head)

Designer:	Arthur Gredington
Height:	5 ½", 14.0 cm
Colour:	Yellow and purple dress, red cape, white collar
Issued:	1955 - 1967
Series:	Snow White and the Seven Dwarfs (Series One)

Back Stamp	Beswick Number	Price			
		U.S. $	Can. $	U.K. £	Aust. $
Beswick Gold	1332B	550.00	775.00	350.00	850.00

SNOW WHITE AND THE SEVEN DWARFS
ROYAL DOULTON SERIES 1997 - 2002

SW 1 / SW 9
SNOW WHITE™
Style Three

Designer:	Amanda Hughes-Lubeck
Height:	5 ¾", 14.6 cm
Colour:	Yellow and blue dress, red cape, white collar
Issued:	SW 1 1997 in a limited edition of 2,000
	SW 9 1998 - 2002
Series:	Snow White and the Seven Dwarfs (Series Two)

Back Stamp	Doulton Number	Price			
		U.S. $	Can. $	U.K. £	Aust. $
Doulton/Disney 60th	SW 1	300.00	400.00	150.00	425.00
Doulton/Disney	SW 9	150.00	225.00	100.00	250.00

SW 2 / SW 10
DOC™
Style Two

Designer:	Amanda Hughes-Lubeck
Height:	3 ¼", 8.3 cm
Colour:	Red tunic, brown trousers, yellow hat, green book
Issued:	SW 2 1997 in a limited edition of 2,000
	SW 10 1998 - 2002
Series:	Snow White and the Seven Dwarfs (Series Two)

Back Stamp	Doulton Number	Price			
		U.S. $	Can. $	U.K. £	Aust. $
Doulton/Disney 60th	SW 2	85.00	120.00	50.00	125.00
Doulton/Disney	SW 10	50.00	70.00	30.00	75.00

SW3 / SW11
GRUMPY™
Style Two

Designer:	Shane Ridge
Height:	3 ½", 8.9 cm
Colour:	Dark rust tunic and trousers, brown hat, light brown basket
Issued:	SW 3 1997 in a limited edition of 2,000
	SW 11 1998 - 2002
Series:	Snow White and the Seven Dwarfs (Series Two)

Back Stamp	Doulton Number	Price			
		U.S. $	Can. $	U.K. £	Aust. $
Doulton/Disney 60th	SW 3	85.00	120.00	50.00	125.00
Doulton/Disney	SW 11	50.00	70.00	30.00	75.00

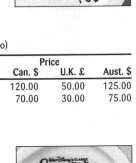

SW 4 / SW 12
HAPPY™
Style Two

Designer:	Amanda Hughes-Lubeck
Height:	3 ½", 8.9 cm
Colour:	Brown and orange tunic, light blue trousers with black belt and a yellow hat
Issued:	SW 4 1997 in a limited edition of 2,000
	SW 12 1998 - 2002
Series:	Snow White and the Seven Dwarfs (Series Two)

Back Stamp	Doulton Number	Price U.S. $	Can. $	U.K. £	Aust. $
Doulton/Disney 60th	SW 4	85.00	120.00	50.00	125.00
Doulton/Disney	SW 12	50.00	70.00	30.00	75.00

SW 5 / SW 13
DOPEY™
Style Two

Designer:	Shane Ridge
Height:	3 ½", 8.9 cm
Colour:	Yellow coat and trousers, purple hat, black belt
Issued:	SW 5 1997 in a limited edition of 2,000
	SW 13 1998 - 2002
Series:	Snow White and the Seven Dwarfs (Series Two)

Back Stamp	Beswick Number	Price U.S. $	Can. $	U.K. £	Aust. $
Doulton/Disney 60th	SW 5	85.00	120.00	50.00	125.00
Doulton/Disney	SW 13	50.00	70.00	30.00	75.00

SW 6 / SW 14
SNEEZY™
Style Two

Designer:	Warren Platt
Height:	3 ½", 8.9 cm
Colour:	Light brown tunic, dark brown trousers, black belt
Issued:	SW 6 1997 in a limited edition of 2,000
	SW 14 1998 - 2002
Series:	Snow White and the Seven Dwarfs (Series Two)

Back Stamp	Doulton Number	Price U.S. $	Can. $	U.K. £	Aust. $
Doulton/Disney 60th	SW 6	85.00	120.00	50.00	125.00
Doulton/Disney	SW 14	50.00	70.00	30.00	75.00

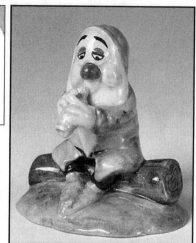

SW 7 / SW 15
SLEEPY™
Style Two

Designer:	Warren Platt
Height:	3 ½", 8.9 cm
Colour:	Beige tunic, dark brown trousers, green hat and a yellow bottle
Issued:	SW 7 1997 in a limited edition of 2,000
	SW 15 1998 - 2002
Series:	Snow White and the Seven Dwarfs (Series Two)

Back Stamp	Doulton Number	Price U.S. $	Can. $	U.K. £	Aust. $
Doulton/Disney 60th	SW 7	85.00	120.00	50.00	125.00
Doulton/Disney	SW 15	50.00	70.00	30.00	75.00

SW 8 / SW 16
BASHFUL™
Style Two

Designer:	Amanda Hughes-Lubeck
Height:	3 ½", 8.9 cm
Colour:	Dark yellow tunic, light brown trousers, green hat
Issued:	SW 8 1997 in a limited edition of 2,000
	SW 16 1998 - 2002
Series:	Snow White and the Seven Dwarfs (Series Two)

Back Stamp	Doulton Number	Price U.S. $	Can. $	U.K. £	Aust. $
Doulton/Disney 60th	SW 8	85.00	120.00	50.00	125.00
Doulton/Disney	SW 16	50.00	70.00	30.00	75.00

SW 17
DOPEY™ BY CANDLELIGHT

Designer:	Shane Ridge
Height:	3 ½", 8.9 cm
Colour:	Green
Issued:	1998 - 2002
Series:	Snow White and the Seven Dwarfs

Back Stamp	Doulton Number	Price U.S. $	Can. $	U.K. £	Aust. $
Doulton/Disney	SW 17	60.00	80.00	35.00	90.00

SW 18
BASHFUL'S™ MELODY

Designer:	Graham Tongue
Modeller:	Graham Tongue
Height:	3 ½", 8.9 cm
Colour:	Blue
Issued:	1998 - 2002
Series:	Snow White and the Seven Dwarfs

Back Stamp	Doulton Number	Price			
		U.S. $	Can. $	U.K. £	Aust. $
Doulton/Disney	SW 18	60.00	80.00	35.00	90.00

SW 19
DOC™ WITH LANTERN

Designer:	Warren Platt
Modeller:	Warren Platt
Height:	3 ½", 8.9 cm
Colour:	Red and yellow
Issued:	1999 - 2002
Series:	Snow White and the Seven Dwarfs

Back Stamp	Doulton Number	Price			
		U.S. $	Can. $	U.K. £	Aust. $
Doulton/Disney	SW 19	60.00	80.00	35.00	90.00

SW 20
GRUMPY'S™ BATHTIME

Designer:	Shane Ridge
Modeller:	Shane Ridge
Height:	3 ½", 8.9 cm
Colour:	White, brown, red and yellow
Issued:	1999 - 1999
Series:	Snow White and the Seven Dwarfs

Back Stamp	Doulton Number	Price			
		U.S. $	Can. $	U.K. £	Aust. $
Doulton/Disney	SW 20	175.00	250.00	100.00	275.00

Note: Serial numbered

SW 21
DOPEY'S™ FIRST KISS

Designer:	Disney
Modeller:	Shane Ridge
Height:	5 ¼", 13.3 cm
Colour:	Yellow, blue, red and green
Issued:	2000 in a limited edition of 2,000
Series:	1. Disney Classics
	2. Tableau

Back Stamp	Doulton Number	Price			
		U.S. $	Can. $	U.K. £	Aust. $
Doulton/Disney	SW 21	250.00	350.00	150.00	375.00

WINNIE THE POOH

BESWICK SERIES 1968-1990

2193
WINNIE THE POOH™

Designer:	Albert Hallam
Height:	2 ½", 6.4 cm
Colour:	Golden brown and red
Issued:	1968 - 1990
Series:	Winnie The Pooh

Back Stamp	Beswick Number	Price U.S. $	Can. $	U.K. £	Aust. $
Beswick Gold	2193	150.00	200.00	95.00	225.00
Beswick Brown	2193	125.00	175.00	80.00	200.00

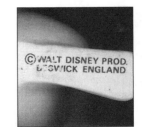

2196
EEYORE™

Designer:	Albert Hallam
Height:	2", 5.0 cm
Colour:	Grey with black markings
Issued:	1968 - 1990
Series:	Winnie The Pooh

Back Stamp	Beswick Number	Price U.S. $	Can. $	U.K. £	Aust. $
Beswick Gold	2196	125.00	175.00	75.00	200.00
Beswick Brown	2196	100.00	150.00	65.00	175.00

2214
PIGLET™

Designer:	Albert Hallam
Height:	2 ¾", 7.0 cm
Colour:	Pink and red
Issued:	1968 - 1990
Series:	Winnie The Pooh

Back Stamp	Beswick Number	Price U.S. $	Can. $	U.K. £	Aust. $
Beswick Gold	2214	150.00	200.00	95.00	225.00
Beswick Brown	2214	125.00	175.00	80.00	200.00

2215
RABBIT™

Designer:	Albert Hallam
Height:	3 ¼", 8.3 cm
Colour:	Brown and beige
Issued:	1968 - 1990
Series:	Winnie The Pooh

Back Stamp	Beswick Number	Price			
		U.S. $	Can. $	U.K. £	Aust. $
Beswick Gold	2215	175.00	250.00	110.00	275.00
Beswick Brown	2215	150.00	225.00	95.00	250.00

2216
OWL™

Designer:	Albert Hallam
Height:	3", 7.6 cm
Colour:	Brown, white and black
Issued:	1968 - 1990
Series:	Winnie The Pooh

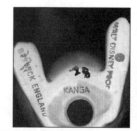

Back Stamp	Beswick Number	Price			
		U.S. $	Can. $	U.K. £	Aust. $
Beswick Gold	2216	125.00	175.00	75.00	200.00
Beswick Brown	2216	100.00	150.00	65.00	175.00

2217
KANGA™

Designer:	Albert Hallam
Height:	3 ¼", 8.3 cm
Colour:	Dark and light brown
Issued:	1968 - 1990
Series:	Winnie The Pooh

Back Stamp	Beswick Number	Price			
		U.S. $	Can. $	U.K. £	Aust. $
Beswick Gold	2217	150.00	200.00	95.00	225.00
Beswick Brown	2217	125.00	175.00	80.00	200.00

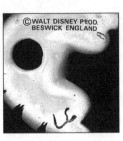

2394
TIGGER™

Designer:	Graham Tongue
Height:	3", 7.6 cm
Colour:	Yellow with black stripes
Issued:	1971 - 1990
Series:	Winnie The Pooh

Back Stamp	Beswick Number	Price			
		U.S. $	Can. $	U.K. £	Aust. $
Beswick Gold	2394	275.00	375.00	175.00	400.00
Beswick Brown	2394	200.00	275.00	135.00	300.00

2395
CHRISTOPHER ROBIN™
Style One

Designer:	Graham Tongue
Height:	4 ¾", 12.1 cm
Colour:	Yellow, blue and white
Issued:	1971 - 1990
Series:	Winnie The Pooh

Back Stamp	Beswick Number	Price			
		U.S. $	Can. $	U.K. £	Aust. $
Beswick Gold	2395	275.00	375.00	175.00	400.00
Beswick Brown	2395	250.00	350.00	150.00	375.00

WINNIE THE POOH
ROYAL DOULTON SERIES 1996 to the present

WP 1
WINNIE THE POOH™ AND THE HONEY POT

Designer:	Warren Platt
Height:	2 ½", 6.5 cm
Colour:	Yellow bear, red jersey, red-brown honey pot
Issued:	1996 - 1999
Series:	Winnie the Pooh and Friends from the Hundred Acre Wood

Back Stamp	Doulton Number	Price			
		U.S. $	Can. $	U.K. £	Aust. $
BK-1	WP 1 / 70th	80.00	115.00	50.00	125.00
BK-2	WP 1	40.00	60.00	25.00	65.00

WP 2
POOH™ AND PIGLET™ THE WINDY DAY

Designer:	Martyn Alcock
Height:	3 ¼", 8.3 cm
Colour:	Yellow bear, pink piglet with green suit, light brown base
Issued:	1996 - 2002
Series:	Winnie the Pooh and Friends from the Hundred Acre Wood

Back Stamp	Doulton Number	Price			
		U.S. $	Can. $	U.K. £	Aust. $
BK-1	WP 2 / 70th	80.00	115.00	50.00	125.00
BK-2	WP 2	50.00	75.00	30.00	85.00

WP 3
WINNIE THE POOH™ AND THE PAW-MARKS

Designer:	Warren Platt
Height:	2 ¾", 7.0 cm
Colour:	Yellow bear, red jersey
Issued:	1996 - 1997
Series:	Winnie the Pooh and Friends from the Hundred Acre Wood

Back Stamp	Doulton Number	Price			
		U.S. $	Can. $	U.K. £	Aust. $
BK-1	WP 3 / 70th	80.00	115.00	50.00	125.00
BK-2	WP 3	65.00	90.00	40.00	95.00

WP 4
WINNIE THE POOH™ IN THE ARMCHAIR

Designer:	Shane Ridge
Height:	3 ¼", 8.3 cm
Colour:	Yellow bear, pink armchair
Issued:	1996 - 1998
Series:	Winnie the Pooh and Friends from the Hundred Acre Wood

Back Stamp	Doulton Number	Price			
		U.S. $	Can. $	U.K. £	Aust. $
BK-1	WP 4 / 70th	75.00	100.00	45.00	110.00
BK-2	WP 4	55.00	80.00	35.00	90.00

WP 5
PIGLET™ AND THE BALLOON

Designer:	Warren Platt
Height:	2 ¾", 7.0 cm
Colour:	Pink piglet, green suit, blue balloon, light brown base
Issued:	1996 - 1998
Series:	Winnie the Pooh and Friends from the Hundred Acre Wood

Back Stamp	Doulton Number	Price			
		U.S. $	Can. $	U.K. £	Aust. $
BK-1	WP 5 / 70th	75.00	100.00	45.00	110.00
BK-2	WP 5	55.00	80.00	35.00	90.00

WP 6
TIGGER™ SIGNS THE RISSOLUTION

Designer:	Martyn Alcock
Height:	1 ¾", 4.5 cm
Colour:	Yellow and black
Issued:	1996 - 2000
Series:	Winnie the Pooh and Friends from the Hundred Acre Wood

Back Stamp	Doulton Number	Price			
		U.S. $	Can. $	U.K. £	Aust. $
BK-1	WP 6 / 70th	75.00	100.00	45.00	110.00
BK-2	WP 6	55.00	80.00	35.00	90.00

WP 7
EEYORE'S™ TAIL

Designer:	Shane Ridge
Height:	3 ½", 8.9 cm
Colour:	Grey donkey with black markings, pink bow
Issued:	1996 - 1999
Series:	Winnie the Pooh and Friends from the Hundred Acre Wood

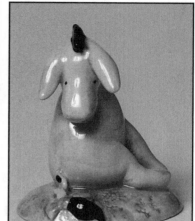

Back Stamp	Doulton Number	Price			
		U.S. $	Can. $	U.K. £	Aust. $
BK-1	WP 7 / 70th	75.00	100.00	45.00	110.00
BK-2	WP 7	50.00	75.00	30.00	85.00

WP 8
KANGA™ AND ROO™

Designer:	Martyn Alcock
Height:	3 ½", 8.9 cm
Colour:	Dark and light brown kangaroos
Issued:	1996 - 1998
Series:	Winnie the Pooh and Friends from the Hundred Acre Wood

Back Stamp	Doulton Number	Price			
		U.S. $	Can. $	U.K. £	Aust. $
BK-1	WP 8 / 70th	90.00	125.00	55.00	135.00
BK-2	WP 8	50.00	75.00	30.00	85.00

WP 9
CHRISTOPHER ROBIN™
Style Two

Designer:	Shane Ridge
Height:	5 ½", 14.0 cm
Colour:	White and blue checkered shirt, blue shorts, black wellingtons, red-brown hair
Issued:	1996 - 2001
Series:	Winnie the Pooh and Friends from the Hundred Acre Wood

Back Stamp	Doulton Number	Price			
		U.S. $	Can. $	U.K. £	Aust. $
BK-1	WP 9 / 70th	80.00	115.00	50.00	125.00
BK-2	WP 9	50.00	75.00	30.00	85.00

WP 10
CHRISTOPHER ROBIN™ AND POOH™

Designer:	Shane Ridge
Height:	3 ¼", 8.5 cm
Colour:	Light blue shirt and shorts, black boots, reddish brown hair, yellow bear
Issued:	1996 - 1997
Series:	Winnie the Pooh and Friends from the Hundred Acre Wood

Back Stamp	Doulton Number	Price			
		U.S. $	Can. $	U.K. £	Aust. $
BK-1	WP 10 / 70th	125.00	175.00	80.00	190.00
BK-2	WP 10	80.00	115.00	50.00	125.00

WP 11
POOH™ LIGHTS THE CANDLE

Designer:	Graham Tongue
Height:	3 ½", 8.9 cm
Colour:	Yellow bear with white candle and hat
Issued:	1997 - 1998
Series:	Winnie the Pooh and Friends from the Hundred Acre Wood

Back Stamp	Doulton Number	Price			
		U.S. $	Can. $	U.K. £	Aust. $
BK-2	WP 11	40.00	60.00	25.00	65.00

WP 12
POOH™ COUNTING THE HONEYPOTS

Designer:	Martyn Alcock
Height:	3 ½", 8.9 cm
Colour:	Yellow bear, brown honeypots
Issued:	1997 - 1999
Series:	Winnie the Pooh and Friends from the Hundred Acre Wood

Back Stamp	Doulton Number	Price			
		U.S. $	Can. $	U.K. £	Aust. $
BK-2	WP 12	50.00	75.00	30.00	85.00

WP 13
PIGLET™ PICKING THE VIOLETS

Designer: Graham Tongue
Height: 2 ½", 6.4 cm
Colour: Pink, light and dark greens
Issued: 1997 - 2000
Series: Winnie the Pooh and Friends
from the Hundred Acre Wood

Back Stamp	Doulton Number	Price			
		U.S. $	Can. $	U.K. £	Aust. $
BK-2	WP 13	40.00	60.00	25.00	65.00

WP 14
EEYORE'S™ BIRTHDAY

Designer: Martyn Alcock
Height: 2 ¾", 7.0 cm
Colour: Grey and black
Issued: 1997 - 2002
Series: Winnie the Pooh and Friends
from the Hundred Acre Wood

Back Stamp	Doulton Number	Price			
		U.S. $	Can. $	U.K. £	Aust. $
BK-2	WP 14	40.00	60.00	25.00	65.00

WP 15
EEYORE™ LOSES A TAIL

Designer: Martyn Alcock
Height: 4", 10.1 cm
Colour: Pink, yellow, grey,
green and brown
Issued: 1997 in a limited edition of 5,000
Series: 1. Tableau
2. Winnie the Pooh and Friends
from the Hundred Acre Wood

Back Stamp	Doulton Number	Price			
		U.S. $	Can. $	U.K. £	Aust. $
Doulton	WP 15	300.00	450.00	175.00	475.00

WP 16
POOH'S™ BLUE BALLOON (MONEY BOX)

Designer:	Shane Ridge
Height:	4 ¼", 10.8 cm
Colour:	Yellow bear, pink pig wearing green suit, white balloon with dark blue rope
Issued:	1997 - 1998
Series:	Winnie the Pooh and Friends from the Hundred Acre Wood

| Back Stamp | Doulton Number | Price | | | |
		U.S. $	Can. $	U.K. £	Aust. $
Doulton	WP 16	80.00	115.00	50.00	125.00

WP 17
WOL™ SIGNS THE RISSOLUTION

Designer:	Martyn Alcock
Height:	3 ¾", 9.5 cm
Colour:	Grey and black
Issued:	1998 in a special edition of 2,500
Series:	Winnie the Pooh and Friends from the Hundred Acre Wood

| Back Stamp | Doulton Number | Price | | | |
		U.S. $	Can. $	U.K. £	Aust. $
Doulton	WP 17	250.00	350.00	150.00	375.00

WP 18
WINNIE THE POOH™ AND THE PRESENT

Designer:	Graham Tongue
Height:	3 ¾", 9.5 cm
Colour:	Yellow and brown
Issued:	1999 - 2002
Series:	Winnie the Pooh and Friends from the Hundred Acre Wood

| Back Stamp | Doulton Number | Price | | | |
		U.S. $	Can. $	U.K. £	Aust. $
Doulton	WP 18	40.00	60.00	25.00	65.00

WP 19
WINNIE THE POOH™ AND THE FAIR-SIZED BASKET

Designer:	Graham Tongue
Height:	2 ¾", 7.0 cm
Colour:	Yellow bear, brown basket
Issued:	1999 - 2002
Series:	Winnie the Pooh and Friends from the Hundred Acre Wood

Back Stamp	Doulton Number	Price			
		U.S. $	Can. $	U.K. £	Aust. $
Doulton	WP 19	40.00	60.00	25.00	65.00

WP 20
THE MORE IT SNOWS, TIDDELY POM™

Designer:	Shane Ridge
Height:	3 ¼", 8.3 cm
Colour:	Yellow, red, pink and green
Issued:	1999-2002
Series:	Winnie the Pooh and Friends from the Hundred Acre Wood

Back Stamp	Doulton Number	Price			
		U.S. $	Can. $	U.K. £	Aust. $
Doulton	WP 20	55.00	80.00	35.00	90.00

WP 21
SUMMER'S DAY PICNIC™

Designer:	Warren Platt
Length:	2 ½", 5.7 cm
Colour:	Blue, yellow and green
Issued:	1998 in a limited editionof 5,000
Series:	1. Tableau
	2. Winnie the Pooh and Friends from the Hundred Acre Wood

Back Stamp	Doulton Number	Price			
		U.S. $	Can. $	U.K. £	Aust. $
Doulton	WP 21	200.00	275.00	125.00	325.00

WP 22
I'VE FOUND SOMEBODY JUST LIKE ME™

Designer:	Martyn Alcock
Length:	5 ¼", 13.3 cm
Colour:	Yellow, black, blue and white
Issued:	1999 in a limited edition of 5,000
Series:	1. Tableau
	2. Winnie the Pooh and Friends from the Hundred Acre Wood

Back Stamp	Doulton Number	Price			
		U.S. $	Can. $	U.K. £	Aust. $
Doulton	WP 22	200.00	275.00	125.00	300.00

WP 23
RABBIT™ READS THE PLAN

Designer:	Martyn Alcock
Height:	4 ½", 11.9 cm
Colour:	Grey rabbit, pink inner ears
Issued:	1999 - 1999
Series:	Classic Pooh

Back Stamp	Doulton Number	Price			
		U.S. $	Can. $	U.K. £	Aust. $
Doulton	WP 23	50.00	75.00	30.00	85.00

WP 24
HOW SWEET TO BE A CLOUD™ (CLOCK)

Designer:	Warren Platt
Height:	4 ½", 11.9 cm
Colour:	Blue, white, yellow and red
Issued:	2000 - 2000
Series:	Classic Pooh

Back Stamp	Doulton Number	Price			
		U.S. $	Can. $	U.K. £	Aust. $
Doulton	WP 24	125.00	175.00	70.00	200.00

WP 25
EEYORE™ NOSE TO THE GROUND

Designer:	Martyn Alcock
Height:	3 ¾", 9.5 cm
Size:	Large
Colour:	Grey and black
Issued:	2000 in a limited edition of 2,000
Series:	Large Size

Back Stamp	Doulton Number	Price			
		U.S. $	Can. $	U.K. £	Aust. $
Doulton	WP 25	125.00	175.00	80.00	200.00

WP 26
PIGLET™ PLANTING A HAYCORN

Designer:	Martyn Alcock
Height:	3 ¾", 9.5 cm
Size:	Large
Colour:	Pink, green and brown
Issued:	2000 in a limited edition of 2,000
Series:	Large Size

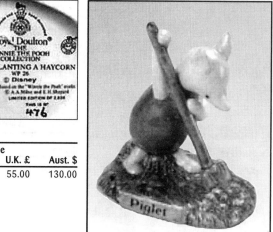

Back Stamp	Doulton Number	Price			
		U.S. $	Can. $	U.K. £	Aust. $
Doulton	WP 26	85.00	120.00	55.00	130.00

WP 27
TIGGER™ LOVES TIGGER LILIES

Designer:	Martyn Alcock
Height:	4 ¼", 10.8 cm
Size:	Large
Colour:	Brown, black and red
Issued:	2000 in a limited edition of 2,000
Series:	Large Size

Back Stamp	Doulton Number	Price			
		U.S. $	Can. $	U.K. £	Aust. $
Doulton	WP 27	125.00	175.00	70.00	200.00

WP 28
POOH BEGAN TO EAT™

Designer:	Shane Ridge
Height:	3 ¾", 9.5 cm
Size:	Large
Colour:	Yellow and green
Issued:	2000 in a limited edition of 2,000
Series:	Large Size

Back Stamp	Doulton Number	Price			
		U.S. $	Can. $	U.K. £	Aust. $
Doulton	WP 28	125.00	175.00	80.00	200.00

WP 29
PIGLET AND THE HONEY POT™

Designer:	Amanda Hughes-Lubeck
Height:	2 ½", 6.4 cm
Colour:	Pink, green, grey and yellow
Issued:	2000 - 2002
Series:	Classic Pooh

Back Stamp	Doulton Number	Price			
		U.S. $	Can. $	U.K. £	Aust. $
Doulton	WP 29	50.00	75.00	30.00	85.00

WP 30
TIGGER PLAYS BALL™

Designer:	Warren Platt
Height:	3", 7.6 cm
Colour:	Brown, black and yellow
Issued:	2000 - 2002
Series:	Classic Pooh

Back Stamp	Doulton Number	Price			
		U.S. $	Can. $	U.K. £	Aust. $
Doulton	WP 30	100.00	150.00	60.00	170.00

WP 31
THE BRAIN OF POOH™

Designer:	Amanda Hughes-Lubeck
Height:	4", 10.1 cm
Colour:	Black, grey, yellow and green
Issued:	2000 in a limited edition of 5,000
Series:	Classic Pooh

Back Stamp	Doulton Number	Price			
		U.S. $	Can. $	U.K. £	Aust. $
Doulton	WP 31	300.00	425.00	195.00	450.00

WP 32
CHRISTOPHER READS TO POOH™

Designer:	Shane Ridge
Height:	3 ½", 8.9 cm
Colour:	Yellow, red, white and black
Issued:	2001 (time limited)
Series:	Classic Pooh

Back Stamp	Doulton Number	Price			
		U.S. $	Can. $	U.K. £	Aust. $
Doulton	WP 32	135.00	185.00	85.00	200.00

WP 33
POOH™ AND THE PARTY HAT

Designer:	Amander Hughes-Lubeck
Height:	2 ¾", 7.0 cm
Colour:	Yellow bear, red hat, pale blue ribbon
Issued:	2001-2002
Series:	Classic Pooh

Back Stamp	Doulton Number	Price			
		U.S. $	Can. $	U.K. £	Aust. $
Doulton	WP 33	65.00	90.00	40.00	95.00

WP 34
GOING SLEDGING™

Designer:	Shane Ridge
Height:	4", 10.1 cm
Colour:	Blue, yellow, red, brown, green and grey
Issued:	2001 in a limited edition of 5,000
Series:	Classic Pooh

Back Stamp	Doulton Number	Price			
		U.S. $	Can. $	U.K. £	Aust. $
Doulton	WP 34	200.00	275.00	125.00	300.00

WP 35
WOL™ AND THE HONEYPOT

Designer:	Warren Platt
Height:	3 ¼", 8.3 cm
Colour:	Grey, white, brown and tan
Issued:	2001 - 2002
Series:	Classic Pooh

Back Stamp	Doulton Number	Price			
		U.S. $	Can. $	U.K. £	Aust. $
Doulton	WP 35	60.00	90.00	35.00	110.00

WP 36
UNDER THE NAME MR. SANDERS™

Designer:	Unknown
Height:	3", 7.6 cm
Colour:	Yellow bear, brown log
Issued:	2001 - 2002
Series:	Classic Pooh

Back Stamp	Doulton Number	Price			
		U.S. $	Can. $	U.K. £	Aust. $
Doulton	WP 36	60.00	90.00	35.00	110.00

WALT DISNEY
WINNIE THE POOH

WINNIE THE POOH AND
THE HONEY POT

POOH AND PIGLET THE WINDY DAY

WINNIE THE POOH AND
THE PAW-MARKS

WINNIE THE POOH
IN THE ARMCHAIR

PIGLET AND THE BALLOON

TIGGER SIGNS THE RISSOLUTION

EEYORE'S TAIL

KANGA AND ROO

WALT DISNEY
WINNIE THE POOH

CHRISTOPHER ROBIN
Style Two

CHRISTOPHER ROBIN AND POOH

POOH LIGHTS THE CANDLE

POOH COUNTING THE HONEY POTS

PIGLET PICKING THE VIOLETS

EEYORE'S BIRTHDAY

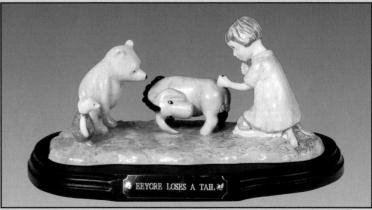

EEYORE LOSES A TAIL

WALT DISNEY
WINNIE THE POOH

POOH'S BLUE BALLOON (MONEY BOX)

WOL SIGNS THE RISSOLUTION

WINNIE THE POOH AND
THE PRESENT

WINNIE THE POOH AND
THE FAIR-SIZED BASKET

THE MORE IT SNOWS, TIDDELY POM

SUMMER'S DAY PICNIC

I'VE FOUND SOMEBODY
JUST LIKE ME

RABBIT READS THE PLAN

WALT DISNEY
WINNIE THE POOH

HOW SWEET TO BE A CLOUD
(CLOCK)

EEYORE NOSE TO THE GROUND

PIGLET PLANTING A HAYCORN

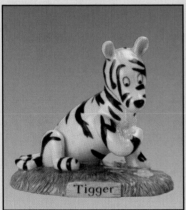

TIGGER LOVES TIGGER LILIES

POOH BEGAN TO EAT

PIGLET AND THE HONEY POT

TIGGER PLAYS BALL

THE BRAIN OF POOH

POOH AND PARTY HAT

WALT DISNEY
WINNIE THE POOH

WOL AND THE HONEYPOT

UNDER THE NAME MR. SANDERS

ALL THE FLOWERS ARE
WAKING UP (SPRING)

SUMMER IS FULL
OF FLUTTERY SURPRISES (SUMMER)

LOVE MAKES ALL YOUR
BOTHERS DISAPPEAR

A PRESENT FOR ME? HOW GRAND!

A LITTLE TREE TRIMMING IS IN ORDER, THE MOST PERFECT TREE IN ALL THE
WOOD, CHRISTOPHER DRESSES THE TREE

SOMETIMES AUTUMN
TICKLES YOUR NOSE (AUTUMN)

WALT DISNEY
WINNIE THE POOH

OH DEAR, BATH TIMES HERE!

TIGGER'S SPLASH TIME

A LITTLE SPONGE FOR A
LITTLE PIGLET

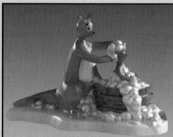

A CLEAN LITTLE ROO IS BEST!

TOOT TOOT WENT THE WHISTLE

A CLEAN BEAR IS A HAPPY BEAR

A SLEEPY DAY IN THE
HUNDRED ACRE WOOD

WHO'S CAKE? POOH'S CAKE?

EEYORE MADE A WINTERY WISH
(WINTER)

BOUNCY BOUNCY BOO-TO-YOU!

WALT DISNEY
WINNIE THE POOH

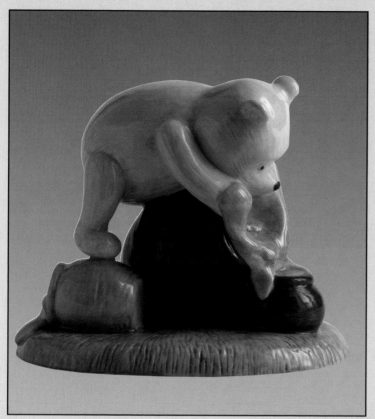

ISN'T IT FUNNY HOW A BEAR LIKES HONEY

WHERE DOES THE WIND COME FROM? (top)
RUM-TUM-TUM WINNIE ON HIS DRUM (bottom)

A BIG NOISE FOR A LITTLE PIGLET

IT'S HONEY ALL THE WAY DOWN

WALT DISNEY
PETER PAN

PETER PAN
Style Two

TINKER BELL
Style Two

WENDY

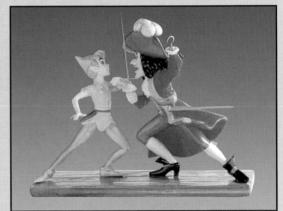

THE DUEL

CAPTAIN HOOK

TIC TOC CROCODILE

HEADING FOR SCULL ROCK

WP 37
ALL THE FLOWERS ARE WAKING UP (Spring)™

Designer:	Warren Platt
Height:	3", 7.6 cm
Colour:	Yellow bear, grey pot with pink flowers
Issued:	2002 to the present
Series:	1. Classic Pooh
	2. Four Seasons

Back Stamp	Doulton Number	Price			
		U.S. $	Can. $	U.K. £	Aust. $
Doulton	WP 37	N/I	N/I	25.00	N/I

WP 38
SUMMER IS FULL OF FLUTTERY SURPRISES (Summer)™

Designer:	Warren Platt
Height:	2 ½", 6.4 cm
Colour:	Pink, green and lilac
Issued:	2002 to the present
Series:	Four Seasons

Back Stamp	Doulton Number	Price			
		U.S. $	Can. $	U.K. £	Aust. $
Doulton	WP 38	N/I	N/I	22.50	N/I

WP 39
LOVE MAKES ALL YOUR BOTHERS DISAPPEAR™

Designer:	Shane Ridge
Height:	2 ¼", 5.7 cm
Colour:	Yellow, red, white and green
Issued:	2002 to the present
Series:	Love and Friendship

Back Stamp	Doulton Number	Price			
		U.S. $	Can. $	U.K. £	Aust. $
Doulton	WP 39	N/I	N/I	25.00	N/I

WP 40
A PRESENT FOR ME? HOW GRAND!™

Designer:	Shane Ridge
Height:	3 ¼", 8.3 cm
Colour:	Yellow bear, red gift box, purple ribbon
Issued:	2002 - 2002
Series:	Birthday Collection

Back Stamp	Doulton Number	Price			
		U.S. $	Can. $	U.K. £	Aust. $
Doulton	WP 40	N/I	N/I	25.00	N/I

WP 41
A LITTLE TREE TRIMMING IS IN ORDER™

Designer:	Martyn Alcock
Height:	3 ¾", 9.6 cm
Colour:	Yellow bear, blue nightshirt and cap, red tree ornament
Issued:	2002 - 2002
Series:	Christmas Collection

Back Stamp	Doulton Number	Price			
		U.S. $	Can. $	U.K. £	Aust. $
Doulton	WP 41	N/I	N/I	25.00	N/I

Note: Set with The Most Perfect Tree in all the Wood (WP 42) and Christopher Dresses the Tree (WP 57).

WP 42
THE MOST PERFECT TREE IN ALL THE WOOD™

Designer:	Martyn Alcock
Height:	4 ¾", 12.1 cm
Colour:	Green tree, red and purple decorations
Issued:	2002 - 2002
Series:	Christmas Collection

Back Stamp	Doulton Number	Price			
		U.S. $	Can. $	U.K. £	Aust. $
Doulton	WP 42	N/I	N/I	25.00	N/I

Note: Set with A Little Tree Trimming is in Order (WP 41) and Christopher Dresses the Tree (WP 57).

WP 43
SOMETIMES AUTUMN TICKLES
YOUR NOSE™ (Autumn)

Designer:	Shane Ridge
Height:	3", 7.6 cm
Colour:	Tan, black, pink, green and brown
Issued:	2002 to the present
Series:	Four Seasons

Back Stamp	Doulton Number	Price			
		U.S. $	Can. $	U.K. £	Aust. $
Doulton	WP 43	N/I	N/I	25.00	N/I

WP 44
EEYORE™ MADE A WINTERY WISH (Winter)

Designer:	Shane Ridge
Height:	3 ¼", 8.3 cm
Colour:	Grey, white and pink
Issued:	2002 to the present
Series:	Four Seasons

Back Stamp	Doulton Number	Price			
		U.S. $	Can. $	U.K. £	Aust. $
Doulton	WP 44	N/I	N/I	25.00	N/I

WP 45
WHO'S CAKE? POOH'S™ CAKE?

Designer:	E. H. Shephard
Height:	3 ¼", 8.3 cm
Colour:	Pink piglet wearing a green suit; pink, white and yellow cake
Issued:	2003 - 2003
Series:	Birthday Collection

Back Stamp	Doulton Number	Price			
		U.S. $	Can. $	U.K. £	Aust. $
Doulton	WP 45	N/I	N/I	25.00	N/I

WP 46
I LOVE YOU SO MUCH BEAR™

Designer:	E. H. Shephard
Height:	4", 10.1 cm
Colour:	Yellow, pink and green
Issued:	2003 to the present
Series:	Love and Friendship

Back Stamp	Doulton Number	Price			
		U.S. $	Can. $	U.K. £	Aust. $
Doulton	WP 46	N/I	N/I	35.00	N/I

WP 47
TOOT TOOT WENT THE WHISTLE™

Designer:	E. H. Shephard
Height:	3 ¼", 8.3 cm
Colour:	Yellow bear, black train, red and black train station, grey train tracks
Issued:	2003 to the present

Back Stamp	Doulton Number	Price			
		U.S. $	Can. $	U.K. £	Aust. $
Doulton	WP 47	N/I	N/I	30.00	N/I

WP 48
ANY HUNNY LEFT FOR ME?™

Designer:	E. H. Shephard
Height:	4", 10.1 cm
Colour:	Yellow bear, blue and brown honey pots
Issued:	2003 to the present

Back Stamp	Doulton Number	Price			
		U.S. $	Can. $	U.K. £	Aust. $
Doulton	WP 48	N/I	N/I	30.00	N/I

WP 49
A CLEAN BEAR IS A HAPPY BEAR™

Designer:	E. H. Shephard
Height:	3 ¼", 8.3 cm
Colour:	Yellow bear and ducks, brown washtub, blue and white bubbles, green towel
Issued:	2003 to the present
Series:	Bathtime Collection

Back Stamp	Doulton Number	Price			
		U.S. $	Can. $	U.K. £	Aust. $
Doulton	WP 49	N/I	N/I	25.00	N/I

WP 50
PRESENTS AND PARTIES™

Designer:	E. H. Shephard
Height:	4 ¼", 10.8 cm
Colour:	Yellow bear, blue hat, green gift box with pink ribbon, white cake
Issued:	2003 to the present
Series:	Birthday Collection

Back Stamp	Doulton Number	Price			
		U.S. $	Can. $	U.K. £	Aust. $
Doulton	WP 50	N/I	N/I	30.00	N/I

WP 51
A LITTLE SPONGE FOR A LITTLE PIGLET™

Designer:	E. H. Shephard
Height:	3 ¼", 8.3 cm
Colour:	Pink piglet wearing green suit, brown washtub, blue and white bubbles, grey bucket
Issued:	2003 to the present
Series:	Bathtime Collection

Back Stamp	Doulton Number	Price			
		U.S. $	Can. $	U.K. £	Aust. $
Doulton	WP 51	N/I	N/I	25.00	N/I

WP 52
BOUNCY BOUNCY BOO-TO-YOU!™

Designer:	E. H. Shephard
Height:	3 ¼", 8.3 cm
Colour:	Orange and black tiger, green, yellow and blue toy box
Issued:	2003 to the present

Back Stamp	Doulton Number	Price			
		U.S. $	Can. $	U.K. £	Aust. $
Doulton	WP 52	N/I	N/I	30.00	N/I

WP 53
A SLEEPY DAY IN THE HUNDRED ACRE WOOD™

Designer:	E. H. Shephard
Height:	4 ¾", 12.1 cm
Colour:	Grey and black donkey, yellow bear, brown and black tiger, pink piglet wearing a green suit
Issued:	2003 to the present

Back Stamp	Doulton Number	Price			
		U.S. $	Can. $	U.K. £	Aust. $
Doulton	WP 53	N/I	N/I	70.00	N/I

WP 54
A CLEAN LITTLE ROO™ IS BEST!

Designer:	E. H. Shephard
Height:	4 ¾", 12.1 cm
Colour:	Brown kangaroos, brown washtub, blue and white bubbles
Issued:	2003 to the present
Series:	Bathtime Collection

Back Stamp	Doulton Number	Price			
		U.S. $	Can. $	U.K. £	Aust. $
Doulton	WP 54	N/i	N/I	30.00	N/I

WP 55/56
PUSH...PULL! COME ON POOH™ (Bookends)

Designer:	E. H. Shephard
Height:	4 ¾". 12.1 cm
Colour:	Left: Grey rabbit, brown, blue, pink and yellow honey pots
	Right: Grey donkey, brown and black tiger, pink piglet
Issued:	2003 in a limited edition of 2,000 pairs

Back Stamp	Doulton Number	Price			
		U.S. $	Can. $	U.K. £	Aust. $
Doulton	WP 55/56	N/I	N/I	80.00	N/I

WP 57
CHRISTOPHER™ DRESSES THE TREE

Designer:	E. H. Shephard
Height:	4 ¾", 12.1 cm
Colour:	Green sweater, blue trousers, red scarf, red and white hat, black boots
Issued:	2003 to the present
Series:	Christmas Collection

Back Stamp	Doulton Number	Price			
		U.S. $	Can. $	U.K. £	Aust. $
Doulton	WP 57	N/I	N/I	25.00	N/I

Note: Set with A Little Tree Trimming (WP 41) and The Most Perfext Tree in all the Wood (WP 42).

WP 58
TIGGER'S™ SPLASH TIME

Designer:	E. H. Shephard
Height:	4", 10.1 cm
Colour:	Orange and black striped tiper, brown washtub
Issued:	2003 to the present
Series:	Bathtime Collection

Back Stamp	Doulton Number	Price			
		U.S. $	Can. $	U.K. £	Aust. $
Doulton	WP 58	N/I	N/I	30.00	N/I

WP 59
OH DEAR BATHTIME'S HERE!™

Designer:	E. H. Shephard
Height:	2 ¾", 7.0 cm
Colour:	Grey and black donkey, brown basket
Issued:	2003 to the present
Series:	Bathtime Collection

Back	Doulton	Price			
Stamp	Number	U.S. $	Can. $	U.K. £	Aust. $
Doulton	WP 59	N/I	N/I	30.00	N/I

WP 60
ISN'T IT FUNNY HOW A BEAR LIKES HONEY™

Designer:	E. H. Shephard
Height:	4 ¼", 10.8 cm
Colour:	Yellow bear, blue and purple honey pots
Issued:	2003 to the present

Back	Doulton	Price			
Stamp	Number	U.S. $	Can. $	U.K. £	Aust. $
Doulton	WP 60	N/I	N/I	25.00	N/I

WP 61
IT'S HONEY ALL THE WAY DOWN™

Designer:	E. H. Shephard
Height:	4 ¼", 10.8 cm
Colour:	Yellow bear, brown tree trunk
Issued:	2003 to the present

Back	Doulton	Price			
Stamp	Number	U.S. $	Can. $	U.K. £	Aust. $
Doulton	WP 61	N/I	N/I	30.00	N/I

WP 62
WHERE DOES THE WIND COME FROM?™

Designer:	E. H. Shephard
Height:	3 ¼", 8.3 cm
Colour:	Yellow bear, red and blue kite
Issued:	2003 to the present

Back Stamp	Doulton Number	Price			
		U.S. $	Can. $	U.K. £	Aust. $
Doulton	WP 62	N/I	N/I	25.00	N/I

WP 63
RUM-TUM-TUM WINNIE™ ON HIS DRUM

Designer:	E. H. Shephard
Height:	3 ¼", 8.3 cm
Colour:	Yellow bear, green, red and blue drum
Issued:	2003 to the present

Back Stamp	Doulton Number	Price			
		U.S. $	Can. $	U.K. £	Aust. $
Doulton	WP 63	N/I	N/I	25.00	N/I

WP 64
A BIG NOISE FOR A LITTLE PIGLET™

Designer:	E. H. Shephard
Height:	3", 7.6 cm
Colour:	Pink piglet, green suit and yellow cymbals
Issued:	2003 to the present

Back Stamp	Doulton Number	Price			
		U.S. $	Can. $	U.K. £	Aust. $
Doulton	WP 64	N/I	N/I	25.00	N/I

WIND IN THE WILLOWS

AW1
TOAD™
Style One

Designer:	Harry Sales
Modeller:	David Lyttleton
Height:	3 ½", 8.9 cm
Colour:	Green toad, yellow waistcoat and trousers, white shirt, red bowtie
Issued:	1987 - 1989

Back Stamp	Beswick Number	Price			
		U.S. $	Can. $	U.K. £	Aust. $
AW1	2942	100.00	150.00	65.00	165.00

AW2
BADGER™
Style One

Designer:	Harry Sales
Modeller:	David Lyttleton
Height:	3", 7.6 cm
Colour:	Black and white badger, salmon dressing gown
Issued:	1987 - 1989

Back Stamp	Beswick Number	Price			
		U.S. $	Can. $	U.K. £	Aust. $
AW2	2940	80.00	115.00	50.00	125.00

AW3
RATTY™
Style One

Designer:	Harry Sales
Modeller:	David Lyttleton
Height:	3 ½", 8.9 cm
Colour:	Blue dungarees, white shirt
Issued:	1987 - 1989

Back Stamp	Beswick Number	Price			
		U.S. $	Can. $	U.K. £	Aust. $
AW3	2941	80.00	115.00	50.00	125.00

AW4
MOLE™
Style One

Designer:	Harry Sales
Modeller:	David Lyttleton
Height:	3", 7.6 cm
Colour:	Dark grey mole, brown dressing gown
Issued:	1987 - 1989

Back Stamp	Beswick Number	Price			
		U.S. $	Can. $	U.K. £	Aust. $
AW4	2939	150.00	200.00	90.00	225.00

AW5
PORTLY™
(Otter)

Designer:	Unknown
Modeller:	Alan Maslankowski
Height:	2 ¾", 7.0 cm
Colour:	Brown otter, blue dungarees, green and yellow jumper, green shoes
Issued:	1988 - 1989

Back Stamp	Beswick Number	Price			
		U.S. $	Can. $	U.K. £	Aust. $
AW5	3065	250.00	375.00	150.00	400.00

AW6
WEASEL GAMEKEEPER™

Designer:	Unknown
Modeller:	Alan Maslankowski
Height:	4", 10.1 cm
Colour:	Brown weasel, green jacket, trousers and cap, yellow waistcoat
Issued:	1988 - 1989

Back Stamp	Beswick Number	Price			
		U.S. $	Can. $	U.K. £	Aust. $
AW6	3076	250.00	375.00	150.00	400.00

WIW 1
ON THE RIVER™ (Mole and Rat)

Designer:	Warren Platt
Modeller:	Warren Platt
Size:	3 ½" x 6 ½", 8.9 cm x 16.5 cm
Colour:	Yellow, black, blue and red
Issued:	2000 in a limited edition of 1,908
Series:	Tableau

Back Stamp	Beswick Number	Price			
		U.S. $	Can. $	U.K. £	Aust. $
WIW 1	—	250.00	375.00	150.00	400.00

WIW 2
TOAD™
Style Two

Designer:	Warren Platt
Modeller:	Warren Platt
Height:	4 ¾", 12.1 cm
Colour:	Orange-brown coat trimmed with dark brown, brown trousers, grey gloves
Issued:	2000 in a limited edition of 2,000 (C of A)
Comm. by:	Doulton-Direct

Back Stamp	Beswick Number	Price			
		U.S. $	Can. $	U.K. £	Aust. $
WIW 2	—	70.00	100.00	45.00	110.00

WIW 3
BADGER™
Style Two

Designer:	Warren Platt
Modeller:	Warren Platt
Height:	5 ½", 14.0 cm
Colour:	Red dressing-gown, blue and white striped pyjamas
Issued:	2000 in a limited edition of 2,000 (C of A)
Comm. by:	Doulton-Direct

Back Stamp	Beswick Number	Price			
		U.S. $	Can. $	U.K. £	Aust. $
WIW 3	—	70.00	100.00	45.00	110.00

WIW 4
RATTY™
Style Two

Designer:	Warren Platt
Modeller:	Warren Platt
Height:	5", 12.7 cm
Colour:	Mustard coat, yellow knickers and waistcoat, white shirt, red tie, brown shoes
Issued:	2001 in a limited edition of 2,000 (C of A)
Comm. by:	Doulton-Direct

Back Stamp	Beswick Number	Price			
		U.S. $	Can. $	U.K. £	Aust. $
WIW 4	4038	70.00	100.00	45.00	110.00

WIW 5
MOLE™
Style Two

Designer:	Warren Platt
Modeller:	Warren Platt
Height:	4 ½", 11.9 cm
Colour:	Blue coat and trousers, yellow waistcoat, white shirt, black shoes
Issued:	2001 in a limited edition of 2,000 (C of A)
Comm. by:	Doulton-Direct

Back Stamp	Beswick Number	Price			
		U.S. $	Can. $	U.K. £	Aust. $
WIW 5	4039	70.00	100.00	45.00	110.00

WIW 6
WASHERWOMAN TOAD™

Designer:	Warren Platt
Modeller:	Warren Platt
Height:	3 ½", 8.9 cm
Colour:	Rose-pink dress, pale pink bonnet, white shawl, black shoes, brown washtub
Issued:	2001 in a limited edition of 2,000
Comm. by:	Doulton-Direct

Back Stamp	Beswick Number	Price			
		U.S. $	Can. $	U.K. £	Aust. $
WIW 4	4152	70.00	100.00	45.00	110.00

INDICES

ALPHABETICAL INDEX

MODEL NUMBER INDEX

3197	Mittens and Moppet
3200	Gentleman Mouse Made a Bow
3219	Foxy Reading Country News
3220	Lady Mouse Made a Curtsy
3234	Benjamin Wakes Up
3242	Peter and the Red Pocket Handkerchief, First Version, First Variation
3251	Miss Dormouse
3252	Pigling Eats His Porridge
3257	Christmas Stocking
3278	Mrs. Rabbit Cooking
3280	Ribby and the Patty Pan
3288	Hunca Munca Spills the Beads
3317	Benjamin Ate a Lettuce Leaf
3319	And This Pig Had None
3325	No More Twist
3356/1	Peter Rabbit, Second Version, First Variation
3356/2	Peter Rabbit, Second Version, Second Variation
3372/1	Mr. Jeremy Fisher, Second Version, First Variation
3372/2	Mr. Jeremy Fisher, Second Version, Second Variation
3373/1	Jemima Puddle-Duck, Second Version, First Variation
3373/2	Jemima Puddle-Duck, Second Version, Second Variation
3398/1	Mrs. Rabbit, Third Version, First Variation
3398/2	Mrs. Rabbit, Third Version, Second Variation
3403/1	Benjamin Bunny, Fourth Version, First Variation
3403/2	Benjamin Bunny, Fourth Version, Second Variation
3405/1	Tom Kitten, Second Version, First Variation
3405/2	Tom Kitten, Second Version, Second Variation
3437/1	Mrs. Tiggy-Winkle, Second Version, First Variation
3437/2	Mrs. Tiggy-Winkle, Second Version, Second Variation
3449/1	Tailor of Gloucester, Second Version, First Variation
3449/2	Tailor of Gloucester, Second Version, Second Variation
3450/1	Foxy Whiskered Gentleman, Second Version First Variation
3450/2	Foxy Whiskered Gentleman, Second Version Second Variation
3473	Peter in Bed
3506	Mr. McGregor
3533	Peter Ate a Radish
3591	Peter with Postbag
3592/1	Peter and the Red Pocket Handkerchief, Second Version, First Variation
3592/2	Peter and the Red Pocket Handkerchief, Second Version, Second Variation
3597	Peter with Daffodils
3646	Mrs. Rabbit and Peter, First Version
3719	Tom Kitten in the Rockery
3739	Peter Rabbit Gardening
3786	Jemima and Her Ducklings
3789	Mrs. Tiggy-Winkle Washing
3888	Sweet Peter Rabbit
3893	Squirrel Nutkin, Second Version
3894	Hunca Munca Sweeping, Second Version
3919	Jeremy Fisher Catches a Fish
3931	Johnny Town-Mouse Eating Corn
3940	Peter in the Watering Can
3946	Yock-Yock in the Tub
3976	Timmy Willie Fetching Milk
3978	Mrs. Rabbit and Peter, Second Version
4014	Farmer Potatoes
4015	Mrs. Tittlemouse, Style Two
4020	Tabitha Twitchit and Miss Moppet, Second Version
4030	This Pig Had a Bit of Meat
4031	Amiable Guinea-Pig, Style Two
5190	Peter and the Red Pocket Handkerchief, First Version, Second Variation
P4074	Hunca Munca, Style Two
P4075	Peter Rabbit Digging
P4210	Two Gentlemen Rabbits
P4217	Peter on his Book
P4234	Mrs. Tiggy-Winkle Buys Provisions
P4236	Head Gardener, The
PS1277	Foxy Whiskered Gentleman, First Version, Second Variation

Character Jugs

2959	Old Mr. Brown
2960	Mr. Jeremy Fisher
3006	Peter Rabbit
3088	Jemima Puddle-Duck
3102	Mrs. Tiggy-Winkle
3103	Tom Kitten

Plaques

2082	Jemima Puddle-Duck
2083	Peter Rabbit, First Version
2085	Tom Kitten
2594	Jemima Puddle-Duck with Foxy Whiskered Gentleman
2650	Peter Rabbit, Second Version
2685	Mrs. Tittlemouse

Tableau

3672	Hiding From the Cat
3672	Mrs. Rabbit and the Four Bunnies
3790	Ginger and Pickles
3792	Mittens, Tom Kitten and Moppet
3867	Mrs. Tiggy-Winkle and Lucie
3930	Peter and Benjamin Bunny Picking Up Onions
3983	Duchess and Ribby
P4155	Flopsy and Benjamin Bunny
P4160	Peter and Benjamin Picking Apples
P4161	Flopsy, Mopsy and Cottontail, Style Two
P4169	My Dear Son Thomas
P4901	Kep and Jemima

Stands

1531	Tree Lamp Base
2295	Display Stand

Studio Sculptures

SS1	Timmy Willie
SS2	Flopsy Bunnies
SS3	Mr. Jeremy Fisher
SS4	Peter Rabbit
SS11	Mrs. Tiggy-Winkle
SS26	Yock Yock (In the Tub)
SS27	Peter Rabbit (In the Watering Can)

BEDTIME CHORUS

1801	Pianist
1802	Piano
1803	Cat - Singing
1804	Boy without Spectacles
1805	Boy with Spectacles
1824	Dog - Singing
1825	Boy with Guitar
1826	Girl with Harp

BESWICK BEARS

BB001	William
BB002	Billy
BB003	Harry
BB004	Bobby
BB005	James
BB006	Susie
BB007	Angela
BB008	Charlotte
BB009	Sam
BB010	Lizzy
BB011	Emily
BB012	Sarah

JILL BARKLEM'S BRAMBLY HEDGE

DBH 1	Poppy Eyebright, Style One
DBH 2	Mr. Apple, Style One
DBH 3	Mrs. Apple, Style One
DBH 4	Lord Woodmouse, Style One
DBH 5	Lady Woodmouse, Style One
DBH 6	Dusty Dogwood, Style One

DBH 7	Wilfred Toadflax, Style One
DBH 8	Primrose Woodmouse
DBH 9	Old Mrs Eyebright
DBH 10A	Mr. Toadflax, Style One, First Version
DBH 10B	Mr. Toadflax, Style One, Second Version
DBH 10C	Mr. Toadflax, Style One, Third Version
DBH 11	Mrs. Toadflax
DBH 12	Catkin
DBH 13	Old Vole
DBH 14	Basil, Style One
DBH 15	Mrs. Crustybread
DBH 16	Clover
DBH 17	Teasel
DBH 18	Store Stump Money Box
DBH 19	Lily Weaver, Style One
DBH 20	Flax Weaver, Style One
DBH 21	Conker
DBH 22	Primrose Entertains
DBH 23	Wilfred Entertains
DBH 24	Mr. Saltapple, Style One
DBH 25	Mrs. Saltapple, Style One
DBH 26	Dusty and Baby
DBH 30	The Ice Ball
DBH 31	Lord Woodmouse, Style Two
DBH 32	Lady Woodmouse, Style Two
DBH 33	Primrose Picking Barries
DBH 34	Wilfred Carries the Picnic
DBH 35	Wilfred and the Toy Chest (Money Box)
DBH 36	Poppy Eyebright, Style Two
DBH 37	Dusty Dogwood, Style Two
DBH 38	Basil, Style Two
DBH 39	Mr. Saltapple, Style Two
DBH 40	Mrs. Saltapple, Style Two
DBH 41	Pebble
DBH 42	Shell
DBH 43	Shrimp
DBH 44	The Bride and Groom
DBH 45	Happy Birthday Wilfred
DBH 46	Mr. Toadflax, Style Two
DBH 47	Mrs. Apple, Style Two
DBH 48	Heading Home
DBH 49	Wilfred's Birthday Cake
DBH 50	Where are Basil's Trousers?
DBH 51	Dusty's Buns
DBH 52	Mrs. Toadflax Decorates Cake
DBH 53	Mr. Apple, Style Two
DBH 54	Lily Weaver, Style Two
DBH 55	Flax Weaver, Style Two
DBH 56	Wilfred Toadflax, Style Two
DBH 57	On the Ledge
DBH 58	Lily Weaver Spinning
DBH 59	Tea at Hornbeam Tree
DBH 60	A Cheerful Blaze
DBH 61	Shooting the Rapids

THE CAT'S CHORUS

CC1	Purrfect Pitch
CC2	Calypso Kitten
CC3	One Cool Cat
CC4	Ratcatcher Bilk
CC5	Trad Jazz Tom
CC6	Catwalking Bass
CC7	Feline Flamenco
CC8	Bravura Brass
CC9	Fat Cat
CC10	Glam Guitar

COMPTON & WOODHOUSE
Teddy Bears

–	Archie
–	Benjamin
–	Bertie
–	Henry

COUNTRY COUSINS

PM2101	Sweet Suzie "Thank You"
PM2102	Peter "Once Upon A Time"
PM2103	Harry "A New Home for Fred"
PM2104	Michael "Happily Ever After"
PM2105	Bertram "Ten Out of Ten"
PM2106	Leonardo "Practice Makes Perfect"
PM2107	Lily "Flowers Picked Just For You"
PM2108	Patrick "This Way's Best"
PM2109	Jamie "Hurrying Home"
PM2111	Mum and Lizzie "Let's Get Busy"
PM2112	Molly and Timmy "Picnic Time"
PM2113	Polly and Sarah "Good News!"
PM2114	Bill and Ted "Working Together"
PM2115	Jack and Daisy "How Does Your Garden Grow?"
PM2116	Alison and Debbie "Friendship is Fun"
PM2119	Robert and Rosie "Perfect Partners"
PM2120	Sammy "Treasure Hunting"

DAVID HAND'S ANIMALAND

1148	Dinkum Platypus
1150	Zimmy Lion
1151	Felia
1152	Ginger Nutt
1153	Hazel Nutt
1154	Oscar Ostrich
1155	Dusty Mole
1156	Loopy Hare

ENGLISH COUNTRY FOLK

ECF 1	Huntsman Fox
ECF 2	Fisherman Otter
ECF 3	Gardener Rabbit, First Variation
ECF 4	Gentleman Pig, First Variation
ECF 5	Shepherd Sheepdog
ECF 6	Hiker Badger, First Variation
ECF 7	Mrs. Rabbit Baking, First Variation
ECF 8	The Lady Pig, First Variation
ECF 9	Hiker Badger, Second Variation
ECF 10	Gentleman Pig, Second Variation
ECF 11	The Lady Pig, Second Variation
ECF 12	Gardener Rabbit, Second Variation
ECF 13	Mrs. Rabbit Baking, Second Variation

ENID BLYTON'S NODDY COLLECTION

3676	Big Ears
3678	Noddy
3679	Mr. Plod
3770	Tessie Bear
–	Noddy and Big Ears

EXPRESS NEWSPAPERS LTD.
Rupert Bear

2694	Rupert Bear, Style One
2710	Algy Pug
2711	Pong Ping
2720	Bill Badger, Style One
2779	Rupert Bear Snowballing
–	Bill Badger, Style Two
–	Edward Trunk
–	Podgy Pig
–	Rupert Bear, Style Two
–	Rupert Bear and Algy Pug Go-Carting
–	Rupert with Satchel

FOOTBALLING FELINES

FF2	Mee-Ouch
FF3	Kitcat
FF4	Dribble
FF5	Thrown In
FF6	Referee: Red Card

HANNA-BARBERA

The Flintstones

3577	Pebbles Flintstone
3579	Bamm-Bamm Rubble
3583	Wilma Flintstone
3584	Betty Rubble
3587	Barney Rubble
3588	Fred Flintstone
3590	Dino

Top Cat

3581	Top Cat
3586	Choo-Choo
3624	Fancy Fancy
3627	Benny
3671	Officer Dibble
3673	Spook
3674	Brain

HARRY POTTER

HP 1	The Remembrall Recovery
HP 2	Harry Casts a Magical Spell
HP 3	Hermoine Studies For Potions Class
HP 4	Ron Follows the Weasley Family Tradition
HP 5	Professor Severus Snape
HP 6	Headmaster Albus Dumbledore
HP 7	Wizard-in-training
HP 8	The Friendship Begins
HP 9	Harry's 11th Birthday
HP 10	Struggling Through Potions Class
HP 11	Slytherin or Gryffindor
HP 12	Ron and Scrabbers
HP 13	Hermoine Learns to Levitate
HP 14	Professor McGonagall
HP 15	Professor Quirrell
HP 16	Hedwig
HP 17	The Birth of Norbert
HP 18	The Mirror Holds the Answer
HP 19	The Journey to Hogwarts
HP 20	Madame Hooch
HP 21	Professor Sprout
HP 22	Harry Potter Playing Quidditch
HP 23	Dobby
HP 24	Dursley Family
HP 25	Whomping Willow
HP 26	Rescue in the Forbidden Forest

THE HERBS

H 1	Parsley the Lion
H 2	Bayleaf the Gardener
H 3	Dill the Dog
H 4	Sage the Owl

HIPPOS ON HOLIDAY

HH1	Grandma
HH2	Grandpa
HH3	Ma
HH4	Pa
HH5	Harriet
HH6	Hugo

JANE HISSEY'S OLD BEAR AND FRIENDS

OB4601	Old Bear
OB4602	Time For Bed
OB4603	Bramwell Brown Had A Good Idea
OB4604	Don't Worry, Rabbit
OB4605	The Long Red Scarf
OB4606	Waiting For Snow
OB4607	The Snowflake Biscuits
OB4608	Welcome Home Old Bear
OB4609	Ruff's Prize
OB4610	Time For A Cuddle, Hug Me Tight
OB4611	Don't Forget Old Bear
OB4612	Hold on Tight
OB4613	Resting with Cat
OB4614	Looking For A Sailor
OB4615	Too Much Food
OB4616	Nest of Socks
OB4617	Snow Decorations
OB4618	Storytime
OB4619	Duck
OB4620	Up, Up and Away

JOAN WALSH ANGLUND

2272	Anglund Boy
2293	Anglund Girl with Doll
2317	Anglund Girl with Flowers

KITTY MACBRIDE

2526	A Family Mouse
2527	A Double Act
2528	The Racegoer
2529	A Good Read
2530	Lazybones
2531	A Snack
2532	Strained Relations
2533	Just Good Friends
2565	The Ring
2566	Guilty Sweethearts
2589	All I Do is Think of You

LITTLE LIKEABLES

LL1	Family Gathering (Hen and Two Chicks)
LL2	Watching the World Go By (Frog)
LL3	Hide and Sleep (Pig and Two Piglets)
LL4	My Pony (Pony)
LL5	On Top of the World (Elephant)
LL6	Treat Me Gently (Fawn)
LL7	Out at Last (Duckling)
LL8	Cats Chorus (Cats)

LITTLE LOVABLES

LL1	Happy Birthday
LL2	I Love You
LL3	God Loves Me
LL4	Just For You
LL5	To Mother
LL6	Congratulations
LL7	Passed
LL8	Happy Birthday
LL9	I Love You
LL10	God Loves Me
LL11	Just For You
LL12	To Mother
LL13	Congratulations
LL14	Passed
LL15	Happy Birthday
LL16	I Love You
LL17	God Loves Me
LL18	Just For You
LL19	To Mother
LL20	Congratulations
LL21	Passed
LL22	(No Name) Also called 'Happy Birthday'
LL23	(No Name) Also called 'I Love You'
LL24	(No Name) Also called 'God Loves Me'
LL25	(No Name) Also called 'Just for You'
LL26	(No Name) Also called 'To Mother'
LL27	(No Name) Also called 'Congratulations'
LL28	(No Name) Also called 'Passed'
LL29	To Daddy
LL30	Merry Christmas
LL31	Good Luck
LL32	Get Well Soon
LL33	Please
LL34	Please
LL35	Prototype for I Love Beswick
LL36	I Love Beswick

NORMAN THELWELL

Earthenware Series 1981-1989

2704A	An Angel on Horseback, First Variation
2704B	An Angel on Horseback, Second Variation
2769A	Kick-Start, First Variation
2769B	Kick-Start, Second Variation
2789A	Pony Express, First Variation
2789B	Pony Express, Second Variation

Resin Studio Sculptures 1985-1985

SS7A	I Forgive You, First Variation
SS7B	I Forgive You, Second Variation
SS12A	Early Bath, First Variation
SS12B	Early Bath, Second Variation

Earthenware Series 2001 to date

NT 1	Losing Hurts
NT 2	Powerfull Hindquarters are a Distinct Advantage
NT 3	Exhausted
NT 4	Choosing Good Feet
NT 5	Excessive Praise
NT 6	Suppling Excerises
NT 7	Body Brush
NT 8	Detecting Ailments
NT 9	Ice Cream Treat
NT 10	Ideal Pony for a Nervous Child
NT 11	So Treat Him Like a Friend
NT 12	He'll Find You

NURSERY RHYMES COLLECTION

DNR 1	Humpty Dumpty
DNR 2	Little Miss Muffet
DNR 3	Old Mother Hubbard
DNR 4	The Cat and the Fiddle
DNR 5	Old King Cole

PADDINGTON BEAR CO. LTD.

Resin Series 1996-1998

PB1	Paddington at the Station, Style One
PB2	Paddington Bakes a Cake
PB3	Paddington Decorating
PB4	Paddington Surfing
PB5	Paddington Gardening
PB6	Paddington Bathtime
PB7	Paddington the Golfer
PB8	Paddington the Musician
PB9	Paddington at Christmas Time
PB10	Paddington Marmalade Sandwich
PB11	Paddington Going to Bed
PB12	Paddington the Fisherman

Ceramic Series 1999

–	Paddington at the Station, Style Two

THE PIG PROMENADE

PP 1	John the Conductor (Vietnamese Pot Bellied Pig)
PP 2	Matthew the Trumpet Player (Large White Pig)
PP 3	David the Flute Player (Tamworth Pig)
PP 4	Andrew the Cymbal Player (Gloucester Old Spotted Pig)
PP 5	Daniel the Violinist (Saddleback Pig)
PP 6	Michael the Bass Drum Player (Large Black Pig)
PP 7	James The Triangle Player (Tamworth Piglet)
PP 8	Richard the French Horn Player
PP 9	Christopher the Guitar Player
PP 10	George
PP 11	Thomas
PP 12	Benjamin

PUNCH AND JUDY

–	Judy
–	Punch

ST. TIGGYWINKLES

TW1	Henry Hedgehog (Standing)
TW2	Harry Hedgehog (Sitting)
TW3	Fred Fox
TW4	Bob Badger
TW5	Rosie Rabbit
TW6	Sarah Squirrel
TW7	Daniel Duck
TW8	Oliver Owl
TW9	Friends
TW10	A Helping Hand
TW11	Deborah Dormouse
TW12	Monty Mole
TW13	Franchesca Fawn

THE SNOWMAN GIFT COLLECTION

DS 1	James, Style One
DS 2	The Snowman, Style One
DS 3	Stylish Snowman
DS 4	Thank You Snowman
DS 5	Snowman Magic Music Box
DS 6	Cowboy Snowman
DS 7	Highland Snowman
DS 8	Lady Snowman
DS 9	Bass Drummer Snowman
DS 10	Flautist Snowman
DS 11	Violinist Snowman
DS 12	Pianist Snowman
DS 13	Snowman's Piano
DS 14	Cymbal Player Snowman
DS 15	Drummer Snowman
DS 16	Trumpeter Snowman
DS 17	Cellist Snowman
DS 18	Snowman Musical Box
DS 19	Snowman Money Box
DS 20	The Snowman Tobogganing
DS 21	The Snowman Skiing
DS 22	The Snowman Snowballing
DS 23	Building the Snowman
–	James, Style Two
–	James, Style Three (James Builds a Snowman)
–	The Snowman, Style Two
–	The Snowman, Style Three (James Builds a Snowman)
–	Dancing in the Snow
–	Snowman and James, The Adventure Begins
–	Dressing the Snowman
–	The Journey Ends
–	Walking in the Air (Wall Plaque)

SPORTING CHARACTERS

SC1	Fly Fishing
SC2	Last Lion of Defence
SC3	It's a Knockout
SC4	Sloping Off
SC5	A Round with Foxy
SC6	Out for a Duck

TEDDY BEARS

4130	Henry
4131	Edward
4132	George
4133	William

THUNDERBIRDS

3337	Lady Penelope
3339	Brains
3344	Scott Tracy
3345	Virgil Tracy
3346	Parker
3348	The Hood

TRUMPTONSHIRE

4054	PC McGarry
4055	Windy Miller
4063	Captain Flack
4065	Dr. Mopp
4066	The Mayer
4067	Mrs. Honeyman
4184	Mrs. Dingle
4185	Jonathan Bell
4186	Mickey Murphy
4187	Mrs. Cobbit

TURNER ENTERTAINMENT

3547	Droopy
3549	Jerry
3552	Tom

The Wizard of Oz

3709	Scarecrow
3731	Lion
3732	Dorothy
3738	Tinman

20TH CENTURY ADVERTISING CLASSICS

AC 1	Father William
AC 2	Golly
AC 3	Sir Kreemy Knut
AC 4	Fox's Polar Bear
AC 5	Player's 'Hero' Sailor
AC 6	John Ginger
AC 7	The Milky Bar Kid
AC 8	Guinness Toucan
MCL 1	Penfold Golfer
MCL 2	Dunlop Caddie
MCL 3	Big Chief Toucan
MCL 5	P..P..P..Pick Up A...Penguin
MCL 6	Christmas Toucan
MCL 7	Seaside Toucan
—	Bisto Kids
—	Tony the Tiger
—	His Master's Voice 'Nipper'

WALT DISNEY CHARACTERS

101 Dalmatians

DM 1	Cruella De Vil, Style One
DM 2	Penny
DM 3	Penny and Freckles
DM 4	Rolly
DM 5	Patch, Rolly and Freckles
DM 6	Pongo
DM 7	Perdita
DM 8	Lucky
DM 9	Patch in Basket
DM 10	Lucky and Freckles on Ice
DM 11	Pups in the Chair

Disney Characters

1278	Mickey Mouse, Style One
1279	Jiminy Cricket, Style One
1280	Pluto, Style One
1281	Goofy, Style One
1282	Pinocchio, Style One
1283	Donald Duck, Style One
1289	Minnie Mouse, Style One
1291	Thumper, Style One

Disney Princess Collection

HN 3677	Cinderella
HN 3678	Snow White, Style Two
HN 3830	Belle
HN 3831	Ariel, Style One
HN 3832	Jasmine
HN 3833	Aurora

Disney Showcase Collection

Alice in Wonderland

AW1	Alice, Style Four
AW2	Made Hatter, Style Three
AW3	March Hare
AW4	White Rabbit, Style Three
AW5	Cheshire Cat, Style Four

The Jungle Book

JB 1	Mowgli
JB 2	Baby Elephant
JB 3	Baloo
JB 4	Bagheera
JB 5	Shere Khan
JB 6	Floating Along
JB 7	King Louie

The Little Mermaid

LM 1	Ariel, Style Two
LM 2	Flounder
LM 3	Sebastian
LM 4	Ursula
LM 5	Scuttle

Peter Pan
Second Series 2002 to date

PAN 1	Peter Pan, Style Two
PAN 2	Tinker Bell, Style Two
PAN 3	The Duel
PAN 4	Captain Hook
PAN 5	Wendy
PAN 6	Tic Toc Crocodile
PAN 7	Heading For Skull Rock

Disney Villains Collection

HN 3839	Cruella de Vil, Style Two
HN 3840	Maleficent
HN 3847	The Queen
HN 3848	The Witch

Fantasia

FAN1	Buckets of Mischief
FAN2	Follow Me
FAN3	Noah's Helper
FAN4	Heart on a String
FAN5	A Flower and His Heart

Film Classics Collection

CN 1	Cinderella, The Dress of Dreams
FC 1	Bambi
FC 2	Thumper, Style Two
FC 3	Dumbo
FC 4	Pinocchio, Style Two
FC 5	Jiminy Cricket, Style Two
FC 6	Timothy Mouse
FC 7	Lady
FC 8	Tramp

Mickey Mouse Collection

MM1	Mickey Mouse, Style Two
MM2	Minnie Mouse, Style Two
MM3	Donald Duck, Style Two
MM4	Daisy Duck
MM5	Goofy, Style Two
MM6	Pluto, Style Two
MM7	Mickey Mouse, Style Two
MM8	Minnie Mouse, Style Two
MM9	Donald Duck, Style Two
MM10	Daisy Duck
MM11	Goofy, Style Two
MM12	Pluto, Style Two

Peter Pan
First Series 1953-1965

1301	Nana
1302	Smee
1307	Peter Pan, Style One
1312	Tinker Bell, Style One

Snow White and the Seven Dwarfs
First Series 1954-1967

1325	Dopey, Style One
1326	Happy, Style One
1327	Bashful, Style One
1328	Sneezy, Style One
1329	Doc, Style One
1330	Grumpy, Style One
1331	Sleepy, Style One
1332A	Snow White, Style One, First Version
1332B	Snow White, Style One, Second Version

Snow White and the Seven Dwarfs
Second Series 1997 - 2002

SW 1	Snow White, Style Three
SW 2	Doc, Style Two
SW 3	Grumpy, Style Two
SW 4	Happy, Style Two
SW 5	Dopey, Style Two
SW 6	Sneezy, Style Two
SW 7	Sleepy, Style Two
SW 8	Bashful, Style Two
SW 9	Snow White, Style Three
SW 10	Doc, Style Two
SW 11	Grumpy, Style Two
SW 12	Happy, Style Two
SW 13	Dopey, Style Two
SW 14	Sneezy, Style Two
SW 15	Sleepy, Style Two
SW 16	Bashful, Style Two
SW 17	Dopey by Candlelight
SW 18	Bashful's Melody
SW 19	Doc with Lantern
SW 20	Grumpy's Bathtime
SW 21	Dopey's First Kiss

Winnie the Pooh
First Series 1968 - 1990

2193	Winnie the Pooh
2196	Eeyore
2214	Piglet
2215	Rabbit
2216	Owl
2217	Kanga
2394	Tigger
2395	Christopher Robin, Style One

Winnie the Pooh
Second Series 1996 to the present

WP 1	Winnie the Pooh and the Honey Pot
WP 2	Pooh and Piglet The Windy Day
WP 3	Winnie the Pooh and the Paw-Marks
WP 4	Winnie the Pooh in the Armchair
WP 5	Piglet and the Balloon
WP 6	Tigger Signs the Rissolution
WP 7	Eeyore's Tail
WP 8	Kanga and Roo
WP 9	Christopher Robin, Style Two
WP 10	Christopher Robin and Pooh
WP 11	Pooh Lights The Candle
WP 12	Pooh Counting the Honeypots
WP 13	Piglet Picking the Violets
WP 14	Eeyore's Birthday
WP 15	Eeyore Loses a Tail
WP 16	Pooh's Blue Balloon Money Box
WP 17	Wol Signs the Rissolution
WP 18	Winnie the Pooh and the Present
WP 19	Winnie the Pooh and the Fair-sized Basket
WP 20	The More it Snows, Tiddely Pom
WP 21	Summer's Day Picnic
WP 22	I've Found Somebody Just Like Me
WP 23	Rabbit Reads the Plan
WP 24	How Sweet to be a Cloud (Clock)
WP 25	Eeyore Nose to the Ground
WP 26	Piglet Planting a Haycorn
WP 27	Tigger Loves Tigger Lilies
WP 28	Pooh Began to Eat
WP 29	Piglet and the Honey Pot
WP 30	Tigger Plays Ball
WP 31	The Brain of Pooh
WP 32	Christopher Reads to Pooh
WP 33	Pooh and the Party Hat
WP 34	Going Sledging
WP 35	Wol and the Honeypot
WP 36	Under the Name Mr. Sanders
WP 37	All the Flowers are Waking Up (Spring)
WP 38	Summer if Full of Fluttery Surprises (Summer)
WP 39	Love Makes All Your Botthers Disappear
WP 40	A Present For Me? How Grand!
WP 41	A Little Tree Trimming is in Order
WP 42	The Most Perfect Tree in all the Wood
WP 43	Sometimes Autumn Tickles Your Nose (Autumn)
WP 44	Eeyore Made a Wintery Wish (Winter)
WP 45	Who's Cake? Pooh's Cake?
WP 46	I Love You So Much Bear
WP 47	Toot Toot Went the Whistle
WP 48	Any Hunny Left For Me?
WP 49	A Clean Bear is a Happy Bear
WP 50	Presents and Parties
WP 51	A Little Sponge for a Little Piglet
WP 52	Bouncy Bouncy Boo-to-You
WP 53	A Sleepy Day in the Hundred Acre Wood
WP 54	A Clean Little Roo is Best
WP55/56	Push...Pull! Come on Pooh (Bookends)
WP 57	Christopher Dresses the Tree
WP 58	Tigger's Splash Time
WP 59	Oh Dear Bathtime's Here!
WP 60	Isn't it Funny How a Bear Likes Honey
WP 61	It's Honey all the Way Down
WP 62	Where Does the Wind Come From?
WP 63	Rum-Tum-Tum Winnie on his Drum
WP 64	A Big Noise for a Little Piglet

WIND IN THE WILLOWS

AW1	Toad, Style One
AW2	Badger, Style One
AW3	Ratty, Style One
AW4	Mole, Style One
AW5	Portly (Otter)
AW6	Weasel Gamekeeper
WIW1	On the River (Mole and Rate)
WIW2	Toad, Style Two
WIW3	Badger, Style Two
WIW4	Ratty, Style Two
WIW5	Mole, Style Two
WIW	Washerwoman Toad

Royal Doulton Shops

ROYAL DOULTON SHOPS – CANADA

C2 - 3625 Shaganappi Trail NW
Calgary, AB
T3A 0E2

West Edmonton Mall
8882 - 170th Street
Edmonton, AB T5T 3J7

Coquitlam Centre
2929 Barnet Highway
Port Coquitlam, BC V3R 5R5

Guildford Town Centre
Surrey, BC
V3R 7C1

Polo Park Shopping Centre
1485 Portage Ave.
Winnipeg, MB R3G 0W4

477 Paul Street
Champlain Place
Dieppe, NB E1A 4X4

1381 Regent Street
Fredericton, NB
E3C 1A2

Micmac Mall
21 Micmac Blvd.
Dartmouth, NS B3A 4K7

White Oaks Mall
1105 Wellington Road
London, ON N6E 1V4

Markville Shopping Centre
5000 Highway #7
Markham, ON L3R 4M9

Pickering Town Centre
1355 Kingston Road
Pickering ON L1V 1B8

Fairview Mall
1800 Sheppard Avenue East
Willowdale, ON M2J 5A7

ROYAL DOULTON FACTORY SHOPS – ENGLAND

Cheshire Oaks Outlet Village, Unit 106
Kinsey Road, Ellesmere Port
Cheshire L65 9LA

167 Picadilly
London
W1V 9DE

Nile Street
Burslem, Stoke-on-Trent
Staffordshire ST6 2AJ

Forge Lane, Etruria
Stoke-on-Trent
Stafffordshire ST1 5NN

Victoria Road
Fenton, Stoke-on-Trent
Staffordshire ST4 2PJ

Lawley Street
Longton, Stoke-on-Trent
Staffordshire ST3 2PH

ROYAL DOULTON SHOPS – UNITED STATES

Dester Hills Premium Outlets
48650 Seminole Dr.
Building C, Suite 152,
Cabazon, CA 92230

Camarillo Premium Outlets
740 Ventura Blvd., Suite 530
Camarillo, CA 93010

Premium Outlets – Gilroy
681 Leavesley Road
Suite B290
Gilroy, CA 95020

Factory Stores at Vacaville
352 Nut Tree Rd.
Vacaville, CA 95687

Clinton Crossing Premium Outlets
20 Killingworth Turnpike, Ste. 530
Clinton, CT 06413

Ocean Outlets
1772 Ocean Outlets
Rehoboth, DE 19971

Gulf Coast Factory Stores
5501 Factory Shops Blvd.
Ellenton, Fl 34222

Miromar Outlets
10801 Corkscrew Rd. Suite 366
Estero, Fl 33928

The Orlando Crossings
5563 International Drive
Orlando, Fl, 32819

Belz Factory Outlet World
500 Belz Outlet Blvd. Suite 80
St. Augustine, Fl 32084

Prime Outlets - Colhoun
455 Belwood Rd., Suite 20
Calhoun, GA 30701

North Georgia Premium Outlets
800 Highway 400, Suite 250
Dawsonville, GA 30534

Lighthouse Place Premium Outlets
403 Lighthouse Place
Michigan City, IN 46360

Kittery Outlet Center
Route 1
Kittery, ME 03904-2505

Prime Outlets - Birch Run
12240 S. Beyer Rd., Suite E80
Birch Run, MI 48415

Shoppes on the Parkway, Ste. 10
Blowing Rock, NC 28605

Factory Stores of America
1209 Industrial Park Drive, Suite 400
Smithfield, NC 27577

Liberty Village Premium Outlets
34 Liberty Village
Flemington, NJ 08822

Belz Factory Outlet World
7400 Las Vegas Blvd. South, Suite 244
Las Vegas, NV 89123

Woodbury Common Premium Outlets
161 Marigold Court
Central Valley, NY 10917

Tanger Outlet Center
Riverhead II, Tanger Drive,
Suite # 1012
Riverhead, NY 11901

Ohio Factory Shops
8150 Factory Shops Blvd.
Jeffersonville, OH 43128

Factory Stores at Lincoln City
1500 SE East Devil's Lake Rd., Ste. 303
Lincoln City, OR 97367

Prime Outlets at Grove City
1911 Leesburg-Grove City Rd.
Suite 210, P.O. Box 1014
Grove City, PA 16127

Tanger Outlet Center
501 Stanley K. Tanger Blvd.
Lancaster, PA 17602-1467

The Crossings Outlet Center
1000 Rte 611, Suite A-23
Tannersville, PA 18372

Myrtle Beach Factory Stores
4638 Factory Stores Blvd. EE 150
Myrtle Beach, SC 29579

Belz Factory Outlet
2655 Teaster Lane, Suite 26
Pigeon Forge, TN 37683

Prime Outlets – Conroe
1111 League Line Rd. Suite 112
Conroe, TX 77303

Tanger Factory Outlet Centre
4015 Interstate 35 South
Suite 402
San Marcos, TX 78666

Potomac Mills
2700 Potomac Mills Circle
Suite 976
Prince William, VA 22192

Prime Outlets - Williamsburg
5699-50 Richmond Rd
Williamsburg, VA 23188

Prime Outlets – Burlington
288 Fashion Way, Store #5
Burlington, WA 98233

ROYAL DOULTON | Visit our website at:
www.royaldoulton.com

THE
ROYAL DOULTON
COMPANY
INTERNATIONAL COLLECTORS CLUB

If you do not *belong* you cannot *receive*:

- A Complimentary Figure
- Exclusive Offers only for Members
- Quarterly Gallery Collector Magazine
- Free Historical Enquiry Service
- Free Entry to our Visitor Centre

Juliet Bunnykins
DB254
Complimentary gift

Charmed
HN4445
Complimentary gift

JOIN THE CLUB

2003 ANNUAL MEMBERSHIP
You may visit a shop opposite
or our website at: www.royaldoulton.com

340